Education and the Common Good

Robin Barrow has been one of the leading philosophers of education for more than forty years. This book is a critical but appreciative examination of his work by some of the leading philosophers of education at work today, with responses from Professor Barrow. It will focus on his work on curriculum, the analytic tradition in philosophy, education and schooling, and his use of Greek philosophy to enrich current debates in the subject. This work will be of interest to all those who have been influenced by his contributions to educational and philosophical debate.

John Gingell is Reader in Philosophy at the University of Northampton. He has published articles in learned journals and the following jointly authored books: Key Concepts in the Philosophy of Education, Modern Political Theory, Philosophy and Educational Policy, In Defence of High Culture

Routledge International Studies in the Philosophy of Education

Education and the Common Good

Essays in Honor of Robin Barrow

Edited by John Gingell

Routledge
Taylor & Francis Group
NEW YORK   LONDON

First published 2014
by Routledge
711 Third Avenue, New York, NY 10017

and by Routledge
2 Park Square, Milton Park, Abingdon, Oxon OX14 4RN

*Routledge is an imprint of the Taylor & Francis Group,
an informa business*

© 2014 Taylor & Francis

The right of John Gingell to be identified as the author of the editorial
material, and of the authors for their individual chapters, has been asserted
in accordance with sections 77 and 78 of the Copyright, Designs and
Patents Act 1988.

Library of Congress Cataloging-in-Publication Data
   Education and the common good : essays in honor of Robin Barrow /
edited by John Gingell.
      pages cm. — (Routledge international studies in the philosophy of
education ; 31)
   Includes bibliographical references and index.
  1. Barrow, Robin—Influence.   2. Education—Philosophy.   I. Gingell,
John, editor of compilation.   II. Barrow, Robin, honoree.
   LB880.B342E38 2014
   370.1—dc23
   2013030893

ISBN13: 978-0-415-51834-5 (hbk)
ISBN13: 978-1-315-86687-1 (ebk)

Typeset in Sabon
by IBT Global.

SUSTAINABLE FORESTRY INITIATIVE
Certified Sourcing
www.sfiprogram.org
SFI-01234
SFI label applies to the text stock

Printed and bound in the United States of America
by IBT Global.

Contents

A Very Short Introduction

For anybody who has been interested in the Philosophy of Education over the last forty years the work of Robin Barrow should need no introduction. Robin's numerous books and articles have touched and enlightened vast areas of the subject. If you wanted to know, for instance, why we should be suspicious of the claims of the de-schoolers and free-schoolers then you went to his *Radical Education*; if you wondered about the merits of large scale empirical research into teaching styles, then you read *Giving Teaching Back to Teachers*; if you were puzzled by the explosion of skills talk over the last few years, then you consulted his work on the subject. There are very few areas of the subject about which he has had nothing to say. This is not, of course, to say that he has always been right in his opinions— although he often has—or that his views have remained the same over the years—they have changed, sometimes for the better and sometime for the worse. It is to say that when Robin turned his attention to a subject in print his opinion was always worth paying attention to. It would be invariably well written—as one of the contributors shows, Robin has always been a joy to read—it would always be well argued and it would be to the point. The mark of a good philosopher, of education and anything else, is not that their views are a substitute for your own judgement but that such views force you to consider and reconsider such judgement in the light of what has now been said. That what they say matters! On this criterion Robin has been an enormously important figure in his chosen fields throughout the many years of his career. And, despite what he says in his end piece, it is why this volume is fully deserved.

As with Robin Barrow, the contributors to this volume should be familiar to any one who has taken an interest in the Philosophy of Education over the last forty years. The scope of their work, and their different areas of expertise, bears testimony to the reach of Robin's work. Their combined status within the profession is evidence of the respect that Robin's work has garnered over the years. But, as should be clear to anyone that reads the essays that follow, this is no mere exercise in hagiography; rather a continuing engagement with what he has to say. One of the notable things about the essays is the obvious affection which many of the authors show towards Robin. To have a career in which one is respected by one's peers and where such respect is accompanied by friendship, is to be fortunate indeed. And this is exactly the position of Robin Barrow at this time. Aristotle would approve.

In organising what follows I have departed a little from tradition at times. The actual order of the essays was a question of judgement and, whilst I was always aware that there might be alternative reasonable arrangements, I think that the order given does make sense. Whilst most of the essays directly engage with Robin's work one of them, that of Ian Gregory, is a response to another, that of Ruth Jonathan. I did of course ask all concerned whether they were happy with this and they all were. Robin's section at the end of the book is partly a response to the essays before; partly, a meditation on his own life and work; and partly, some thoughts—often critical—about the academic environment which some of us find ourselves in at the present day. This last part may be thought a little indulgent by some. However, if we are going to celebrate the work of notable figure in the academic world it is surely defensible to include that figure's thoughts on that world. As I said above I think Robin thoroughly deserves a volume like this and it has been my deep pleasure to know him and his work over the years.

John Gingell

Acknowledgements

I would like to thank David Wall and Michael Watters for their help in editing this book. Without them the task would have been much more onerous than in fact it actually was.

1 The Philosopher and the Writer

Richard Smith

ARGUMENT AND STYLE

In philosophy the matter of the language which is its vehicle—which is a clumsy way of putting it, and immediately sets up a distinction which I want to question—is central in a way that would not be the case to the same extent in other disciplines. There is first of all the question of whether philosophy is best carried out through speech or in writing: a question to which Plato is often supposed to have given a definitive answer, both in the legend of the origins of writing in the *Phaedrus* (274b5ff.) and in his choice of the dialogue form. From this can be traced many elements of philosophy as it has been practiced in Anglophone countries in modern times. There is for instance the idea that philosophy is most nearly itself in live argument and disputation, in which one interlocutor (a revealing term: one who takes part in a conversation) defends a claim while another attempts to reveal its flaws. This can be traced all the way to the traditional Oxford tutorial, where the undergraduate student reads aloud the essay that he or she has written and then attempts to justify its arguments against the criticisms of the tutor. Its influence lingers in the practice of submitting a conference paper (a *paper*, we call it) and then summarising it orally (which we call *speaking to it*) in the live conference session. Before going any further we might note that, in what may seem a contrast to this tradition, Plato's dialogues are written, and that they are carefully, even artfully, constructed; a point which is often conveniently forgotten.

This prejudice in favour of the oral is closely connected with a preference for, or commitment to, the analytic style of philosophy as against what is usually called the 'Continental' style, that is to say the style favoured by non-Anglophone philosophers from Continental Europe and those influenced by them. I say more about this distinction below. Here it is enough perhaps to characterise the analytic tradition as emerging from the logical positivism of the 1930s and 1940s, especially as mediated through such Anglophone philosophers as A. J. Ayer, and as constituting the standard approach to academic philosophy in the Anglophone countries for the last half century. Its practitioners see themselves as bringing clarity to replace muddle and confusion, and they aspire to clarity in their own writing and lecturing. Their prose style is by intention plain and unadorned. They may not always notice that this is a distinctive *style*, but it is not stylistically neutral. It has much in common with the style of ordinary conversation, and for the most part its devotees see themselves as eschewing the figurative and the poetic. These latter ways of writing, they might say, are often the source of philosophical confusion. It is thus related to their prose style that they are quick to spot common fallacies, such as an undistributed middle (all terriers are dogs, everyone in this room owns a dog, so everyone in this room owns a terrier) or a category mistake (such as supposing that all talk of the mind must be the same as talk of the brain). When philosophy of education started to establish itself as a subject area (or subdiscipline of philosophy: not much turns on the distinctions here, in my view) in the UK in the 1960s under the leadership of such figures as Richard Peters, Paul Hirst, and Robert Dearden, it was analytic philosophy that it took as its model.

Robin Barrow of course places himself squarely in this tradition, as the title of one of his papers reminds us: 'The Need for Philosophical Analysis in a Postmodern Era' (1999). Here he argues for the importance of 'a *specific* understanding of philosophical analysis' (p. 415, my emphasis), but there is nothing, I think, in his understanding of it that other prominent followers of that tradition, whether in philosophy of education or in philosophy more widely, would take substantial issue with. Since I shall offer below some criticisms of philosophy practiced exclusively in this tradition I begin by acknowledging some of its many strengths; and since many of those are displayed to virtuoso effect by Robin Barrow himself it is hard to do better than quote him at sufficient length to display some of the central features of his style. When in 2006 as founding editor of the journal *Ethics and Education* I sought to establish that this was to be a journal of some quality, Barrow was one of the people I approached to contribute to the first issue. His article is called 'Moral Education's Modest Agenda', and it was everything I hoped it would be. Here he is towards the end of the article making the classical move of distinguishing moral education from various practices which sometimes make false claims to the title.

> The main task in moral education is to clear the ground of all the irrelevant and inappropriate practices and ideas that have hitherto been wished upon us. We have to throw out systems of behaviour modification, because to condition people to behave in certain ways is not to educate them and does not allow them to act freely nor, therefore, morally. We have to fight against the indoctrination that is still prevalent throughout the world, not least in fundamentalist Christian communities, which closes people's minds around an impoverished set of unprovable and exclusionary rules that, again, are not themselves moral and that prevent the development of a moral understanding. We have to chase values clarification, and all other programs that similarly suggest

that the important things are being sincere and articulating one's views rather than holding coherent and rationally justifiable views, out of the schools. We have to challenge the contemporary tendency to impose remedies, such as therapy, drugs and counselling, on people, rather than tackling the causes of the problems. Moralizing, whether directly or indirectly by means, for example, of carefully censored texts, is anathema to a true moral education. Developmental theories, which are still a staple part of teacher education in North America, continue to contribute to a wholly misleading picture of what morality is and how one should morally educate the young, essentially because they treat people as physical entities with brains but without minds, and because they treat moral education as a matter of seizing upon and reinforcing allegedly natural stages of development. Similarly, one cannot overestimate the harm that has been and to some extent still is being done to the spread of true moral understanding by the insidious influence of political and moral correctness. (Barrow 2006, pp. 12–13)

There is much to admire here. First, not to be underestimated and certainly not to be taken for granted on the part of academics working in the field of education, is the irreproachable grammar. Varied in its structures and with a fluency suggestive of speech, its qualities include a number of rhetorical devices (this by no means constitutes a criticism: I return to this below). We might note the simplicity and forcefulness of the opening sentence, which commands the reader's assent partly by suggesting that reader and writer will be at one in what they identify as 'inappropriate practices and ideas'. The second sentence is more complex, and just as the complexity builds towards the end it is cut short by the brevity of the assertion that not to act freely is to act non-morally. Something similar occurs in the fourth sentence, which ends 'out of the schools'. The next sentence contains a near-classic tricolon, 'therapy, drugs and counselling', any sense of glibness counteracted by avoiding the common device of having the terms increase in number of syllables (such as 'friends, Romans, countrymen'). The long sentence beginning 'Developmental theories' makes sophisticated points almost in passing: for example that it makes no sense to think of human beings as purely physical beings ('with brains but without minds'), and that the supposedly 'natural stages of development' are not natural and are therefore not inevitable at all. The reader is here treated with respect, as one on whom these sketches of important theoretical ideas will not be wasted, and for whom the long and fairly demanding sentence in which they are set will not present an obstacle. The final sentence, when read aloud or vocalised internally, invites the inclusion of pauses, of an almost Churchillian nature, depending on just how Churchillian one can be without parody: after 'Similarly', at various points up to and including 'being done', after 'true moral understanding' and 'insidious influence'. Thus the paragraph concludes with a sentence of steady and magisterial force. I do not mean to imply that the rhetorical qualities here are contrived, or even deliberate. Rather they are, I would say, simply the way language naturally falls from the pen of someone with a traditional, literary, and linguistic as well as philosophical (and in Barrow's case classical) education.

Admirable too, I would say, is the unmistakeable presence here of *argument*. I say 'unmistakeable', yet I have come across readers of philosophy written in this style who complain that they are being presented with mere assertion—readers who thus miss both the compression of complex arguments at various points (such as the distinction Barrow makes between minds and brains) and the implicit invitation here to join in the discussion, to respond, to argue back. How different this is from what one might call the standard academic journal article on any aspect of education, where the writer cannot make the most banal point without supporting it with a string of citations. Barrow offers no detailed citations (although Kant, Hume, and Mill are mentioned in passing, and Plato makes several appearances), and there is thus no list of references at the end. It is interesting to imagine the reaction of those refereeing for a standard academic journal. Barrow—would they perceive this?—has the courage to speak for himself, and we readers are implicitly invited to lay aside the devices by which we insulate ourselves from the uncomfortable business of engaging face-to-face, as it were, with an intelligent human being in argument about things that matter, and speak for ourselves in turn. We encounter someone with a profound concern for education, and stand to be educated by him.

This point about the absence of citation and reference is worth developing a little. Nicholas Burbules (2012, np) and others have argued that the academic conventions of citation carry particular and substantial implications for how we think of knowledge. For example, one of the standard functions of citation is to refer to an empirical study that sets out certain facts or at least what are claimed to be facts. If, say, in writing an article on equality in education I were to note that more equal societies do better for all their citizens on a range of indicators (better educational outcomes, less crime, greater mutual trust . . .), it would be natural to cite Wilkinson and Pickett's book, *The Spirit Level* (2009). However particular styles of citation, notably APA (American Psychological Association), which employ name of author(s) and date, 'become in standard use the documentation of a fact . . . such usage reinforces the idea that research is about the examination and testing of empirical claims, and that citation is a process of buttressing those claims through referencing supporting studies' (Burbules). The citation of name and date even becomes identified with the familiar claim or fact that it is supposed to support, as is the case with Wilkinson and Pickett above. When we also see that the APA manual sets out how a research article should be formatted (Literature Review, Methods, Results, Discussion) it is clear that research which follows these conventions is being conceived essentially as empirical, even quasi-psychological, rather than as philosophical, conceptual, or, as I want to say, argumentative and thoughtful. The discovery and reporting of facts and correlations has become hegemonic.

Thus Barrow's style here (and in a good deal of his other published writings) is not a side issue. It is of a piece with his commitment to thoughtful argument. It constitutes an act of resistance to the increasing assumption that educational research that is not empirical is not really research. That assumption is steadily making itself at home, both in Anglophone universities and elsewhere. A colleague in a British university (not my own), a philosopher of education, heard his specialism described by his head of department at a departmental meeting as 'Alchemy, or whatever it is you do.' Another colleague in a different university was told by one of his department's 'managers' that his philosophical research was 'hobby research'. From a third university again, this time not a philosopher of education but a philosophically inclined social scientist, being interviewed for a professorship, was asked by the chair of the Appointing Committee: 'You have told us all about your ideas and theories. Now what about actual research?' No doubt there are other factors at work here: for instance it is rare for philosophical research to attract external funding, while this is relatively easy for even the most banal empirically based educational research projects. Funding can be measured and becomes a proxy for quality. Psychology always looks as if it is bound to be at least relevant, and probably important, to education, even if its claims do not always survive critical scrutiny. Much more could be said about all this. Barrow himself has of course developed some of these points in his 1984 book, *Giving Teaching Back to Teachers*.

Finally, in the extract above I admire Barrow's steady assertion that there is such a thing as 'true moral understanding', which I read less as part of a strategy to discover some Platonic Form, valid for all time, than as the insistence that for the things we value—education, justice, equality, and friendship, for example—it is an endless and vital undertaking to distinguish the true from the false, the genuine from the fake, the false from the spurious. I called this above a 'classical' move, in the context of Barrow's distinction between true moral education and practices which only pretend or seem to be that. In the *Gorgias* Plato has Socrates investigate what Holland (1980, pp. 33–34) calls 'the problem of spurious semblances, of the difference between worthwhile pursuits and their time-serving substitutes'. For Plato (or Socrates: certainly for the 'Socrates' of the *Gorgias*) the difference is between *dialektiké*, which is, roughly, philosophy understood as an educational practice, and mere rhetoric, or persuasive speech making. The latter is nothing more than snake oil, an appeal—like certain forms of cookery—to what people like or can be got to like rather than to what is good for them.

> The reason why rhetoric could not be a form of education was that it had nothing to do with knowledge, and the reason why it had nothing to do with knowledge was that it involved no criticism of received opinions, no putting of statements to the test, no insistence that an account

be given of the nature of anything, no sifting the true from the false or distinguishing reality from appearance. Instead, success was its sole concern and efficacy its standard of excellence. (ibid., p. 19)

This seems to me to catch the philosophical spirit of Robin Barrow as it runs through everything he has written. And how we need this kind of philosophical spirit in our time, as we always need it! The mark of a good school now, it seems, is that the children pass the tests and the school passes its inspection: success and efficacy are the sole standard of excellence, which is understood mainly or entirely as what moves it up the league tables. Undergraduate students of education and other students of social science in their first year are generally astonished—and usually delighted—to discover in my classes that education has from time to time been theorised in more exalted terms, as the widening of horizons, as the expanding of the mind, as learning to speak the Oakeshottian 'conversations of mankind'. Even as they learn this, however, their degree courses are being rewritten to reduce the demand that students acquire knowledge or criticise received opinions (to echo Holland's words above), including their own existing opinions: this is being done to make their courses easier, in the hope of better results in the National Student Satisfaction Survey. Universities in England are now becoming funded according to market principles, and accordingly sell themselves with videos in which young people leer at each other as they stroll across the thoroughly modern campus—just a little ivy and Georgian brickwork to add a touch of class—between coffee shops and up-to-the-minute IT facilities. In the market appearance *is* reality if it brings in the consumers, since the market admits no other criterion of quality than what appeals and can be sold. And since they are now consumers students must naturally be given what they want rather than what is good for them, their received opinions pandered to and flattered. This is to be the fate of the university. We should pause to register this extraordinary development. The university, generally until now thought of as a place dedicated to the pursuit and testing of knowledge, of 'putting of statements to the test' (Holland's words again), and still in the view of many one of the few places left among the beleaguered public services of England dedicated to 'sifting the true from the false or distinguishing reality from appearance', is apparently to give its customers what they want, as if it was just one more commercial outlet dealing in boutique clothing or electronic gadgets.

This is one reason why philosophy, and Barrow's way of doing philosophy, still matter.

CLARITY AND OTHER VIRTUES

The purpose of this second section is not to offer substantial criticisms of Barrow's way of doing philosophy, as if to balance the appreciation expressed in the first section. What is admirable in it is still to be admired. The purpose is rather to ask if the strengths of analytic philosophy, both in general and in the case of Robin's preferred version of it, cannot be achieved without drawbacks and limitations, just as there cannot be light without shadow. We might start with the idea of clarity. The demand for clarity is one corollary of the analytic philosopher's commitment to doing away with muddle, and Barrow names clarity as first among 'the criteria that govern the quality of a concept' (1999, p. 427), and thus by implication as foremost among the aims of conceptual analysis. I can see nothing to be said for muddle. However the idea of clarity is not as straightforward as it may seem, and repays investigation (repays philosophical analysis, one might say).

First, it is not always noticed that talk of clarity is metaphorical. In the case of water, from which the metaphor appears to derive, clarity consists in the fact that you can see through the water to rocks and fish below the surface, or to the coral beneath the surface of the sea. Thus clear language enables you to see down to the realities beneath. The clarity of the sentence 'the earth goes round the sun' lies in the way it allows you access to the truth that the earth does indeed go round the sun, that of the sentence 'Kennedy was assassinated in Dallas in 1963' similarly (though the reality of assassination as opposed to, say, simple murder makes for complications). Things become more difficult, though, with 'Today is Monday'. There is no such thing as a Monday, lurking beneath the limpid water. That today is Monday seems instead to be a matter of it being neither Sunday nor Tuesday nor any other of the days of the week. This simple point lies behind the idea that the meaning of language is constituted less by its accurate representation of how things are down there under the water than by systems of difference. Meaning and truth are, at least in significant part, a function less of the relationship between language and anything else, such as the submarine 'reality', than of the endless and shifting web of language itself. If it is true that Kennedy was *assassinated*, rather than simply *shot*, this is a matter of what the dictionary tells us about how the verb 'to assassinate' is used—it is used in the case of the illicit killing of statesmen and political leaders—and cannot be read off from some notional ideal video of 'the events themselves'. (It is often noted that a dictionary offers an excellent image of how language has meaning: in an endless web where each definition consists of words, to be looked up where necessary in other parts of the dictionary.) Some of course go so far as to complain that simplistic ideas of clarity are used to *fix* meaning: that the apparently unobjectionable securing of stability through the metaphor of seeing through the water to things that are as surely there, as are the fish and the coral, has a way of turning into a different kind of fix—in which meanings are nailed down in the way it suits particular power groups. (We might think of the difference between 'Mau Mau terrorists killed many Kenyans and British settlers in the 1950s' and the same sentence with 'freedom fighters' replacing 'terrorists'. Of course 'British settlers' could be put differently too.)

The commitment to clarity has one particular and odd consequence. From its origins in logical positivism there seems to come the idea that language that is clear will be language of a certain kind. It turns its back against the figurative and the metaphorical, as I noted above—or it thinks it does, in the case of 'clarity'—and prefers what it thinks of as a plain and unadorned style. In doing this it frequently adopts the language and style of science, as if the best language for philosophical analysis was the language of a scientific report. Two examples from texts on the philosophy of education will help to make the point. In the first the writer is distinguishing love from other emotions, including hate:

> The evaluations made by a man P who hates his neighbour Q are such as these: 1. He wants to avoid Q; he wishes to see him come to grief; when he meets him, he has an inclination to say rude things to him—and so on. And he does so, normally, because 2. He thinks or knows or assumes—i.e. apprehends—that Q has done something which P considers to be evil against him, or that Q as what P seems to be a despicable character, or something of the sort . . . (Pitcher 1972, p. 383)

In the second example the writer is analysing the concept of teaching.

> Even though teaching may not be intentional, we have argued that an important point of being able to say that B was taught *X* by A is to locate responsibility for B's learning *X*. To say, 'No one taught *X to* B', is either to deny that anyone is to be held responsible for B's learning *X*, or perhaps to suggest that B taught him/herself and is the only one to be held responsible. (Kleinig 1982, p. 29)

To repeat: if the opposite of clarity is muddle and confusion then the value of clarity is self-evident (clear, one might say). But clarity all too readily becomes fetishised and one result of this is the adoption of a particular kind of writing style, an adoption which is not always conscious. It is typical of this style to aim for the elimination of metaphor, and to value what its adherents seem to think of as a tough-minded use of argumentation that imitates the unadorned style in which a scientific experiment might be written up and its results expressed. Here we might recall that another of the roots of analytic philosophy lies in the attempt undertaken by such philosophers as Frege and Russell to create an ideal notation that would free thought from the grip of ordinary language and the confusions to which it is prone. One outcome of this project, however, which is now widely regarded as having been ill-conceived, is the residue in the writings of analytic philosophers of quasi-scientific prose in which unacknowledged metaphors from mathematics and algebra are perhaps the most vivid evidence that a particular kind of rhetoric has made itself at home.[1] These roots go deep: they can be traced back without difficulty at least as far as Descartes, for whom geometry supplied the model that all sound knowledge should aspire to, on the grounds that it attains the highest degree of certainty.

Along with this yearning for the tropes of science and mathematics analytic philosophers, especially those working in the field of education, are prone to a further commitment, tending at times to approach the status of dogma. This is to regard philosophical analysis as a body of skills and techniques, which can be brought to bear on statements and arguments from a wide range of literature, even where the philosopher is not particularly knowledgeable about the specific subject matter. Category mistakes, for instance, such as moving incautiously between talk of the mind and talk of the brain (see above), can often be identified in the writings of neuroscientists and sociobiologists. The fallacy of moving between claims about what is empirically the case and non-empirical claims about what *must be* the case can be found in much recent work on happiness and well-being. (Typical claims might be: 'Here are some of the things that make people happy: a sense of belonging, sufficient income to live on, opportunities for exercise and play . . . if this woman commits herself to writing a novel in a garret, half-starved and in isolation, or this man risks his life to work among lepers, it *must be* because it makes them happy.') When British philosophy of education was at what some regard as its acme, some thirty years ago, conferences seemed to be patrolled by philosophers in search of such fallacies, eager to pounce on an incautious naturalistic fallacy (the so-called fallacy of deriving an 'ought' from an 'is': even then not obviously fallacious: see e.g., Frankena 1939) or on a case of 'because it is trivially true it must be importantly true' (for instance, the idea that because it is true that children enjoy play therefore the whole of the curriculum should be based on play).

These are indeed fallacies and there are others, and people were right to draw attention to them. But there was one particularly unfortunate result of the fetishising of analytic philosophy in this style. The first was that it became seen in many quarters as an almost exclusively destructive discipline, putting forward no substantial theses of its own but concentrating on mounting a critique of the efforts of others. In this it was in many respects again the natural heir of earlier philosophy. Here is Wittgenstein, writing in the *Tractatus* (§ 6.53), whose decimal notation exemplifies the other legacy I noted above:

> The right method of philosophy would be this: To say nothing except what can be said, *i.e.* the propositions of natural science, *i.e.* something that has nothing to do with philosophy: and then always, when someone else wished to say something metaphysical, to demonstrate to him that he had given no meaning to certain signs in his propositions. This method would be unsatisfying to the other—he would not have the feeling that we were teaching him philosophy—but it would be the only strictly correct method.

A short example from Barrow himself, who is in my view usually one of the least of the offenders in this respect, will serve as an illustration. Here he is, in his critique of 'postmodernism', complaining that Jean-Francois Lyotard 'regards postmodernism as a theory that involves "an incredulity towards meta-narratives"' (Barrow 1999, p. 419; it is noticeable that this is the only place in the entire article where Barrow actually quotes one of the 'postmodernists' that he takes issue with). The problem here, Barrow thinks, is that 'since, in his [Lyotard's] terms, "meta-narrative" is a synonym for "theory" and "incredulity" a *soi-disant* phrase for "denial"', this means that this is a theory that denies theory.' But an attentive reading of Lyotard's text reveals that metanarrative is not a synonym for theory in general. Metanarratives are those over-arching ideas (hence 'meta') that emerged from the Enlightenment and that we in the west have largely taken for granted: progress, capitalism, the emancipation of the human spirit, and the hegemony of science and scientific knowledge. Incidentally, 'incredulity' is not a synonym or elegant variation for 'denial'. 'Incredulity' registers what Lyotard thinks we experience as the continual pull of these metanarratives even as we begin to lose our faith in, say, capitalism (even if Lyotard did not live to see the financial crises of recent years) or worry that the consequences of trying to export western notions of progress to the developing world have been mixed. To convict Lyotard of crudely asserting the equivalent of *p* and *not-p* is too simple and altogether too quick.

Many of the reservations I have expressed here about analytic philosophy can be brought together by observing that the analytic philosopher usually makes a sharp distinction between philosophy and other forms of writing, particularly rhetoric. There is, it is generally supposed, excellent warrant for this in Plato, who often represents Socrates as mounting a critique of rhetoric, in the person for instance of Lysias (in the *Phaedrus*) and Gorgias in the dialogue that bears his name (as noted above). Yet in the *Gorgias* Socrates observes a distinction between good rhetoric and bad. In the *Protagoras* Socrates says that Protagoras would justly make the kinds of criticism of him that he commonly makes of the sophists, the travelling salesman, as we have been taught to think of them, of the skills and tricks of rhetoric in classical Greece. The distinction between philosophy (hard-edged, rigorous, 'scientific' in its language) and more figurative forms of language, tending towards poetry at one extreme, is however hard to maintain in the face of the extended poetic passages and rhapsodic myths of the *Republic* (the myth of Er, and the analogies of Sun, Cave, and Divided Line, are two of the more obvious examples) or of parts of, say, the *Phaedrus* (the story of the cicadas, the analogy of the charioteer, the story of Theuth and the invention of writing).

I have written elsewhere (Smith 2008) about the extreme difficulty of giving any coherent account of the distinction between rhetoric and philosophy, and of the contradictions into which those philosophers who have addressed the subject tend to fall. Collingwood, for instance, writes that the philosopher should adopt a 'plain and modest' style, while at the same time he praises 'the classical elegance of Descartes, the lapidary phrases of Spinoza, the tortured metaphor-ridden periods of Hegel' (1933, p. 213). In one remarkable passage, which I also quoted in my 2008 paper, he writes:

> The principles on which the philosopher uses language are those of poetry; but what he writes is not poetry but prose. From the point of view of literary form, this means that whereas the poet yields himself to every suggestion that his language makes, and so produces word-patterns whose beauty is a sufficient reason for their existence, the philosopher's word-patterns are constructed only to reveal the thought which they express, and are valuable not in themselves but as a means to that end. The prose-writer's art is an art that must conceal itself, and produce not a jewel that is looked at for its own beauty but a crystal in whose depths the thought can be seen without distortion or confusion; and the philosophical writer in especial follows the trade not of a jeweller but of a lens-grinder. He must never use metaphors or imagery in such a way that they attract to themselves the attention due to his thought; if he does that he is writing not prose, but, whether well or ill, poetry; but he must avoid this not by rejecting all use of metaphors and imagery, but by using them, poetic things themselves, in the domestication of prose: using them just so far as to reveal thought, and no further. (ibid., pp. 214–215)

The paradox of writing about the philosopher as jeweller or lens-grinder, while at the same time declaring that the philosopher 'must never use metaphors or imagery in such a way that they attract to themselves the attention due to his thought' is obvious enough. To bring this chapter round to one of the points with which I began it (in itself a familiar enough rhetorical device), Collingwood seems to be undone here by an ambition to separate language from thought, to distinguish writing philosophy from thinking it, explicitly referring to the search for a 'principle which must be followed in learning to write philosophy, as distinct from learning to think it' (1933, p. 213), in his commitment to the idea of a language that reveals thought rather than distorting it—as if there could be philosophical thought independently of language.

It should be clear now why I wrote above that to identify and describe Barrow's *rhetoric* does not imply criticism. Far from it: all philosophical writing is rhetorical, in the sense that I have been using this word here, and Barrow's rhetorical style—his writerly style, for those still uncomfortable with the idea of rhetoric—bears favourable comparison with many writers in the twentieth-century analytic tradition, whether they write about education or other topics. A degree of self-consciousness of this on Barrow's part might well have formed an obstruction in the deep well of fluent, classical prose that distinguishes him. On the other hand it might have given him more sympathy with writers in a different tradition, such as Jacques Derrida and Jean-François Lyotard, who have embraced this point with enthusiasm: who have released their readers a little to use language, as they do, with a degree of playfulness and irony that is itself a challenge to many of the current educational tendencies that Barrow would no doubt repudiate—the prevalence of the language of economics and neo-liberalism, the assumption that all good educational research will be 'scientific', and the substitution of the demands of performativity for serious thought about the proper ends of education.

NOTES

1. Barrow's writings are for the most part refreshingly free of this tendency. There are just a few examples in some of his earlier works, e.g., Barrow (1976), pp. 70–71, 82.

REFERENCES

Barrow, R. (1976) *Common Sense and the Curriculum*, London: Allen & Unwin.
———. (1984) *Giving Teaching Back to Teachers: A Critical Introduction to Curriculum Theory*, Sussex: Wheatsheaf.
———. (1999) 'The Need for Philosophical Analysis in a Postmodern Era', *Interchange* 30(4), pp. 415–432.
———. (2006) 'Moral Education's Modest Agenda', *Ethics and Education* 1(1), pp. 3–13.
Burbules, N. (2012) 'The Paradigmatic Differences between Name/Date and Footnote Styles of Citation', *Vlaanderen Fund for Scientific Research: Philosophy and History of the Discipline of Education—Evaluation and Evolution of the Criteria for Educational Research*, Leuven, Belgium, November 2012.
Collingwood, R. G. (1933) *An Essay on Philosophical Method*, Oxford: Clarendon Press.
Frankena, W. (1939) 'The Naturalistic Fallacy', Mind 48, pp. 464–477.
Holland, R. F. (1980) *Against Empiricism: On Education, Epistemology and Value*, Oxford: Blackwell.
Kleinig, J. (1982) *Philosophical Issues in Education*, London: Croom Helm.
Pitcher, G. (1972) 'Emotion', in *Education and the Development of Reason*, ed. R. Dearden, P. Hirst and R. S. Peters, London: Routledge & Kegan Paul.
Smith, R. (2008) 'To School with the Poets: Philosophy, Method and Clarity', *Paedogogica Historica* 44(6), pp. 635–645.
Wilkinson, R. and K. Pickett (2009) *The Spirit Level: Why More Equal Societies Almost Always Do Better*, London: Allen Lane.
Wittgenstein, L. (1963) *Tractatus Logico-Philosophicus*, London: Routledge & Kegan Paul.

2 Barrow, Utilitarianism, and Education

John Gingell

Since Robin Barrow's first book in the philosophy of education, *Plato, Utilitarianism and Education* (Barrow 1975), he has consistently defended a Utilitarian approach to educational problems. The upper case is, I think, important here. A quick trawl of the Internet under 'utilitarianism and education' reveals a large number of people who believe that this type of education is designed to provide an education which has as its main aim the production of people who can contribute directly to the, largely, economic activities of our society. Such an education would, it is feared, downgrade, or completely ignore, the study of such things as literature and history because these things have no obvious economic outcomes and promote vocational and technical subjects which seem to be geared to such economic ends. I have no doubt that there may be people who think that the role of education is simply to service the economic activities of our society (indeed one of the contributors to this book, David Carr, includes in his sections on philosophical and educational schools of thought exactly such a view (Carr, this volume)), but Barrow is not of this ilk. Indeed, Barrow in *Giving Teaching Back to Teachers* (Barrow 1984, Ch. 4, Sec. 2) says of this idea, 'A view that will not die, although it has been killed more often than it knows, is that the solution to the problem of establishing a worthwhile curriculum lies in seeking out content that is useful or relevant' (p. 76) before killing this idea once again. And in *Common Sense and the Curriculum* (Barrow 1976, Ch. 3, Sec. 2) he spends some time attacking, to my thinking, completely successfully, Macintyre's interpretation of Utilitarian educational thought along such lines. Barrow's actual position, both on Utilitarianism and on its relevance to education, is neatly summed up in the same chapter:

> Utilitarianism, in the sense that I intend, is grounded in the premise that what matters ideally is a world in which everyone is happy, that is to say a world in which people are not depressed, anxious, alienated, frustrated, burdened by a sense of guilt or inadequacy, bored, angry or, more generally, miserable. What matters in practice, therefore, is the attempt by a community to minimise such states of mind as these, which are logically

incompatible with happiness, by such means that are available. The question of the moral acceptability of various possible means is likewise judged by reference to the ideal of happiness. The two most obvious and potent means of striving towards the ideal are the formulation of rules of conduct and the provision of a suitable education. Education should seek to develop individuals in such a way that they are in a position to gain happiness for themselves, while contributing to the happiness of others, in a social setting that is designed to maintain and promote the happiness of all so far as possible.[1] (1976, p. 86)

On the back of this central idea, Barrow goes on to develop a curriculum for all which includes: health training and education, moral training, numeracy, and literacy in the Primary stage; natural sciences, mathematics, religion, fine arts, history, and literature in the Secondary stage (with the last two carrying on in the next stage); vocational and social studies and various options in the Tertiary stage; and philosophy in the Quaternary stage. Whilst one might wonder about the details and the emphasis of this curriculum—I, for instance, was critical of Barrow's later attempt to defend his emphasis on literature and history in terms of the development of intelligence (see Gingell and Brandon 2001, Ch. 5, section on Intelligence)—no one in their right mind could think that Barrow's work on the curriculum is simply an account of the economic uses for education or schooling. However, although it is a common, but important, mistake to confuse Utilitarianism as Barrow spells it out with a narrow idea of economic utility, it is also the case that Barrow's use of Utilitarian theory to examine the practices of education, for example, the curriculum and the general practices of schooling, provides him with an important advantage over some of the other theories that have been applied to education. Utilitarianism is, as Barrow makes clear, a general theory of social, economic, and individual value. As such it can question any and all of the practices and institutions of a given society—or, indeed, of a given world order—in terms of their propensity to produce happiness—or, decrease misery—and commend those that do such things and condemn those that do not. Thus, any thoughts that Utilitarians have on education must, or should be, located within this nexus of social value. So questions about our system of education are, of necessity, located within a web of value that can be applied to our society as such. That is, that educational questions are simply part of a consideration of our values in general, whether these be applied to individuals or social and political matters. And that this gives such a theory advantage can be seen by considering some of the alternative educational theories that have been on offer.

Without doubt the dominant theory of educational philosophy when *Common Sense and the Curriculum* was published was that associated with the work of Richard Peters. In his enormously influential book *Ethics and Education* (1966), and for many years following, Peters argued that 'education' in its full sense was to be distinguished by three complex criteria. First, that 'education', in this sense, has a necessary implication that something valuable or worthwhile is going on. There may be secondary senses, for example, an anthropological sense where we refer to, say, 'Spartan education', or a sense in which we wish to repudiate a certain set of practices, as when we say, 'he had a rotten education', where the term does not involve commendation, but in its primary sense it must; it would, argued Peters, involve a contradiction to say that someone had been educated but had not changed for the better. But this value that Peters sees as necessarily involved in education must not be thought of as instrumentally connected to the practices of education. Education is not valuable because it leads to some valuable end, for example, getting a good job or becoming happy, it is valuable in and for itself. The second criterion for 'education' was that it must involve the acquisition of a body of knowledge and understanding which surpasses mere skill, know-how, or the collection of information. Such knowledge and understanding must involve the principles which underlie skills, procedural knowledge, and information, and must transform the life of the person being educated both in terms of his general outlook and in terms of his becoming committed to the standards inherent in the areas of his education. He must also develop a cognitive perspective whereby the learning of any specialism, for example, in science or maths, is seen in the context of the place of this specialism in a coherent view of life in general. Third, the processes of education must involve an understanding of what is being learned and what is required for such learning so, for instance, it could not be the result of indoctrination or conditioning, and must involve some minimal voluntary participation in such processes.

The world of the educated person, according to Peters, has cognition at its heart—although he makes it clear that he sees such cognition as having links to such things as character development and the emotions—but it is also a public world, for the structures of cognition are, by and large, those structures of thought and awareness which are contained within modes of thought such as science, history, mathematics, and aesthetic awareness which the person being educated inherits from past ages. And it is within this world of thought that the question of worthwhile-ness which is raised by Peters's first criterion gets answered. There, Peters drew a distinction between activities that are extrinsically worthwhile, that is, valuable because they lead to some other valuable end, and those that are intrinsically worthwhile, that is, valuable in and for themselves, with education securely tied to the latter. But it also turns out, according to Peters, that such activities can be justified as 'educational' activities because it is only in the context of activities such as science, literary appreciation, history, and philosophy that the question of the justification of educational activities can be asked and answered. Thus Peters's ultimate argument for the content of education is a transcendental deduction from those pursuits and activities which, according to him, must be presupposed in asking and answering the question 'Why do this rather

than that?'—for example, those activities presupposed by the process of justification as such. Peters was not the only philosopher of education to propose that education was made up of intrinsically worthwhile activities; the
same conclusion, with rather different arguments, was proposed by Hirst
(1965) and White (1973). All such attempted justifications of education face
at least two significant problems when compared to Barrow's Utilitarianism.
First, the arguments of all of these theorists regarding the intrinsic worthwhile-ness of education seem weaker than Barrow's notion that happiness
is the only thing that is intrinsically worthwhile. Can we, as Peters claims,
only reach such a conclusion from the asking for justification situated within
certain precise activities? What if nobody asks the question? Does this mean
that a justification cannot be offered? Second, and more importantly, one
of the things that Barrow takes into account but these other theorists seem
to ignore is that education is a vast set of enterprises within a society, and
it has to be paid for. Even if education was intrinsically worthwhile why
would this intrinsic worthwhile-ness be something that a modern state had
to raise taxes to pay for? There may be plenty of things that are intrinsically
worthwhile, sexual pleasure, the contemplation of beautiful objects, a decent
national football side, and so on, which we certainly wouldn't expect to be
funded by the state.

So, Barrow's Utilitarian approach has at least as much going for it as
alternative approaches suggested at the same time. What is really needed
are not such complete alternatives but rather an approach that takes
Utilitarianism seriously and thinks it is lacking with regard to education.
Finding such an approach is difficult largely, I suspect, because for most
people—but not most philosophers of education—Utilitarianism provides
a default position with regard to education, that is, they do want to ask
what the activities of education are for, and some account which is couched
in individual and societal happiness would provide a reasonable answer.
However, there is at least one theorist who does satisfy the above require-
ment, and this is Amy Gutmann in 'What's the Use of Going to School?
The Problem of Education in Utilitarianism and Rights Theories' (1982).
Gutmann raises what she takes to be a central problem for Utilitarianism and education and then suggests an alternative approach to education
based on Rights Theory, which avoids this problem. The central problem,
according to Gutmann, is that Utilitarianism must assume that happiness
has to be subjectively defined for each individual. Given this how is it possible for society to prepare children for the pursuit of their own, self-defined
happiness in advance of their having defined it? But, in making this move,
Gutmann seems to be running together at least three different points. It is
certainly not the case that Utilitarians believe that the definition of 'happiness' is subjectively defined. They assume as with any word in a public
language that there is a common meaning roughly shared and understood
by competent users of the language. If this was not the case such concepts
would be unusable. Modern Utilitarians tend to define 'happiness' in terms

of desire or preference satisfaction, that someone is happier to the extent that more of their strongest desires are satisfied. Such a definition may be open to challenge, but such a challenge needs to be fully spelt out, and this is something Gutmann never does. Most relevantly this is not a subjective definition in Gutmann's sense. However, Utilitarians may assume that people are made happy by different things, for example, your happiness may depend upon lying in the sun all day, but such an activity would bore me rigid. But one must not assume, given this degree of subjectivity, that there are not things in general that contribute to the happiness of most people. Moreover, neither can we assume that we lack reliable empirical evidence about what these things are. Of course, such generalisations will not necessarily capture everybody, but who for a moment thought that they would? So for instance, it may be the case that some people are not unhappy being ill, badly fed, badly housed, and inadequately entertained. For most people however, such things would be detrimental to their happiness. But if this is so then it seems perfectly possible for Utilitarianism to suggest a content and manner of education which is likely to promote the future happiness of the children being educated. It might be the case, for instance, that some people would be happier being uneducated, in a society where most are educated, than they would be if they had been subjected to the rigors of education. The notion of, for instance, the illiterate, non-numerate but happy person involves no contradiction as anyone who has seen *Forrest Gump* will know. But the likelihood is that such lacks would—and typically do—leave people unhappy. Ignorance, for most people, is not bliss. So, Barrow's suggestions for a Utilitarian curriculum seem perfectly reasonable. Of course, the details may need arguing through—as there are arguments at the moment for the relative places of, say, foreign languages and history in the English curriculum—but, contrary to Gutmann, the subjectivity she alleges does not, and cannot, undermine the reasonableness of the task itself.

One of Gutmann's secondary points is that Utilitarianism may produce an illiberal and conservative approach to education because according to her the Utilitarian educates children for the way that society is now. But with some of her strictures concerning this, for instance, the notion that education might help to contribute to an individual's capacity for profit-yielding employment and the admission into good company, it is very hard to imagine a society in which such things would not be part of most people's happiness or well-being. Her general point however is easily met. Of course our education system has to deal with society as it is at the moment and will vary according to that society. But, if such a society were to change then there is no reason why education cannot follow such changes. There is likely to be a time lag here, but such a lag simply reflects the vast institutional nature of education in the developed world. Consider, for example, the advances over the last fifteen years of information technology and the ways that such advances have been incorporated within the schooling system in England.

Gutmann's preferred approach to education, based on Rights Theory, is an 'education for freedom'. Her questions are 'does freedom provide a better standard than happiness by which to determine what and how to teach children?' and 'can one derive from the standard of freedom an educational programme that remains neutral among conceptions of the good life?'. For Gutmann,

> Rights Theorists need only determine whether education expands or contracts the opportunities children will have for rational choice in the future. This objective criterion is easier to apply in practice because it does not depend upon a difficult counter-factual assessment of future states of mind: how much happier or sadder would they have been were they uneducated? (Gutmann 1982, p. 268)

But what Gutmann implicitly presents here is a false dichotomy. It is simply not the case that one has to have Utilitarianism or freedom. That Utilitarianism rules out any form of political, or educational, liberalism is false. Indeed in some versions of Utilitarianism, most notably associated with the John Stuart Mill of *On Liberty* (1974), freedom is either a part of, or a necessary means to, happiness, and it is not at all difficult to see why this should be so. If, as Mill seems to argue in *On Liberty*, the happiness of the individual, and of society, generally depends upon free choice, then Utilitarianism must promote such freedom to choose. One of the main themes of philosophy of education in the last twenty years has been the notion that education should contribute to the learner's autonomy, and this is surely a theme that Barrow could easily endorse. There may be again arguments concerning what such autonomy involves (see, e.g., Gingell and Winch 2004, Ch. 7) but the place of rational choice within an overall Utilitarian conception of education seems easy to defend. Gutmann raises the problem of Old Order Amish children in this connection. Her contention is that such children, who may, in line with their parents' wishes, be denied a secondary education, very likely will end up happier than if such an education was forced upon them. However, as she points out, education is not to be promoted for the sake of satisfying the parents' wishes but rather for increasing the opportunities open to the children being educated. It very well might be the case that some children brought up to be ignorant may be as happy in their future lives as those offered a full education. But this is unlikely to be common, and if, as Mill contends, one's personal happiness depends upon satisfying the conditions for rational personal choice, for example, a significant degree of knowledge concerning the options open to one and a degree of rationality which enables one to choose between such options, then a Utilitarian commitment to ensuring that all children have the possibility of reaching such a stage seems reasonable. After all, it might very well be the case in some circumstances that children indoctrinated to have certain beliefs and desires *might* achieve happiness in later life, but this would not be an argument for indoctrination, much less an argument for indoctrination as general policy, and certainly would not be a function of any reasonable Utilitarian prescription for education.

There are problems here which have been pointed out by Ernest Gellner (1964). For as society moves away from a situation in which people's basic wants, for example, for health, freedom, food, shelter, etc. are unsatisfied, it also moves towards a situation where in educational terms we are creating the desires that need to be satisfied rather than merely teaching people how to satisfy those basic wants. But, if this is the case then an education that emphasises the freedom that we talked of above and the type of enculturalisation that is implicit in Barrow's curriculum is certainly defensible. So, for example, being taught, as far as possible, to enjoy the arts and literature seems to raise the possibility of happiness in a way, given our present society, that incurs few costs for oneself and is unlikely to impinge on the potential of others for achieving happiness.

In the last third of her paper, when Gutmann is trying to spell out the implications of an education for freedom, she seems to realise that this alone will not do—that such an education has to come with secondary principles in order to give it any educational flesh. But, what these secondary principles do is to manufacture a situation where Gutmann's curriculum and a Utilitarian curriculum are easily compatible. It might be possible to talk of a Rights curriculum which could detach itself from Utilitarian considerations, but it can only do this if it becomes in some way educationally unacceptable. So, for instance, we can see this if we take the educational prescriptions of one of Gutmann's influences. John Rawls in *Political Liberalism* (1993) suggests some of the educational implications of his theory. He rejects an education based upon the educational promotion of liberal values and defends instead a much weaker version of education, which requires not an espousal of such values, but:

> Far less. It will ask that the children's education includes such things as the knowledge of their constitutional and civic rights so that, for example, they know that liberty of conscience exists in their society and that apostasy is not a legal crime, all this to ensure that their continued membership when they come of age is not based simply on ignorance of their basic rights or fear of punishment for offences that do not exist. Moreover, their education should also prepare them to be fully cooperating members of a society and enable them to be self-supporting; it should also encourage the political virtues so that they want to honour the fair terms of social cooperation in their relation with the rest of society. (1993, pp. 199–200)

But note, the first part of Rawls's prescription could be satisfied by a notice on the school notice board which outlines the children's basic legal rights (much in the way that factories in England used to display copies of the

Factory Act on their notice boards). However, no sensible person could think this a sufficient recommendation for education or a real way of giving the children the real experience of the possibility of choice. The awareness that Rawls talks about here may be one of the conditions for a reasonable education, but it could only fulfil this role if embodied in educational processes which stressed an active commitment to autonomy. If this is all that Gutmann means by an education for freedom, then it fails because it is hardly an education at all. However, if we look at Rawls's last sentence this is far more ambiguous and, in fact, sits ill with the first part. This seems to imply some content to education and an encouragement of the liberal virtues, which aim to produce people who value liberalism rather than simply tolerate it. The problem here is a deep one for those like Rawls and Gutmann who espouse a political and educational liberalism. Their fear is that such liberalism becomes a version of the good life rather than a neutral position which adjudicates between different conceptions of the good. But, unless children are taught to value such liberal virtues it is likely that such liberalism simply disappears, and we are left with competing and contending conceptions of what is good. In other words, such liberalism, if it is to survive must, at the very least, try to inculcate the values of choice and freedom, and therefore it must take upon itself at least some of the baggage that liberals may try to avoid. In doing so it does provide the possibility of reasonable prescriptions for education but only at the cost of losing its complete and pure neutrality, and this is what gives Utilitarianism an anchor within such a conception.

So Utilitarianism is a possible player within the game of educational thought. In Barrow's case his Utilitarianism is not explicitly spelt out in his important works, such as *Radical Education* (1978), *The Philosophy of Schooling* (1981), and *Giving Teaching Back to Teachers* (1984); however, such works, although they are not part of a defence of Utilitarianism within education, can easily be seen as compatible with such an approach. It is also the case that the version of Utilitarianism which is applied may vary from time to time. Barrow in the works cited above is explicitly defending a Benthamite approach to the problems. We have suggested that this needs to be supplemented by some of Mill's later thought but there is little wrong with this. As I said above, if such a position is to be rejected, at least in the way Gutmann *tries* to do it, then reasons must be given for its rejection and some alternative be explicitly defended.

So far I have simply argued that Utilitarianism can function as a theory applied to education. And, it might be thought that this is all a Utilitarian philosopher *qua* philosopher can properly do. But a Utilitarian educationalist can go much further than this. It is worth saying a little about the history of Utilitarianism in defence of this position. Jeremy Bentham saw his role not as simply providing a theory for others to put into use but as something that would make him the most practically benevolent person of all time. And, following this, he not only wrote about and preached the doctrine but also wanted to put it into practice by, for instance, helping to set up the Mechanics Institutes and University College London. The fame of the theory spread not simply because it was taken up by other philosophers but because it was taken up by social reformers generally who used it to drive forward the great reforming legislation, for example, concerning child labour, sanitation, housing, education, and the suffrage of the nineteenth century (Perkin 1969). It is at least arguable that what was going on here was not merely a concern for the general happiness in an abstract sense but, rather, reformers noting the types of things that made people unhappy and trying to remedy these, and we may do the same with education. Thus, even if we have with Barrow's suggestion above a defensible account of a Utilitarian curriculum, this should only be one strand of our educational concerns. As far as education in England is concerned it seems to be the case that the notion of a National Curriculum, as Barrow and others suggested, has come to be and will in some form remain. It is likely that the elements and emphasis of this will continue to be argued about. But, this now does not seem to be our main educational problem. That, as far as I am concerned, has to do with the differential outcomes for children within our educational system. For instance, it is a national disgrace, and should be seen as such, that nearly a fifth of our children leave primary school functionally illiterate and non-numerate. What this means, of course, is that for such children the notion of a secondary school national curriculum simply has little purchase. Given that they cannot access the elements of such a curriculum, for them the curriculum does not apply.

It is also the case that if we look at the progress of children throughout our secondary schools such progress has enormously different outcomes in terms of academic success rates. So, for instance, children in the best independent and state schools are more or less assured of acquiring five A-C grade GCSE passes in their final year of compulsory education. For children in the worst schools, chances of such a success are very small indeed. It is worth emphasising that the gap here is not simply a technical matter but a chasm that separates those that the education system serves well and those it serves ill. But this chasm should be unsurprising when we note what has just been said about literacy and numeracy at the end of primary education. It may seem to some, for instance, those who are at the moment talking about reintroducing a system of schooling which separates the academic children from the rest, that such results simply mirror the inherent capabilities of different children. However, there is research evidence to suggest that this is simply not the case. In a long-term research exercise targeted at children in a socially deprived area of the British Isles illiteracy has simply been eradicated (MacKay 2006). If this is possible then the differential outcomes mentioned above are not questions concerning individual aptitudes but questions concerning very profound issues of social justice. Our education system is failing a large number of our children, and in doing so affects in very important ways their possibilities for general well-being. Whether this is a strictly philosophical question may be open to debate; however, it is certainly the case that this has profound educational consequences, and as far as Barrow is an educationalist as well as a philosopher it is certainly something that he might address. No theory of the curriculum, of whatever philosophical hue, can ignore those structural features of education as it is today which may frustrate its outcomes. Therefore, there is reason to suppose that this is a proper topic for a philosophical educationalist to address.

NOTES

1. This is an early take on Utilitarianism by Barrow, but as the following paper by McNamee makes clear he changes his approach later in his career.

REFERENCES

Barrow, R. (1975) *Plato, Utilitarianism and Education*, London: Routledge & Kegan Paul.
———. (1976) *Common Sense* and *the Curriculum*, London: Allen & Unwin.
———. (1978) *Radical Education*, Oxford: Martin Robertson.
———. (1981) *The Philosophy of Schooling*, Sussex: Wheatsheaf.
———. (1984) *Giving Teaching Back to Teachers*, Sussex: Wheatsheaf.
Gingell, J. and E. Brandon (2001) *In Defence of High Culture*, Oxford: Blackwell.
Gingell, J. and C. Winch (2004) *Philosophy and Educational Policy*, London: Routledge.
Gellner, E. (1964) *Thought and Change*, London: Weidenfeld & Nicolson.
Gutmann, A. (1982) 'What's the Use of Going to School?', in *Utilitarianism and Beyond*, ed. A. Sen and B. Williams, Cambridge: Cambridge University Press.
Hirst, P. (1965) 'Liberal Education and the Nature of Knowledge', *Philosophical Analysis and Education*, ed. R. Archambault, London: Routledge & Kegan Paul.
MacKay, T. (2006) *The West Dunbartonshire Literacy Initiative,* Scotland: West Dunbartonshire Council.
Mill, J. S. (1974) *On Liberty*, first published 1859, London: Dent.
Perkin, H. (1969) *The Origins of Modern English Society, 1780–1880*, London: Routledge & Kegan Paul.
Peters, R. (1966) *Ethics and Education*, London: Allen & Unwin.
Rawls, J. (1993) *Political Liberalism*, New York: Columbia University Press.
White, J. (1973) *Towards a Compulsory Curriculum*, London: Routledge & Kegan Paul.

3   Ethical Theory, Utilitarianism, and Anti-Theory

Mike McNamee

I first met Robin Barrow when I was a graduate student, working generally in the philosophy of education and more specifically in the philosophy of physical education. The first academic conference I attended was in 1987 at the Philosophy of Education Society of Great Britain at Roehampton, London. It was clear even to a novice such as me that he was a driving force, one of the most significant at that time, within the English-speaking tradition of analytic philosophy of education. The sheer depth and quality of his corpus of scholarship before and since that first meeting maintains my faith in that early judgment.

The atmosphere of the conference, indeed the discipline, at that time was adversarial. Robin reveled in it. Not only in presenting his own liberal-utilitarian line, but in attacking, provoking, cajoling others, he brought clarity and rigour to every discussion he was part of whether in the seminar room, the main hall, or the conference bar. In addition to his philosophical acumen, Robin was both warm and intellectually generous. When he examined my doctoral thesis a few years after, he was fair, open-minded, and tough, and despite knowing he would not be inclined to concur wholly with the thesis I presented I had no misgivings about his role as opponent. I had wanted to argue, after MacIntyre, that social practices like sports can contribute to a full and valuable life and ought properly to be thought of as educational, not mere schooling as Robin had maintained (Barrow 1983, pp. 60–61). We had a solid discussion, the doctorate was awarded and we later repaired to a local hostelry to continue the discussion and range on to football, rock and roll, and life. I recall these anecdotes since, in a *fettschrift*, contributors focus on the body of work that the author has developed but less frequently on the character of the person that brought them to life. And I have always found Robin tremendously congenial company. It is, therefore, a signal pleasure to write an essay in honour of his exceptional and sustained contributions to the field of philosophy of education. And in the warmth of that friendship and admiration I shall write of him by his given name.

Despite their differences, Robin is to my mind rightly seen as the philosophical heir to Richard Peters's pioneering efforts in liberal philosophy of education. Peters's *magnum opus*, *Ethics and Education* (1966), brought together themes that have run right through Robin's lifelong scholarship, and it is his ethical posture that I wish to focus on in this chapter. There are several features of his account of ethical theorizing that I wish to critically review. Additionally I also wish to compare and contrast a radically different competitor to his theory—a broadly Wittgensteinian anti-theoretical position—which adopts a similar rejection of the practical imperatives of ethical scholarship. I want also to suggest that his account of utilitarianism is at least congenial to a position on moral authority as ethical expertise, which I believe he would recoil from. Nevertheless, I think it worth exploring in the light of his own ethical writings, which have done more than most to articulate a developed ethical posture for education and educators.

BARROW ON ETHICAL THEORY

Before discussing the relation between utilitarianism and ethical expertise it is necessary first to set out an account of how Robin conceives ethical theory. I take his definitive account to be that laid out in his *Utilitarianism: A Contemporary Statement* (1991) where he lays out and defends his account of the general terrain of ethical theory, and specifically his version of rule utilitarianism.

The landscape of ethics and philosophy has certainly changed since Robin penned his words on ethical theory. His 1991 book *Utilitarianism* finds itself between two important remarks that serve as scholarly bookends. Stephen Toulmin authored an important article in 1982, 'How Medicine Saved the Life of Ethics'. The phase of ordinary language philosophy was, in moral philosophy, notably dull. This is of course not to say there was not merit in clarifying concepts such as 'promise' or 'obligation', and so forth, merely that it seemed to fall short of the traditional philosophical aim of leading others to wisdom and indeed wise choices. Toulmin had noted how the increasing attention from the 1960s onwards to pressing ethical problems had often brought about consensus despite the varying theoretical differences of discussants to meetings such as those that brought about the Belmont Report for the protection of research participants. The rise of medical ethics in North America, at least, led McGee to write an editorial asking 'Will bioethics take the life of philosophy?' for the *American Journal of Bioethics* in 2006. There is no doubt that—in medical ethics at least—there has been a schism between applied ethics (which may or may not approach the subject, at least in part, empirically) and moral philosophy, which employs exclusively conceptual methods in the pursuit of clarificatory goals. Within the philosophy of education, moral philosophical works abound, while there is relatively little work in what might be called applied ethics.

Robin's *Utilitarianism* sits somewhere between these bookends, and firmly within the tradition of moral philosophy for education. He asserts the goal of ethical theory should be an attempt to 'explicate what in ideal circumstances would constitute right conduct, rather than as an attempt to provide unambiguous prescription for conduct in the imperfect world we inhabit.' Additionally, he articulates a second guiding premise: 'the plausibility of a particular theory is to be assessed by reference to such things as its clarity and coherence, *and not in any direct way by reference to how useful it may prove to be as a practical guide to conduct or to how it squares with our sentiments*' (1991, p. 12, emphasis added). This conception can be reasonably located within a particular phase of philosophy's self-conception for most of the twentieth century: Philosophers are neither apt nor obliged to engage directly in commentary upon the messy world of actual lives, but to systematically speculate on how things ought to go in some ideal world. Such a conception will strike contemporary readers— and I am reminded that the ink of these remarks are only two decades dry—as out of sorts with the current approach to philosophy in general and applied ethics in particular. Moreover, his remarks are certainly at odds with the significant progress Utilitarians have made in policy development and critique in such social practices as medicine and health care.

Robin is more specific about what he takes 'ethical theory' not to consist in rather than what it does comprise. It is clear that he is strongly rationalist and anti-religious in respect of ethical theory (and doubtless beyond that too). He explicitly rejects any divine command theory where God is the source of moral authority. And he rejects with equal strength the position that moral judgment and motivation rest upon human feelings and emotions. Irrespective of potential objections from theologians and virtue theorists, it is clear enough to see what he sets his face against here. Nevertheless, his remarks about ethical theories' nature and prerogatives beg certain questions as to the nature of theory and theory–practice relations in ethics and in life.

Theories, whether scientific or literary, he argues, ought not to be bound by the contingencies of life. That either theory may shatter our current preconceptions, received understandings, or prejudices bears not at all upon the satisfactoriness of the theory. Applied to our present concerns he summarizes: 'ethical theory is not to be constructed, nor therefore assessed, by *exclusive* reference to our current values and our capacity to put it into practice' (ibid., emphasis added). The qualifier, 'exclusive' is doing important work in this sentence. Note his expression of an anti-practice prejudice is not identical to his earlier remark quoted above. Moreover the remainder of his chapter is consistent with the former not the latter quotation. Who would seriously hold the position that theory was bound to, or limited—in some constitutive way - to current practice? No-one, I suspect. That an ethical theory ought not to consider in any way how human beings are in the world would be an odd position, perhaps especially odd for a utilitarian whose position is at least naturalist in one sense: what constitutes pleasure and pain, welfare and harm, is closely related to empirical and conceptual matters regarding human nature[1]. Robin writes that ethical theory is 'designed to elaborate on what is involved in acting morally. They are designed to explain in what morality consists.' And makes only the minor concession that 'while such an explanation obviously has *indirect* bearing on our capacity to act morally, it is not in itself any objection to a theory that it does not make it easy for us to exercise that capacity, or that it does not tell us clearly what to do in all conceivable situations' (1991, p. 13).

The weight of his remarks would appear only to rebut those who think that ethical theory be either deductively applied or those that think ethical theory should render decision making a direct or easy process. With respect to the first point it is true that some people will find in ethical theory a kind of comfort blanket. Faced with the exigencies that life throws up, they may resort to a theory that could be applied formulaically: take principle, add situation, decide conclusion, and act accordingly. But few who have considered ethical problems seriously are in favour of such deductivism. And many philosophers and novelists, not just Aristotelians, have thought there to be something odd about a human morality that so distinctly cuts off cognition from volition. Equally, though, it might be thought of as a criticism that an ethical theory had nothing to say about decision making, but rendering that process easy *per se* is not in itself an aim I have ever heard advocated. One might think, then, that Robin was attacking a straw man here. Certainly, many have noted the advantage of utilitarianism is that it does give fairly clear guidance regarding the basis of decision making from a moral point of view (human welfare) and the scope of those affected by it. Just as much complexity as is necessary ought to be advocated in relation to the issue involved: no more or less. Nevertheless, any defender of deontology or virtue ethics would sign up to the position that ethical living is hard and not necessarily made easier by systematic ethical reflection. So it is not clear yet how the account of ethical theory advances any particular theory, or family of theories, such as utilitarianism. Nor is it obvious that his outline advances upon a systematic generalized commonsense morality, as we shall see. After all, as William Blake remarked, 'wisdom is sold in the desolate market place where none can come to buy. . . . ' (*The Four Zoas*). One needs no ethical theory to see and feel the weight of his remark. Perhaps one needs no ethical theory at all, as Wittgensteinians and others have suggested. I shall pursue this possibility further below.

Barrow, like the English philosopher G. E. Moore nearly a hundred years before him, suggests that any attempt to analyze goodness further is in error. He accepts that it cannot so much be explained as recognized; it is the most general word of approval. As we are trained to learn to use the word yellow properly, across a wide variety of objects (and even adjectives: 'yellow-bellied') there is nothing beyond these uses that either bind them or permit further precision without a further specification. Goodness, after Aristotle, is taken by Robin to be a supervenient quality, emerging from persons, things, or states. Thus we understand the locution 'good knife', 'good husband', 'good resolution', and so on. There will be few complaints about this position. Utilitarianism being a teleological theory posits that the good has primacy over the right. And this will of course be deeply contested. What he says here is instructive beyond that particular dichotomous debate. If the act of promise keeping is right it must be because the state of affairs of promises being kept is good. This reveals not only his teleological position but also his rule-utilitarian position specifically. He adds: 'At any rate, my concern here is simply one of clarifying the use of terminology' (1991, p. 19). But of course much more is being done here than *simply* linguistic or conceptual clarification. I say 'simply' here, but it should be clear I do not take this to be a simple exercise in itself. Replacing the word with others, such as 'merely', does not really help either. One might as easily say that acts go to make states of affairs and are primary in a perfectly clear sense, but that would not cohere with his rule-utilitarian stance, for he is not committed to the goodness of every action being subject to a consequential quantification, merely that the general rule underlying the action is morally justified in terms of human goodness or welfare. Still, the aim of ethical theory being clarificatory as to ideal moral living is reinforced in his making the point about the primacy of the good over the right.

In its barest outline, what can be said of most ethical theories is this: that they offer an account of how an agent ought to live their life; that agents may typically choose what they do; that they have an appreciation of the motivating states (if one says 'reasons' here one is already going too far in one—albeit very general—direction) underlying their acts and choices, and that they are responsible for them. What is often thought to be true of modern moral theories like utilitarianism and deontology is that they are impartial, universal, and prescriptive. Robin demurs at least from the last of these widely agreed notions. What then gives ethical theory its purchase, how it delivers upon the 'oughtness' of a norm is not the prescriptivity of its principles. He writes:

> Nor are ethical theories, properly speaking, prescriptive. It is true that morality is a prescriptive domain: moral principles enjoin us to do certain things. But an ethical theory is only incidentally prescriptive, because of its subject matter. The theory itself is essentially descriptive: it explains what makes things right; it gives an account of what is the moral case. It is comparable in this respect, if no other, to medical theory, which is likewise dealing with normative concepts such as health and fitness, but which nonetheless does not in itself prescribe specific practice. (1991, pp. 24–25)

What is at stake here is twofold. First, what counts as theory in relation to ethics? Second, what is the proper way(s) of conceiving theory-practice relations? These issues far outrun the scope of a short chapter such as this but something at least can be drawn from them here.

First, it seems clear that Robin takes the idea of a theory to share persisting features whether in ethics or whether applied to his own example of medicine (1991, pp. 24–25) above, or literature and science before (1991, p. 14), or engineering (1991, p. 30). His line of approach is consistent: Theory is answerable to its own criteria and not the exigencies of life. The salient fact, with respect to present concerns, is that the qualifier 'ethical' as a prefix to 'theory' does not play a role in modifying it (i.e., the conception of theory). He does make one exception to this rule and gives clear justification for it. Robin rejects (1991, p. 31) the idea that ethical theory is like mathematical theory, since the axioms of the latter have universal acceptance unlike in moral matters. Whether this is genuinely true is a matter for philosophers of mathematics, but the idea of universal acceptance by any group of philosophers seems doubtful to me. It strikes me that any *n* of philosophers is at least likely to generate *n+1* views on any serious subject matter at hand.

He goes on then to offer criteria by which any ethical theory, *qua* theory, must aspire to and be evaluated in the light of. The criteria might as easily apply to those fields he has drawn attention to above: engineering, literature, and medicine. I quote him at length:

> What we therefore have to do is apply the tests that we apply to any conceptual question: that is, we have to judge the worth of an ethical theory by reference to the clarity and fullness with which it is explicated, its internal coherence and consistency, and its consistency with other of our rationally held beliefs with which it may come into contact. (. . .) If an ethical theory meets these requirements, then it may be said to be amenable to our rational understanding. Obviously, it may then come into conflict with our sentiments or psychological antipathy. The task of the author of an ethical theory is to force the reader to recognize, by reason, that an entirely coherent package or system that has some undeniable grounding in what he (the reader) does believe about morality is being offered. If that is the case, it may reasonably be pointed out that any remaining psychological objections are just that: psychological. They do not cohere with what has been agreed to be a coherent explication of the implications of one or more agreed starting point; it is they, the psychological objections, that should in reason be abandoned, and not the theory. (1991, p. 31)

Two messages dominate here: First there is an elevation of the rational in human nature and in particular its capacity for systematization. Second, and closely related, there is the reinforcement of a naturalistic prejudice: sentiment is seen as an obstacle to rationality. One must force others by reasons to view things aright (over against those unruly competitors: emotions, feelings, and moods). This philosophical prejudice is buttressed by the distinction between the psychological and the logical. In this posture,

Robin is following John Stuart Mill all the way down. He writes in a foot-note of the standard criticism that utilitarianism is overly demanding and out of kilter with the proclivities of human nature that, following Mill, such criticisms 'are not the fault of the theory but the fault of human beings' (1991, p. 33). Obvious cases of weakness of will notwithstanding, this line of attack is likely to strike many philosophers as, at best, unhelpful. For it would be an odd theory of human living, that it took little or no account of divergences from reality as experienced by, say, a very large number of persons. Robin qualifies Mill's position, writing that the latter had had not made it sufficiently clear that the theory is an ideal against which human conduct and character can and ought to be evaluated.

These joint features, the elevation of the power of systematizing ratio-nality and the weakness of human sensibility, are further reinforced by reference to the role of idealizing in ethical theory and distinguishing those idealizations from practice. Ethical theory is not, as he understands it, answerable to practice where practice may be understood very broadly as a sentiment, an existing code, or a religious authority. Robin does seem to make one concession at least towards application:

> Ethical theories do have crucial relevance to justified conduct in real life, which is of course why they are of pressing practical importance, but it is an indirect relationship—the theory provides the explanation of the idea to which we inadequately strive. (1991, p. 34)

Having so sharply distinguished ethical theory and practice, however, it is difficult to take seriously this claim of 'pressing practical importance' where what can (and ought) to be served up—we are repeatedly told—is an analysis of ideal action and policy. Yet Robin has never been shy of policy critique and development, nor of exhorting teachers this way and that in the face of commonsensical orthodoxy. Shibboleth busting has been one of his favourite professional pursuits, and he is undeniably skilled in the practice. Why then shy away from the kinds of normativity that might be expected of ethical theory? I am reminded of a passage in the writings of Annette Baier on the schism between applied ethics and moral philosophy:

> Can we approve of a division of labor in which the theorists keep their hands clean of real-world applications, and the ones who advise the decision makers, those who do "applied ethics", are like a con-sumer reports service, pointing out the variety of available theories and what costs and benefits each has for a serious user of it? Does the profession of moral philosophy now display that degeneration of a Kantian moral outlook that Hegel portrays, where there are beauti-ful souls doing their theoretical thing and averting their eyes from what is happening in the real world, even from what is happening in the way of "application" of their own theories, and there are those

who are paid to be the "conscience" of the medical, business or legal profession, what Hegel calls the moral *valets*, the professional moral judges? (1989, p. 37)

The import of Baier's anti-theoretical sentiments is manifold. Some who engage in applied ethics (myself included) would reject the characterization she offers of the 'ethicist'—an ugly term of art that technicizes the work of a scholar falling under its description. To be fair it is an accurate description of at least some who ply their trade thus. It is the other half of her probing that is pertinent here. Ought we to think that Robin falls under the former label: a 'beautiful soul' averting his gaze from the real world? To the extent that he insists that ethical theory is restricted to ideal-world-generated duties it seems her criticism hits the mark. But the criticism seems an odd one of a utilitarian, for that theory has attracted widespread support for its empirically minded practicality. And even critics acknowledge widely the in-principle universally applicable decision procedure for moral agents. So, on the one hand it will strike some readers as odd that Robin articulates and defends an account of ethical theory that is abstract in the sense that it is in no way answerable to the world and the messy lives of those inhabit it. On the other hand, what he schematically offers as a systematic check against egoism and caprice and so on, are the evaluative criteria of any theory viz.: clarity, coherence, parsimony, scope, and so on. Is this enough to sustain an *ethical* theory? What then of his utilitarianism?

Since Robin makes clear that he is not defending any and all accounts of utilitarianism but only his own rule-based version, it is necessary to offer a thumbnail sketch here. First, he remarks that his account is not especially detailed. Instead he wants to defend a particular account, though one whose major contours are all he will spell out. He broadly proposes that a utilitarian must aim at complete happiness based on sincere and accurate considerations 'of what overall set of acts would combine to produce complete happiness in ideal circumstances' (1991, p. 45). Happiness is taken to be the end of moral action, and cannot be explained in terms of anything more basic. Moreover, it ought to be distributed such that one would aim at a world in which everyone was completely happy. That is the ideal. And it is literally that with which the utilitarian must concern him or herself. Robin believes that by forcing the role of ethical theory generally, and utilitarianism specifically, to focus on the achievement of the ideal he can rid himself of classical problems such as how the utilitarian will seriously consider issues of the distribution of happiness and avoid simple maximization sums that might include the misery of a number of persons for the greater happiness of some larger number of persons.

And he goes to some lengths to underscore this. So, for example, when faced with uncertainty whether an act, falling under a general rule, will promote happiness he says:

The theory has to be worked out in terms of an ideal. If utilitarianism is correct, then an ideal world would be one in which everyone was completely happy. (1991, p. 45)

Nevertheless, attempting to determine this ideal in terms of formulae (e.g., the greatest happiness of the greatest number) is apparently wrongheaded:

The utilitarian should not allow himself to be driven to accepting any of these formulae as *summary statements of how one should proceed in everyday life*. (1991, p. 46, emphasis added)

Rather,

What the *theory demands* is that we assess what is right by reference to *what kinds of conduct would promote happiness in ideal circumstances*. (ibid., emphasis added)

and finally:

To repeat the main contention once more: in order to understand any ethical theory, *it is necessary to envisage* it first in *the context of an ideal world*, in a situation in which, so to speak, it works; for difficulties that arise in putting it into practice, if they arise from people's wrong conduct or from contingent difficulties in everyday life, rather than incoherence of the theory, cannot reasonably be held against the theory. (1991, pp. 46–47).

To these remarks readers may find themselves asking 'is that really what an ethical theory *must* look like?'; 'why can we not hold it against such a theory that it is too far removed from application?'; and 'is not such a theory impotent?'. Finally, and perhaps most pressing in philosophical terms, if the ethical theorist (and those who would be advised by such) are to work their way towards 'the context of an ideal world', one cannot help but ask what kind of place is this, and further whether some rather more determinate topography might be sketched out. Finally, even if Robin were inclined to make good on these queries, how could we understand the ideal as supplying a *context*? It seems rather to me that the ideal functions so as not to pick out any particular contexts.

That the two chapters I have focused on in his *Utilitarianism* carry no sustained unpacking of examples bears testimony to this final point. It appears that the only answer available is the rather thin one, 'the ideal world one in which all persons are completely happy'. Granted that the notion of an ideal world is not understood tautologically, Robin repeatedly reminds his readers that he is open-minded about his utilitarian solution, rather in the same way a good Popperian is intellectually modest about their scientific conjectures. But that hardly helps us because, as I have said, the ideal is not a *context* at all; it so radically underdetermines our starting point it cannot give us a clear target to aim towards. And part of the reason, I suggest, is that Robin has seriously underloaded ethical theorists in terms of their responsibility to pass on wisdom, just as moral educators might attempt to deepen or enrich the moral sensibilities of their pupils, and how both aim at guidance that is action guiding in some overriding normative sense (and if you do or don't [like Robin] want to call that 'prescriptive' that is fine by me).

Finally, there seems a sense in which if all one is doing is offering some, but not wholly compelling reasons, that in our actions and being we aim at bringing about an ideal world in which all are completely happy, then one wonders if the enumeration of what follows ought really to be called an ethical *theory*. And if the ends of the ideal are such, is the subsequent job of an applied ethicist—as opposed to an ethical theorist—merely to evaluate or predict the best means to that end? If and insofar as this is the case, we might ask ourselves whether ethical theorists are working only part time, and moreover whether it is the job of moral experts within utilitarianism to settle matters impartially and reliably. I suspect, however, that this picture is one that Robin is as unhappy with as I am.

AN ANTI-THEORETICAL ALTERNATIVE

A number of objections to Robin's conception of ethical theory have been touched upon in the foregoing. I cannot offer a full-blown alternative, but only consider in the light of his remarks whether some radically differing alternative might be at least as plausible. To do that, I wish to consider a broadly Wittgensteinian anti-theoretical ethics. What I want to say straight off is that this is not considered as a straightforward rebuttal of Robin's ideas since there are important similarities in their perspectives, which I shall draw out below. And there are important differences too. And one of these differences, drawn out by O'Neil (1986), is their tendency to privilege examples: to explore them in detail for their ethical import they present.

One mark of Wittgensteinian ethics[2] is the rejection of ethical theory understood in the sense of a quasi-scientific theory.[3] The early Wittgenstein, in the *Tractatus* and in the *Lecture on Ethics*, holds that there can be no systematic or truth functional theory of the good life. In the writings of the later Wittgenstein, meaning is understood as a function of use: practice has primacy in spheres of action (including speaking), not theory. And so it must be for ethics too. It would therefore follow that even if theories of ethics were constructible, they would not have authority. It would not be much of a criticism of a problem-centred ethics that its conception was practical. Wittgensteinian writing in ethics has tended to be more reflective but like Robin's ethical theorizing more removed from the task of moral problem solving.

Roy Holland to the effect that the former are "more a matter of registering an experience or marking an encounter, than passing judgement"
(Cited in Gaita, 2004, pxii). Here then is an important contrast in the
task of ethical theorizing: of registering moral experience or encounters. The spirit of these remarks are taken up by Raimond Gaita in his
book *Good and evil* where he marks out three such encounters and
registers three such experiences. They take the form of putting before
the reader ethical exemplars that speak for themselves, in the absence
of any particular theory. He says that his *modus operandi* is "a kind
of testimony" (ibid). While noting the non-neutrality of his writings,
Gaita insists that his philosophical aim is one of understanding not
instruction. He declares that his book is not intended to help readers
answer the Socratic question of how one should live:

> *Good and Evil* is not a book on practical ethics. (. . .) My primary
> aim is to *understand* those encounters and to place them in traditions
> of philosophical thought about morality and concern over the meaning
> of our lives more generally. . . . To understand what moral philosophers
> can be held morally accountable for—what kind of holding to account
> it is—even in the practice of the discipline. I will not be misunderstood,
> then, if I say that the book is resolutely and morally passionately an
> enterprise in metaethics. (. . .) *Good and Evil* invites readers to see
> morality and philosophy from a new perspective; not so much by argu-
> ing for this or for that thesis as by exposing assumptions, showing
> other possibilities and being sceptical about what we often think must
> be the case. (ibid.)

Before offering a sketch of these three 'experiences' or 'encounters', I'd like
to make some methodological points. First, it is not clear how steadfast
the distinction between practical ethics and meta-ethics really is. Though
Robin does not mention it he seems too to accept and implicitly employ
such a distinction. Second, it is far from clear that one can develop a substantive meta-ethical position as he claims by supplying examples that are
motivationally inert? Are they really just being laid out before us to think
of as we may? Third, the claim to originality—'to see morality and philosophy from a *new* perspective' (ibid., emphasis added) is surprisingly odd
given the obviousness of the sources that Gaita follows, both ancient and
modern. Fourth, the task of exposing assumptions is as old as philosophy
itself. And finally, if all that Gaita is doing is 'showing other possibilities'
why ought anyone to see why the moral of his encounters should 'go deep'
with them too.[4] The first and last of these questions are the most pressing in
the light of Robin's commitment that ethical theory ought not to be saddled
with the problem of guiding individual action in any (even relatively) determinate way.

Gaita expresses an idea worked on by Williams (1995) before him: the
difficulty of finding the right tone of voice with which to press home a

philosophical mode for moral thinking at once more natural, untechnical, and yet illuminating and authoritative. He strives for a voice that would render the conclusion of his moral insights, and carefully worked through examples, to be self-evident to the reader. It is as if he thinks that one would be able to see more clearly the moral realities that life presses upon us were we to be unencumbered by, or relieved of, prejudices such as one finds in traditional moral theories.

Gaita's first example is the compassion showed by Mother Teresa to the ill-plighted beggars of Calcutta. He speaks of her as a 'moral saint' and of her compassion as 'saintly goodness'. In her compassion, devoid of condescension as it was, no home can be made for the thoughts that their lives were worthless or that it would have been better had they not been born. What is striking about her example, he suggests, is the purity of her acts. Moreover that purity is cast with humility. Viewing her compassion under this description elevates her acts and character above a more traditional virtue-ethical description. For one might admire Mother Teresa's acts for their courage: for their steadfastness in the face of otherwise helpless adversity. Yet that is not the aspect under which Gaita views her. In a similar vein, he describes in his later book *A Common Humanity* (2000) a nun who attends to abandoned patients with severe mental illnesses. In each case what Gaita wonders at is not an achievement. He writes of the notion of purity:

> We are inescapably judged in its light, that's not because it represents the upper limit on a scale of human achievements, not even if that limit is beyond human achievement. People are sometimes edified by the saying (which often appears on desk calendars) that 'a man's reach must extend beyond his grasp, for what else is heaven for'. That has no application to the purity of Mother Theresa's love. And the Platonic forms are not in that kind of heaven.
>
> The nature of Mother Teresa's compassion is a matter for wonder, but the wonder is not directed at her achievements. Much of what she did was an extraordinary achievement, and we wonder too, although in a different way, at that—at her tireless efforts, her resilience, and so on. Our wonder at these is conditioned by our sense of human possibilities and limitations. (. . .) What I wonder at is a compassion that was without a trace of condescension, even though it was often for people in the most appalling and ineradicable affliction. (. . .) Her compassion is an example of what I have been calling a 'pure' love. I call it that, not because I claim any insight into her motives, but because of what is revealed in its light. (2004, p. 204)

He then goes on to use Simone Weil's metaphor of a torch, whose power is revealed by what it illuminates. On the one hand this is an odd choice of metaphor since it directs our attention away from the object (the torch) and toward what is external to it: its employment reveals the relative value of the torch. Nevertheless, he recognizes that one can adopt a perspective from which any particular person maybe seem to be the mere vessel of goodness. He writes 'there is a sense in which she disappeared from consideration' (2004, p. 205).

Gaita offers a second 'encounter', taken from Hanna Arendt's book *Eichmann in Jerusalem* (1963), which recalls an incident from the Nuremberg trials generally, and Adolf Eichmann's in particular. Although more sober than many of today's public show trials for the perpetrators of mass atrocities, such as the Serbian warlords, Moshe Landau was moved to remind the court that the trial's sole purpose was to see justice done. The fact that the defendant oversaw the mass genocide of Jews does not deflect Landau from his absolute commitment to justice.

While purity maybe an attribute or property both of love and justice it finds no home in the third encounter or experience, which Gaita takes to reveal the reality of morality. In contrast, Gaita draws our attention to an example of what Peter Strawson (1974) described as a 'reactive attitude'. The particular moral notion he uses is the concept of 'remorse'. He writes that the object of his discussion is not the mere psychological reaction to wrongdoing. One might experience this emotion in a shallow or corrupt egoistic way. For example, one might *display* remorse for its instrumental value. Often perpetrators of crimes declare publicly their remorse in order to lessen the penalty or sanction they are about to be given. Of course, this is not remorse proper but a mere simulacrum. It is not immediately clear, then, how Gaita is to draw the distinction between the psychological and the conceptual. Yet it is clear enough what Gaita is after: the notion that remorse is a deeply felt moral emotion that registers on a scale greater in import than regret.

Gaita presents to the reader the story of a Dutch woman acting in resistance to the German occupying force in World War II. The woman, because of her involvement in a plot to kill Hitler, ordered from her house three Jews she had been sheltering there for fear that their presence might scupper what was seen to be the more significant plan. Upon their expulsion, the three Jews are caught and murdered. Her sense of deeply felt remorse is captured in her suffering self-recognition as a murderess. Her remorse registers the wronging of their 'individual preciousness'. The phrase is an explicit analogue of the religious notion that each individual is sacred, or possessed of inherent dignity, because they are made in the image of a God-creator. With respect to the Dutch woman specifically, Gaita notes she is not blameworthy. He draws attention to a fine and important distinction between responsibility and blameworthiness. The two are often it elided, even in moral philosophy. Nevertheless, Gaita stresses the point—and he is surely right in this—that one may be held responsible for acts that one is causally associated with without being morally responsible. His consideration of the circumstances in which she acted as she did leads him precisely to this evaluation. And he is justified too in holding that despite this blame-free responsibility she must bear, he both recognizes and gives warrant to her remorse.

In each of these examples, the ethical import of what goes on is revealed to us in the absence of systematic reflection on the bases of morality. What is the point of raising these examples in the face of Robin's account of ethical theory? Well, first, it seems that there is considerable power in these examples. Second, each takes our attention away from a mere calculation or estimation of consequences of either acts or general rules. Third, each directs our attention to concepts beyond 'happiness' to an appreciation of a broader moral lexicon. Fourth, the kinds of reflection required to make sense of the stories is not a systematizing one. Fifth, each of the stories draws from us a response, properly called ethical, that is not reducible to principles—whether deontological or consquentialist. Life does not wait on ethical theory, and this is a point that Robin and any sane human being for that matter will agree upon. What is the point of ethical theory then, and how might it impinge upon educational life? I shall come to this point presently but before departing in that direction I want to draw one final observation.

Let me remark that there is at least one point of comparison too between Robin's conception of ethical theory and a Wittgensteinian moral philosophy. I noted earlier how Robin eschews the idea that an ethical theory can tell us what to do: that there was a simple relation between theory and practice in ethical matters. This too is the stance of some Wittgensteinians though for different reasons. The latter Wittgenstein[5] famously held that philosophy was a descriptive enterprise, which left everything as it was. The task for the philosopher was perspicuous representation. Take the words of Peter Winch for example:

> Philosophy can no more show a man what he should attach importance to than geometry can show a man where to stand. (1972, p. 191)

One might imagine a game in which geometry might tell us where to stand; indeed in Norman Malcolm's memoir of Wittgenstein, a very similar game is recounted where the players adopt the motions of various planets. But that is not my point. There is an older conception of philosophy, practiced by Socrates and others, where philosophers did not shy away from imparting wisdom by one means or another. That conception was less spectatorial, more engaged, than Robin would permit or recognize. And many Wittgensteinians would sit on the same fence.[6] Robin's insistence that theory is merely 'designed to elaborate on what is involved in acting morally', such that it has only '*indirect* bearing on our capacity to act morally' (1991, p. 13) underlies his conception of moral philosophy as just another branch of disengaged (disembodied?) reason.

If it is fair to ascribe to Robin a spectatorial role for the ethical theorist deploying disengaged reason to construct proper criteria of moral action, then it is also worth emphasizing that by making ethical theory accountable to the criteria of decontextualized theory he seems to be committing the error elegantly described by Stanley Cavell as being 'in denial of the human' (1979, p.XXV). Though Cavell was referring to modern epistemology, Robin's remarks, as noted above (and expanded below in quotation), seem guilty of the same denial:

> The task of the author of an ethical theory is to force the reader to recognize, by reason, that an entirely coherent package or system that has some undeniable grounding in what he (the reader) does believe about morality is being offered. If that is the case, it may reasonably be pointed out that any remaining psychological objections are just that: psychological. They do not cohere with what has been agreed to be a coherent explication of the implications of one or more agreed starting point; it is they, the psychological objections, that should in reason be abandoned, and not the theory. (1991, p. 31)

The idea that one's theory might be right in the face of all natural facts is not merely a case of aversion to the naturalistic fallacy. Rather it is to throw the baby out with the bath water: to denude ethical reflection of a significant component of its subject matter. It risks falling foul of what Richard Wollheim charged Kant with providing: an ethics 'singularly bleached of human psychology' (1984, p. 202).

FINAL QUESTIONS ON ETHICAL THEORY AND MORAL EDUCATION

How, if at all, might ethical theory alter our conception of the moral educational task? First, grant that there are different levels of development. One need not be a Kohlbergian to allow this. One need not believe in the existing of discrete and specifiable stages of moral judgment that one progresses toward in an unlinear fashion or a steady rational awakening to the imperative of moral obligations. One may offer virtue ethical (Tobin 1989) or feminist (Gilligan 1982) accounts of ethical development and maturity just as one may offer deontological ones (Kohlberg 1978). Quite what a utilitarian account would look like I do not know. That it typically embodies a conception of the formal properties of impartiality, prescriptivity, and universality—like deontology—should condition its conception. Each will have its proper critics and adherents who - according to the criteria Robin judges apt to criticize theories (clarity, coherence, elegance, parsimony, and so on)—those ethical theories to be unacceptable or acceptable. The foregoing seems to me uncontroversial. Nevertheless it seems antithetical to Robin *qua* ethical theorist. He is convinced that ethical theories can be rationally superior when properly understood. Yet the philosophical ocean is already well populated by the wrecks as were made by those who had claimed some master rule or virtue or single criterion of goodness or rightness.

How might moral educators, more broadly enamored of ethical reflection in particular cases and general rules (call it philosophical if you will) conceive of their task? Might they not want to broaden the horizons of their learners beyond the present and the particular; or to deepen the wells of the pupils' empathy; to nourish their emerging sense of responsibility by (literary and other) examples and exemplary conducts; to sustain them in righteous indignation when the masses are adopting pernicious attitudes; and so on, and so forth. Quite whether Robin's conception of ethical theory or what I have called a Wittgensteinian one (with the aid of Raimond Gaita) seems to me a moot point. That ethical theory and reflection must conform to standards of reasonableness is one thing; circumscribing what that amounts to in practice is another. Yet moral problems *are* personal problems, though they may of course have greater import beyond individuals. That fact must condition what is to count as an ethical theory.

What would be objectionable, in any event, is the idea that someone might do the hard work of ethical reflection for the learner: that one might borrow so to speak the ethical authority of the example or the theory, contested as they are. What is rich in prospective for Wittgensteinians is the invocation of processes of receptivity, empathy, openness, imaginative sensitivity, and so on, which the nuanced example can provide the moral educator. But these psychological realities are precisely the features that Robin has rejected for ethical theorizing. In the life of an ethical theory such as Robin's utilitarianism, then, one is left to wonder quite how learners will be moved to respond in ways that he determines are right. And what is at odds for Robin and the many ethical theorists he elegantly rejects is precisely the manner in which ethical reflections must take seriously the idea and individuality of human experience while being mindful of those rational checks that he points out so admirably.

NOTES

1. John Harris, the utilitarian philosopher, coined the phrase 'humanimal' to encapsulate the fact that we are one among the animals, not altogether distinct from them. In this regard he was echoing Bentham's famous remark that when considering how to treat animals one ought to enquire whether they can feel pain not whether they can talk rationally, make contracts, and so on.
2. The label is not a straightforward one. Authors such as Roy Holland, Peter Winch, Dick Beardsmore, Dewi Phillips, Howard Mounce, and Cora Diamond would all fall under this loose canopy though their writings range from absolutism to particularism in ethics.
3. It is not of course exclusive to Wittgensteinian writers. Williams (1985) says it with particular force.
4. The phrase to 'go deep' is used throughout *Good and Evil* and is attributable to Rush Rhees (1969, p. 56) as a mode of indicating the moral seriousness of a saying, thing, or context.

5. On whether there are two or three or indeed just one is a moot point. The standard position in the literature is that there is an earlier and a later. For criticism of this see Mounce (2007).
6. I say 'many' but not all. Gaita's writings seem to me to fall outside, or explore the richness of moral life beyond, the descriptivist terrain.

REFERENCES

Baier, A. C. (1989), in *Anti Theory in Ethics and Moral Conservatism*, ed. S. Clarke and E. Simpson Albany: SUNY Press, pp. 29–48.

Barrow, R. (1991) *Utilitarianism*, Aldershot: Edward Elgar.

Blake, W. (1893) *The four Zoas*, accessed at https://tspace.library.utoronto.ca/html/1807/4350/poem169.html 21.9.13

Cavell, S. (1979) *The Claim of Reason: Wittgenstein, Skepticism, Morality and Tragedy*, Oxford: Oxford University Press.

Gaita, R. (2000) *A Common Humanity*, London: Routledge.

———. (2004) *Good and Evil: An Absolute Conception* (2nd edition), London: Routledge

Gilligan, C. (1982) *In a Different Voice*, Cambridge, MA: Harvard University Press.

Harris, J. (2010) 'Transhumanity: A Moral Vision of the 21st Century', in *Ethics and Humanity: Themes from the Philosophy of Jonathan Glover*, ed. N. A. Davis, R. Keshen, and J. McMahan, Oxford: Oxford University Press, pp. 155–174.

Kohlberg, L. (1978) 'Revisions in the Theory and Practice of Moral Development', *New Directions for Child and Adolescent Development* 2, pp. 83–87.

McGee, G. (2006) 'Will Bioethics Take the Life of Philosophy?', *American Journal of Bioethics* 6(5), pp. 1–2.

Mounce, H. (2007) *Metaphysics and the End of Philosophy*, London: Continuum.

O'Neil, O. (1986) 'The Power of Example', *Philosophy* 61(235), pp. 5–29.

Rhees, R. (1969) *Without Answers*, London: Routledge & Kegan Paul.

Strawson, P. F. (1974). Freedom and resentment, and other essays. London: Methuen.

Tobin, B. M. (1989) 'An Aristotelian Theory of Moral Development', *Journal of the Philosophy of Education* 23(2), pp. 195–211.

Toulmin, S. (1982) 'How Medicine Saved the Life of Ethics', *Perspectives in Biology and Medicine*, Baltimore, MD: Johns Hopkins University Press.

Williams, B. A. O. (1972) *Morality: An Introduction to Ethics*, Cambridge: Cambridge University Press.

———. (1985) *Ethics and Limits of Philosophy*, London: Fontana.

———. (1995) 'Replies', in *World, Mind and Ethics: Essays on the Ethical Philosophy of Bernard Williams*, ed. J. E. J. Altham and R. Harrison, Cambridge: Cambridge University Press, 185–245.

Winch, P. (1972) *Ethics and Action*, London: Routledge & Kegan Paul.

Wollheim, R. (1984) *The Thread of Life*, Cambridge MA: Harvard University Press.

4   In Defence of Virtue Teaching

Richard Pring

Robin Barrow's book *Happiness* (1980) provides a useful introduction to Aristotle's key notion of '*eudaimonia*', often translated as 'happiness'—'an activity of the soul in accordance with virtue' (amongst other things). The virtues constitute a way of living— of appraising the value of the many desires and aims which make up daily life. Together they reflect what it means to live a distinctively human life, and thus they might be seen as the end which should direct all other aspects of our lives. They should be embodied in all that we do.

However, virtue is not a word we often use now. Like 'piety', it has a certain medieval odour about it (although plaques on the walls of medieval churches indicate that there were quite a lot of virtuous women around up to the early part of the nineteenth century), and I'm not sure many would, in the twenty-first century, take it as a compliment to be called virtuous, just as they may take exception to being called pious. That is a pity because virtue was a central notion in the *Nichomachean Ethics*, and the moral life, as outlined by Aristotle, was the foundation of the Christian tradition as it became articulated through Aquinas.

Presumably the explanation for the demise of virtue as a significant moral concept has something to do with a reconceptualisation of the moral life—a different way of appraising people and their actions from a moral point of view. One could say that a different philosophical tradition prevails, and this enters into our understanding of the moral life— and (what is professionally more significant) into our understanding of moral education.

In this chapter I expand on these thoughts, and show how (in neglecting virtue) the prevailing view of moral education is based on an impoverished account of the moral life with its mistaken espousal of autonomy as the most important educational aim. Indeed, so much is this the case that autonomy is now taken as a self-evident moral good—both in popular educational literature and in the philosophy of education. And, therefore, I cannot expect to convince many of my argument, but only (perhaps, and if I am fortunate) suggest that here is another way of looking at things.

VIRTUES

Virtues are dispositions. Persons are kind if they are disposed to acting kindly. Someone, however, who does act kindly may not be a kind person. He may be acting with clenched teeth, and from a sense of duty. The smile accompanying the deed might be a forced one, since he knows that smiling is often an adjunct of kindness. The person in question may be kind often, but still not a kind person. He has no inclination to act in the way that kind persons would be expected to act—even though he forces himself to do so. On the other hand, he may become kind by constantly performing kind acts. Eventually he comes to like so acting—the smile comes spontaneously. And why not? Virtue is its own reward. There is some satisfaction, even in adversity, in acting from the appropriate feelings. And so there is good reason, in morally educating, to make sure that young people act regularly as if they were virtuous, even though they may not be acting out of virtue. They may come to like it. And no doubt the justification for making them say 'please' and 'thank you' would be along similar lines. Such verbal responses, though first produced in blind obedience, and then, if you are a lucky parent, mechanically, do embody a set of attitudes which become internalised and which presumably dispose one to act in a certain way.

A disposition is a propensity to act in a certain way in certain circumstances. Of course, these ways and these circumstances can be spelt out only in very general terms, but nonetheless the generalities do point to a form of moral life. Generally this consists of a range of dispositions which enable you to react fairly spontaneously to most situations that are likely to confront you and that involve the possibility of choice. Different circumstances require different kinds of dispositions—hence, the list of virtues that constitutes the good life: chastity in matters of sexual relations, obedience in matters relating to authority, kindness in response to the needs of others, generosity in relation to the goods one has acquired, and thrift in guarding against future misfortunes. The list of such dispositions is long, although some will be seen to be more important than others. Again different social and economic groups will have different lists—not simply in order of priority but in what the lists should contain or omit. For example, magnanimity was important for Aristotle, but does not loom large in current lists of virtues. Humility is a peculiarly Christian virtue, and is nowhere to be found in Homer. Again, virtues change in rank order. When I was a boy, obedience was very important as a virtue. It still plays an important part in the lives of young people for obviously practical reasons, but grandparents (myself included) feel uncomfortable in appealing to it as a basis for action, choosing instead to give reasons (and thus left with no line to fall back on when the reasons are not accepted). Indeed, the obedient child would now no doubt be seen as rather wimpish—it seems to contradict our espousal of autonomy which, so we are told, is the ultimate good. Furthermore, what previously counted as a vice can become a virtue—if it is called by a different name and if we submit to enough media influence. Thus the old biblical vice of greed becomes transformed into enterprise which is a recently arrived virtue. It has always been around as a disposition, but it has only recently been officially legitimised as an aim of education.

To trace the shifts in the lists of virtues (helped in a longitudinal study, let us say, by an opinion poll conducted every five years) would be enlightening and could provide the basis of some interesting sociological and philosophical speculation: sociological, because it might help establish the connection between how the public envisage 'the good person' (and thus 'the good life') and the changing social and economic scene; philosophical, because it stimulates reflection on the interconnections between our moral appraisal of people (and of how they act) and how we come to see them as persons—a view of human nature and of the social and economic framework within which they develop as persons. Thus, to speculate rather carelessly, there would seem to be connections between the importance attached to obedience and a rather hierarchical view of society, which in turn sees many people (children or employees) not to have the capacity to get at the truth or to be able to reason things out for themselves. There would seem to be connections between the demise of greed as a vice and a certain view of 'human nature' and of the economic realities in which that nature is to flourish: namely, first, with regard to human nature, a sense of rational choice (Adam Smith style) in which the main human drive is that of the maximisation of profit and in which reason focuses upon the most efficient means for arriving at such limited objectives; and second, with regard to 'economic realities', the constant need for expansion of general wealth which can only be achieved from the individual pursuit of profit. And so we could go on. The point is that virtues—the approved disposition to act in certain ways in certain circumstances—shift from age to age and from society to society, and that these shifts are often related to underlying views about human nature and about the economic and social realities in which that nature is understood to develop.

Sometimes those shifts (as in the case of greed not becoming greed) can be seen to be quite consciously forced—a political campaign, almost, to reconceptualise our system of moral appraisal to bring it in line with economical realities as they are understood by people in positions to influence things.

But our opinion poll might nonetheless preserve, amongst all these shifts, a certain stability both in its content and in its priorities, because there may be limits to how far one can (with all the political will in the world) change moral appraisals since these must relate to some conception of the good life, and that in turn must relate to some view of human nature which resists all efforts to disguise it. For instance, the virtue of justice or fairness would, I suspect, remain fairly prominent, as would 'courage', 'honesty' (which is not to say that most people would be honest in most circumstances, only that they would recognise honesty in many circumstances as a good thing), and 'loyalty'.

The major point is that virtues as dispositions—though in detail not securing universal agreement—do seem fundamental to our moral appraisals and do seem tied to views (disputed views, maybe) about what it means to be human and the social and economic circumstances in which one acts out a recognisably human life.

To see moral matters in terms of dispositions to act is not to deny any place for deliberation or for reasoning or for decision making. Far from it. The problems that one has to confront in everyday living require just that, for potentially rival dispositions might be called into action—the disposition to be merciful, say, at the same time as the disposition to be just. And also one can sometimes come to question the appropriateness of the dispositions one has acquired for the good life. Has obedience the place in my scheme of things that once it had? And how far should I let compassion override the exercise of retributive justice? The moral life consists in such deliberations—over time, in the context of concrete situations, with the overall pattern of one's life in view, and no doubt with Butler's *Lives of the Saints* at one's elbow.

Indeed, far from dispositions excluding deliberation and reasoning, they provide the necessary base and background for it. Without the disposition to be kind, one may well not see a situation as one requiring one's attention—the young beggar on the street would be seen as just that, unless one was disposed to react to that kind of situation in a particular way. One sees it as a moral issue to be deliberated about (whether to save one's money for another charity, whether to be sternly indifferent to someone who should, in justice to himself, be earning a living) precisely because one is disposed to do so; it falls under, as it were, the category of actions where kind acts are seen as the appropriate ones. The phone hacking by journalists of News Corp would not have been seen by the accused as (with hindsight) a mistake, a miscalculation, a misjudgement of the country's mood, if the newspaper had been in the hands of virtuous people rather than in the hands of calculating pragmatists—for, surely, the honest and considerate person would have, instinctively picked these acts out for the dishonest and inconsiderate behaviours that they were.

A disposition must be accompanied by appropriate emotions. The kind person must have a spontaneous liking for other people and would feel a certain unhappiness when she sees them in distress. The humble person feels no anguish in self-effacement, but enjoys the pleasure others get when the plaudits go in their direction. The thrifty person would feel irritated at others' thoughtless frittering away of their earnings on trivia and would feel mildly sick when her own earnings disappeared as a result of an act of carelessness. Hence, education of the emotions would be an essential part in making people virtuous—giving them what is thought to be the appropriate emotion.

'Appropriateness' is, of course, a tricky term. It sounds as though something significant is being said without very much given away. Hence, the importance in Aristotle and Aquinas of the golden mean. Roughly, that signifies that you can drink but not so much as to make your head spin, or you can eat well but not so much as to make you loosen your belt. Of course, those with such dispositions would readily adapt to circumstances which make different demands—as when you are confronted with an undernourished child and would give away some of what normally you would be eating.

The golden mean sees an emotional response to lie (spontaneously, acceptably, and pleasantly) between deficiency and excess. The courageous person lies between the coward and the foolhardy; the kind person between the cruel and the sentimental softy; the humble person between self-effacement and the braggart. It is a position where one is disposed to act towards others and towards situations in a way that is seen as appropriate, given some overall view of how human beings should so relate to others and to those circumstances (with justice, with respect, etc.), without being prevented from doing so by a deficiency of those feelings that act as a springboard for action or by an excess. Foolhardiness is often confused with courage because it is an excess of the very feeling that enables courageous people to face danger; it is an excess because so strong are the feelings that they get in the way of the reflection which enables one to judge the appropriateness of following the feelings. Thus the courageous, rather than the foolhardy, man may choose not to throw away his life in battle, because the war is lost and he may thus live to fight another day.

It is traditional to distinguish between moral and intellectual virtues—we shall leave aside the cardinal virtues of faith, hope, and charity. What I have been talking about are the moral dispositions to act where feelings either help or get in the way and where these are generally seen to be a good thing. But there are other dispositions that need cultivating, namely, those that pertain to the pursuit of truth. Thus feeling horrified at the destruction of evidence, despising the use of underhand tricks in argument, being open to criticism, would all characterise the intellectually virtuous. They are the sort of virtues which seem logically related to the getting at the truth. And one would expect to see their most clear-cut manifestation in philosophy seminars—though one often does not.

PRUDENCE, CHARACTER, AND SYMPATHY

One of the advantages of being virtuous is that, in most circumstances, one does not have to do too much thinking or to get twisted up in a debilitating internal moral struggle. The right action will generally suggest itself to the well-disposed person. But Aquinas, for one, was not altogether happy with that, and kept a special place for prudence. Prudence seems to be that extra quality that helps one keep things in balance—'in balance', by the way, being an unavoidable notion that once again is parasitic upon some broader view of what constitutes 'the good life'. Blessed Vincent Pallotti, the parish priest of Sant' Andrea della Vale in the Corso Vittorio Emmanu-elle in Rome, never became a saint because the Church, in her wisdom, said he lacked prudence. He was a very virtuous person—exceedingly kind, concerned, humble, pious, but he kept falling asleep in the confessional which caused some consternation to his penitents. He lacked that practical wisdom which guides the balancing of these different good dispositions.

There are other mental categories which are associated with moral and intellectual virtues. They are, first, character— referring to such qualities as perseverance, forcefulness, strength—which in one sense is morally neu-tral in that it can be put at the equal disposal of virtue and vice. Thus Hit-ler had a certain strength of character, and Faust had perseverance (but he lacked the intellectual virtues, wanting knowledge without the achievement of knowledge and without the struggle that is a prerequisite of that achieve-ment). Moral education has offered many recipes for the acquisition of these important character traits—from the learning of irregular Greek verbs and long-distance running, right through to more complex solutions such as the strengthening of the ego. This is an interesting shift because of the changed philosophical position—to that of faculty psychology, whereby (the will) is analogous to a limb that can be strengthened through training or exercise.

A further mental category is what Hume refers to as sympathy. Sympathy is not itself an emotion (or sentiment, to use Hume's word), and thus being sympathetic is not necessarily being virtuous. Rather is it a condition of being virtuous because without sympathy you cannot necessarily identify the emotions in others. Certainly, you lack the capacity for that emotion to make such an impression on you that you come to have it as your own—or share the emotion. This is clearly important in the virtuous person who should feel anger where someone else is suffering gross injustice—but such anger (as opposed to a purely cerebral acknowledgement that someone is being treated unjustly) requires a certain sharing of feelings, the ability to make someone else's ill-treatment one's own.

Reference to Hume is important. Popularly, it is often attributed to Hume that reason is but the slave of the passions and has no place in decid-ing between good and evil. Moral autonomy would be an empty goal if, in freeing pupils from the burden of authority, it did no more than place them in the shackles of uncontrollable passions. But 'reason as the slave of the passions' makes sense where virtues—namely, the dispositions to act with appropriate emotions in appropriate circumstances—become much more central in our moral appraisals. For the morally good person is one who has those dispositions which, upon contemplation, one admires; such admira-tion being clearly connected with certain beliefs about social, economic, and biological conditions of man. Reason has a place but it is partly a subservient one (helping one to sort out the appropriateness of the feelings, given one's beliefs and given the circumstances) and partly a contribution to that important contemplative process through which certain qualities and not others receive admiration. Hume refers to the esteem given to the beneficent person. A rational matter? Well, that depends. It is clearly the case that such a person brings happiness to friends and to others. Would it not be odd if such dispositions were not to receive approval, and the attendant virtues be recognised as contributing to the good life?

To summarise these two sections, there has been a long tradition in philosophy to place 'virtue' at the centre of ethics, and thus the acquisition of virtue at the centre of moral education. Virtues are dispositions and, as such, constitute specifically named feelings and states, which act as a springboard for action in appropriate circumstances. Such dispositions constitute a complex but coherent view of 'the good life', and quite clearly relate to certain underlying views about human nature and about the social and economic conditions in which people have to act. There is a place for moral reasoning, but it is a more subservient place than currently is often attributed to it-deliberative, probing the underlying views about society and man's position in it, delineating clearly the circumstances in which one is acting. And what is approved—the current list of virtues in fashion—is not definitive; it will alter as circumstances change or as insights are gained (and arguments are won) concerning what we understand about persons and what makes them tick. But such alterations take place slowly, and certain emotions (at the hub of the system) look fairly invulnerable because human nature remains fairly constant in many respects. Thus, moral education would consist in helping young people to be strengthened in those virtues, or to acquire them where they are deficient, on the assumption that (even in an ever more complex world) the person with the right dispositions could be expected by and large to act in the right way. Moral education would aim, too, to create that sympathetic capacity and the supportive framework in which this life of virtue might be more comfortably lived out. A person is virtuous if he or she feels comfortable in the exercise of virtue—a pleasant doctrine, to be recommended to all those suffering from moral torment.

That at least was my position at the end of my first year of undergraduate studies. I liked Aristotle, and his subsequent elaboration in Aquinas, because although I had some vices, I reckoned that I had enough virtues to outweigh them. And thus, if good men are to be rewarded in heaven, I felt I had a sporting chance to be counted amongst the saints. Chastity—a virtue then, but not so strongly felt to be so now—was a problem, but I felt that longevity (with its dampening of the passions) would eventually compensate for weakness of will, although I am now coming to see that some other virtues become more difficult to maintain.

AUTONOMY AND THE 'GOOD WILL'

This complacency was shattered in the second year of undergraduate studies when I read Kant's *Groundwork for the Metaphysics of Morals* and, of course, his *Critique of Practical Reason*. For this awakened the medieval debates between rival groups bidding for entry into eternal life. On the one hand, there were those who were 'naturally' nice—they were virtuous indeed: effortlessly setting about their Christian duties, humble of nature, engaged smilingly in charitable deeds, generous in their bounty, readily merciful to the wrongdoer. On the other hand, there were those who were not so well endowed: basically they did not like people (kindness required an effort), anger and irritation had to be subdued (though with difficulty), and pleasures of the flesh were an obvious temptation (though bravely resisted). Why should those with natural endowments of goodness be rewarded at the expense of those with such obvious handicaps? Surely, a fairer divine system required that the rewards should go to those who had achieved something—to those who had had to make an effort (and the harder the effort the better) in acquiring the characteristic qualities of the good person. Surely, the kingdom of heaven should be reserved for them. Not so much what you were, but how you became what you were.

Kant's *Groundwork* starts with the sentence: 'Nothing can possibly be conceived in the world, or even out of it, which can be called good, without qualification, except a good will.' He then goes on to say that what I have referred to as the intellectual and the moral virtues are only conditionally good—conditional upon the extent to which they serve the purposes legislated by 'the good will'. The good will—that is, the practical reason in operation—directed all action according to principles which it (the good will) was prepared to make universal laws of nature, irrespective of the self-interest and the feelings of the person in possession of such a will. The goodness of the good person resided, therefore, not in appropriate feelings—how could those be morally good when their possession lay outside their control?—but in the determination to live according to principles which reason showed anyone, who wasn't prejudiced by his self-interest, would adhere to. Such principles transcended the peculiar interests and wants of any individual. They were what any rational person would subscribe to who did not know his self-interest. Such principles would stand out as major obligations whether one liked them or not, and indeed there seemed to be more merit in acting according to them when one did not like them—for that truly was the test of 'the good will'.

Hence, the morally good life seemed to be turned on its head—from the one where goodness lay in the enjoyment of appropriate feelings to the one where, to the contrary, it was proportionate to the struggle against one's feelings; from the one where concepts such as 'duty', 'obligation', 'must', 'ought' had a minimum role (for they are brought into play only when people need persuading against their inclinations) to one where these became the central moral notions; from one where moral principles lie implicit within a typical social and economic form of life (with its relationships and the accompanying feelings which enable those relationships to flourish) to one where the moral life consists mainly in establishing universalisable principles; from one where practical reasoning plays a subservient role (deliberative, reflective, certainly, but within a set of perceptions largely determined by the feeling reactions to the world as one has been brought up to understand it) to one where practical reasoning is the foremost skill or ability to be fostered (a moral shift from the humble life of Benedict Joseph Labre to that of the canon lawyers—rational creatures every one—who dismissed him as an insignificant and eccentric beggar); from a moral form of life intimately connected with the social and economic environment, in which one lives, to one in which the moral life, based on moral principles, transcends such local factors and would be much the same in Mozambique and Manchester, in Fiji and Finchley, if only we could achieve that growth in practical reasoning, no doubt by using the instructional guide so ably set out for us by that philosopher of education, John Wilson.

It is, of course, a gross act of simplification to lump so many philosophers (with all their subtle arguments) together, but I see this important shift with its subsequent demotion of virtue to be rooted in the philosophy of Kant (although, as I indicated, it was intimated in theological debates, concerning the freedom of the will, of earlier centuries) and to be reflected particularly in the work of R. M. Hare and thence, into philosophy of education and of moral development, in the work of Piaget (1932) and Kohlberg (1971), on the one hand, and in the work of John Wilson (1973), on the other. In Hare's book *Moral Thinking* (1981—over 200 pages) virtues rarely get a mention. There is some concession:

> It is understandable that within the general area of morality marked out by the use of "ought" and "must" (which is not the whole of morality, because the word "good" and the virtue have been left out of the picture).

But this is grudging and arrives only on page 153. Emotions, feelings, and virtues do not get a mention in *Freedom and Reason* (1963). Again, the *Language of Morals* (1952), despite its name, has hardly a place for virtues—indeed, the first mention on page 131, picked out by the index, is the expression 'in virtue of', and the three pages 137 to 139 talk about the virtues of fire extinguishers.

In place, then, of the cultivation of virtues we have the cultivation of autonomy, the person who can 'make up his or her own mind' about matters of right and wrong behaviour through the self-application of universalisable principles that transcend the provincialism of particular traditions of feeling. Feeling has little place in the cultivation of autonomy, except insofar as feeling is an obstacle to be overcome. But it provides no guidance, no indication of what is right and wrong, no indication within a cultural tradition of what it is to be, and grow, as a person in particular social and economic climates. Autonomy indicates (in the moral development programmes of, say, Kohlberg) an undermining of the life of emotions as these are celebrated in those who put virtue at the centre of the moral stage.

For that reason, I believe both the theory and the practice of moral education have been much impoverished in our schools.

REFERENCES

Barrow, R. (1980) *Happiness,* Oxford: Martin Robertson.
Hare, R. M. (1952) *Language of Morals,* Oxford, Oxford University Press.
———. (1963) *Freedom and Reason,* Oxford, Oxford University Press.
——— (1981) *Moral Thinking,* Oxford, Oxford University Press.
Hume, D. (1751/1983) *An Enquiry Concerning the Principles of Morals,* Cambridge, MA, Hackett.
Kant, I. (1785) *Groundwork for the Metaphysics of Morals,* many editions.
———. (1788) *Critique of Practical Reason,* many editions.
Kohlberg, L. (1971) 'Stages of Moral Development as a Basis for Moral Development', in *Moral Education Interdisciplinary Approaches,* C. Beck et al., Toronto: University of Toronto Press.
Piaget, J. (1932) *The Moral Judgement of the Child,* London: Routledge & Kegan Paul.
Wilson, J. (1973) *A Teacher's Guide to Moral Education,* London: Heinemann.

5 Understanding Educational Theory
Reflections on the Work of Robin Barrow and John Darling

David Carr

RADICAL AND PROGRESSIVE EDUCATIONAL THEORY

Robin Barrow has been a notable contributor—following on from his early work on Plato and utilitarianism (Barrow 1975)—to our understanding of past and present educational theories and ideas. That said, the new post-war British analytical philosophy of education, of which Barrow was a leading light, was never generally sympathetic—with at least one honourable exception to whom we shall shortly turn—to more unorthodox conceptions of education of the kind often referred to as 'progressive', 'child-centred', 'radical' (including so-called free-schooling and 'de-schooling'), and the like. To be sure, one of the seminal texts of this period—P. H. Hirst and R. S. Peters's influential work *The Logic of Education* (1970)—does actually propose some reconciliation of the well-worn educational dichotomy of traditionalism and progressivism, claiming that whereas the former is a perspective on educational content the latter is more focused on educational methods. But this claim seems both false and specious. It is certainly false, since some very famous progressive educators—such as A. S. Neill—had absolutely no interest (innovative or otherwise) in educational methods: but it seems also specious insofar as almost everything that Peters and Hirst otherwise wrote about education shows them to have firmly rooted in a liberal-traditionalist ('cultural transmission') view of education that was fairly educationally conservative and largely unsympathetic to more progressive or radical denunciations of conventional conceptions of moral and/or social authority and discipline.

Such 'traditionalist' commitments on the part of Peters, Hirst, and other analytical philosophers, of course, has sometimes been held to belie the purported philosophical neutrality of such writers and to betray the fundamental ideological colours of analytical philosophy as such. However (as Barrow has himself rightly argued), it shows no such thing. It shows only that Peters and Hirst, like other people, had opinions and values and that they sought to support such opinions and values—or even to arrive at them—through reasoned error-free argument. It is such argumentation that inclines them to deep suspicion of alleged progressive claims (though these, it has to be said, are seldom very precisely attributed) that (for example):

the liberty of autonomy can only be fostered by unrestricted freedom; that there can be no authority without coercion; and that education for democracy is the same thing as democratic education. It is such argumentation that leads Barrow to large-scale demolition of a raft of vague and unsupported educational claims on the part of various 'non-traditional' educational theorists and practitioners—such as Jean Jacques Rousseau, A. S. Neill, Paul Goodman, Everett Reimer, Ivan Illich, and Weingartner and Postman—in his impressive work *Radical Education* (Barrow 1978). To be sure, Barrow does try to adopt an even-handed approach to such theorists and is certainly kinder to some (such as Rousseau) than others (such as A. S. Neill): but all are taken to task on familiar philosophical grounds of unsupported assertion, unwarranted generalisation, fallacious argument, incoherence, and self-contradiction. Moreover, despite any difference of detail one might have about his account of this or that particular case, it is mostly difficult to demur from Barrow's overall verdicts.

Still, notwithstanding the prevailing hostility of (British) post-war analytical educational philosophers towards progressive and radical educational trends, there were a few honourable exceptions. Perhaps the most noteworthy of these was John Darling (though, one might also here recall Wilson 1971), a close contemporary of both Barrow and the present author, who taught in the philosophy department of Glasgow University before moving to the University of Aberdeen Department of Education to teach philosophy of education. Prior to his untimely death in 2002, Darling published several insightful papers on the progressive ideas of (particularly) Rousseau and Neill, as well as a longer work entitled *Child-Centred Education and its Critics* (1994), and had attracted considerable attention as an able analytical advocate or apologist for progressive ideas. In the 1980s he organised a landmark Aberdeen conference (to which the present author also contributed) which featured such notable latter-day Scottish progressives as R. F. Mackenzie and Jon Aitkenhead. In this connection, it is noteworthy that—aside from more obvious philosophical and/or ideological differences between Darling and Barrow on such progressive approaches—they take rather different perspectives on particular progressive, radical, or child-centred theorists. Thus, while it seems that Barrow has little or no time for A. S. Neill, he appears to have more respect for Rousseau as a philosopher of occasional insight. On the other hand, Darling clearly deplores what he takes to be Rousseau's extremely manipulative educational theory (also recognised by Barrow), but is highly sympathetic to the emphases of Neill and his followers on personal freedom and/or emancipation.

BEYOND TRADITIONALISM AND PROGRESSIVISM

All the same, as one who was at the time much interested in differences of so-called 'traditional' and 'progressive' educational ideas, and who had found Darling's insights into such approaches of considerable value, I was nevertheless somewhat disappointed by the eventual appearance of *Child-Centred Education and its Critics* (see Carr 1995). Indeed, the precise source of my disappointment was that despite Darling's significant contribution to our critical appreciation of the complexity of progressive and other educational views—for example, of differences between Rousseau and Neill—the book did not much further explore the emerging possibility that far from constituting a unified educational position, the approaches generally referred to as progressive or child-centred might be better understood as a diverse collection of rather different educational ideas or perspectives. In short, just as Barrow had included a range of rather different educational alternatives under the heading of 'radical education' (albeit appreciating real differences between them), Darling appeared to defend a loose composite of non-traditional educational ideas and practices under his heading of 'child-centred education'. In this regard, it seemed too that a timely opportunity for philosophical discrimination between interestingly different educational perspectives had been missed by an educational philosopher who was—on the evidence of previous track record—singularly well placed to undertake this.

In this regard, it seemed especially ironic that Darling first came to my notice with the publication of a paper in *Journal of Philosophy of Education* entitled 'Progressive, Traditional and Radical: A Re-alignment' (Darling 1978). I still think that this paper should have been regarded as a landmark of post-war analytical educational theorising, though—so far as I know—it was never widely noticed (though see Carr 1985). At all events, the paper revisits the well-trodden educational distinction between traditionalism and progressivism, arguing with some ingenuity that it does not—as frequently assumed—exhaust all the theoretical and practical educational possibilities. More precisely, Darling argues that what he calls 'radicalism'—namely, the rejection of traditional institutionalised education by so-called 'de-schoolers'—might be taken to constitute a significant educational alternative to *both* traditionalism or progressivism as these are commonly conceived. In short, Darling points out that although there are respects (such as an emphasis on individual freedom or 'emancipation') in which progressivism and radicalism seem clearly opposed to traditionalism, there are other respects (such as opposition to schooling) in which radicalism is opposed to both traditionalism and progressivism, as well as those in which progressives (laying less emphasis on the instrumental social and economic purposes of education) would also appear opposed to both traditionalists and radicals.

In the present view, irrespective of his particular 'child-centred' allegiances, Darling's paper opened up the interesting possibility of breaking away from the conventional textbook educational theorising that seemed unable to move beyond the received clichés of traditional versus progressive, teacher-centred versus child-centred, authoritarian versus libertarian, and so on. To be sure, it was not just that such 'adversarial' thinking certainly failed to register—as Darling's paper had shown—educational possibilities that could not easily be assimilated to this dichotomy, but that there might actually be differences between theorists and practitioners often lumped together as 'progressive', 'child-centred', or 'libertarian' that were perhaps as significant as any similarities between them. To be sure, these had already begun to emerge in Darling's opposition of A. S. Neill to Rousseau and in the differences Barrow had also observed between Rousseau, Neill, and the 'de-schoolers'. But now, one might ask (see Carr 1985), if there were such significant differences between so-called 'progressive' or 'child-centred' educationalists, might there not also be interesting differences between so-called 'traditional' or 'teacher-centred' educational theorists? Indeed, though one might be tempted to locate both R. S. Peters and Barrow (for example) broadly in the 'traditionalist' camp, there are equally well-known differences between the educational thought of these philosophers which would seem no less significant than any similarities. From this viewpoint, continued use of such terms as 'traditional', 'child-centred', and 'radical' might appear less than helpful: precisely, it might seem better just to abandon the portmanteau labels under which both Darling and Barrow had sought to defend or critique unconventional educational ideas in their respective works *Child-Centred Education* and *Radical Education*.

But is this not a rather trifling criticism? I have admitted that both Darling and Barrow do discriminate between different individual views—so, bearing this in mind, what is there in any book title? There may, however, be a more substantial point at issue here. For it is not just that danger may lie in lumping interestingly different educational theorists under the stale old theoretical headings, but that such headings also risk blurring some theoretically significant *connections*. For example, it is noteworthy that neither Darling nor Barrow (nor, for that matter, any other latter-day educational philosopher I have come across) mentions the defining influence on A. S. Neill of his friend and mentor, the American progressive educator Homer Lane. Indeed, it is hardly any exaggeration to say that there is no idea of substance in Neill that is not to be found in Lane (1928). First, Neill (1968) seems to have followed Lane in his particular interest in difficult, disturbed, or 'problem' children; second, the influence on Neill of (mostly Freudian) psychoanalytical theories and techniques as a means to 'curing' such problems was also derived exclusively from Lane; third, perhaps most significantly, Lane's own progressive school/reformatory *The Little Commonwealth*—with its strong emphasis on the therapeutic effects of freedom—may be regarded as the basic blueprint for Neill's own progressive school of *Summerhill*. But it should also be noted that this particular psychologically influenced perspective on education and educational problems does not end with Lane's disciple Neill, but continued (albeit in the less favourable contexts of state schooling) in the work of Neill's many followers and admirers, such as R. F. Mackenzie, Michael Douane, and Jon

Aitkenhead. In short, Neill's ideas may be contrasted with others (including, according to both Barrow and Darling, Rousseau and Illich), not just as one individual viewpoint against another, but as part of a particular tradition or *school* of educational thought defined by particular and distinctive theoretical (in this case psychotherapeutic) influences and concerns.

PHILOSOPHICAL SCHOOLS OF THOUGHT

With this in mind, we may now turn to a key chapter recently produced by Robin Barrow—under the very title 'Schools of Thought'—for the *Sage Handbook of Philosophy of Education* (Bailey et al., 2010). In this essay, Barrow precisely sets out to consider the pros and cons of focusing on *schools of thought*—rather than on particular educational thinkers or specific educational ideas—for the useful study and teaching of educational philosophy and theory. Briefly, for present purposes, he approaches this question by asking whether the 'isms' of past or present philosophical thought—such as realism, idealism, naturalism, Neoplatonism, pragmatism, utilitarianism, Thomism, Marxism, existentialism, phenomenology, structuralism, post-structuralism, hermeneutics, postmodernism, or whatever—may serve to define or identify anything much in the way of clear or distinctive educational policies or approaches. However, while giving this idea a fair run for its money, Barrow—as might be expected—does a largely thorough demolition job on any such prospect. Moreover, though one suspects that his generally negative view may be partly temperamentally driven by an analytical and liberal philosopher's distrust of parties and ideologies (indeed, while Barrow (2008) admits to membership of the ethical utilitarian club, he also acknowledges the respects in which this compromises his status as a moral philosopher), one cannot help again agreeing with his overall verdict on the possibility as Barrow conceives it.

However, Barrow's case rests essentially on several assumptions. One of these is that the philosophical positions and perspectives he considers seem too vague or open-ended to admit of precise definition for any useful educational purpose. On the one hand, as he says (Bailey et al., 2010, p. 25), in addition to the fact that different advocates of schools of thought often associate this or that school with rather different philosophers, different individuals associated with a given school also often appear to hold rather different views. (Perspectives such as Marxism, for example, are notoriously schismatic.) On the other hand, the various 'isms' themselves are prone to vary in sense from one philosophical context to another. Thus, what may count as 'naturalism', 'idealism', or 'realism' in the context of this (say epistemological) problem or controversy may not so count in that (say ethical or moral) one: one may, for example, be a realist with regard to questions of the objectivity of knowledge, without being what would usually be counted an ethical or moral realist (though, to be sure, it would be difficult to manage this the other way around). But, in any case, it is also difficult to see how many if any of these 'isms' might be clearly matched to particular educational approaches or policies. It is difficult, for example, to see what implications being an epistemic idealist (in any defensible sense of this term) or a moral realist might have for this rather than that position on equality of educational opportunity or comprehensive schooling.

But while one may agree with practically everything that Barrow says here, it seems worth asking whether some other approach to thinking about the study and teaching of educational philosophy and theory in terms of schools of thought might offer more mileage. Indeed, it seems that Barrow offers a very particular—if not fairly idiosyncratic—interpretation of the question of whether there are philosophical schools of educational thought (or, perhaps, educational schools of philosophical thought). Precisely, he seems to construe such theorising in terms of whether it is possible or useful for the purposes of study or teaching of educational theory to try to understand educational ideas, policies, and practices as grounded in or shaped by particular *philosophical* theories or perspectives (the 'isms'). But might we not ask rather whether philosophical enquiry or analysis (which neither Barrow nor myself, if I understand his views correctly, would want to include in any list of 'isms') might assist us to identify a range of interestingly different or distinctive traditions or schools of *educational* thought, policy, or practice defined more in terms of inherently educational issues and criteria? In sum, whereas for Barrow the schools-of-thought question seems to be that of whether educational ideas might be defined by reference to distinctive *philosophical traditions of thought*, it might be asked rather whether the practice of (analytical) philosophy can help us identify distinctive *schools of educational thought*.

SCHOOLS OF EDUCATIONAL THOUGHT

It is in just this sense, of course, that the positions generally referred to as 'traditionalist' and 'progressive' have usually been regarded as opposed educational schools of thought. In this regard, the familiar differences and disagreements between so-called traditionalists and progressives are not about (say): whether we may coherently suppose an objective reality independent of human mind or sense experience; whether there are any rational grounds upon which to regard value judgements or moral actions as true or right; or whether—if there can be such grounds—moral actions are to be considered right in terms of beneficial consequences; but about such issues as: the extent of legitimate authority in education and schooling; the implications of any belief in equality of educational opportunity for common or separate schooling; or whether it is ever right to discipline or punish unruly or deviant behaviour. To be sure, such primarily educational questions *may* be connected (somewhere down the line) with more fundamental metaphysical or epistemological issues—such as when, to take a rather recondite example, the epistemic holism of pragmatists (expressed, for example, in denial of empiricist distinctions between logical and factual truth or fact and value) is held to undermine any traditional organization of the school curriculum in terms of disconnected subjects. But even here, the educational pros and cons of teaching through subject—as opposed to thematic or topic-based—curricula, can usually be appreciated or addressed without undue entanglement with the metaphysical or logical complexities.

The trouble with the traditional–progressive distinction, of course, is not that it is not valid educational theory, but that it is not—despite the general truths it does contain—very *good* educational theory. Indeed, as I have argued in various places down the years (see, for example, Carr 1998, 2003), insofar as the distinction has been almost uniformly misunderstood by past and present educationalists, it has been more trouble than it may seem worth. As already indicated, the Peters–Hirst view that it is basically a distinction between content (curriculum) and methods (pedagogy) is a complete non-starter; some undeniable progressives have been less interested in methods than many traditionalists—and others have been no less interested than traditionalists in content. Again, a highly influential latter-day attempt (Bennett 1976) to interpret traditionalism and progressivism as empirical hypotheses regarding the effectiveness of different educational methods that might be experimentally tested is hardly more promising. Since the criteria by which any such effectiveness might be judged are no less open to controversy than the methods subjected to test, any such approach clearly begs all the important philosophical and/or moral questions: the key differences between traditionalists are clearly here again normative differences of educational ends rather than technical differences of means. But as Darling has also indicated in his 1978 paper, it may also be that traditionalism and progressivism are not exclusive positions that exhaust all theoretical or ideological possibilities: that, to be sure, there may be interesting educational alternatives that lie outside the terms of this worn dichotomy.

That said, the traditional–progressive distinction is not in the present view entirely bogus and may provide a useful starting place for any thinking about the possibility of understanding educational theory in terms of broad schools of thought. As I have argued before (Carr 1998, 2003), the distinction is an essentially normative one (all the way down) that does initially divide educational approaches into two broad groups. At heart, traditionalists are those who take the basic task of education to be that of the passing from one generation to the next of a socioculturally inherited store of wisdom, knowledge, and values. This traditionalist view is well captured in Matthew Arnold's definition of education as the transmission of culture, and of culture as 'the best that has been thought and said in the world' (Gribble 1967, p. 150), as well as strongly implied in R. S. Peters's view of the small child as 'the barbarian at the gates of civilization' (Peters 1959, p. 104). In brief, for traditionalists, education so conceived improves us (morally and otherwise), and we would be much the worse off without it. However, progressives from Rousseau onwards are basically those who want to question this traditionalist assumption on the grounds that the so-called knowledge, wisdom, and values of past inheritance is at best open to question and at worst no more than downright indoctrination. To whatever extent particular individual progressives may disagree about other things— and as we shall shortly see they often disagree about much—they are united in this general suspicion or scepticism about the alleged benefits of cultural inheritance: indeed, we shall here assert as a conceptual truth that if any are entirely innocent of such suspicion, they should not be called 'progressives'.

However, as Darling indicates, this is not to deny that this distinction is clear-cut in the sense that we may confidently place all educationalists on this or that side of this distinction. Thus, for example, while Darling's radicals or 'de-schoolers' share the progressive distrust of the epistemic and moral inheritance of traditional schooling, it is largely what they take to be the hidebound or useless institutionalised forms of such knowledge that they deplore. In this respect, their defence of the individual and social impor-tance of other more instrumentally valuable sorts of knowledge—such as vocational crafts and skills—does not wholly accord with the emphasis of many progressives on the (perhaps expressive or psychotherapeutic) devel-opment of individual personality for its own sake. In this respect, aside from the fact that A. S. Neill continued to pursue the professional career of school headmaster, we may feel some disquiet about any inclination of Darling or Barrow to include Neill among so-called radical educationalists. But there is also the problem of those who also, though commonly regarded as progressives (to the large extent that they would require all past knowl-edge claims to be submitted to criticism and evidence), also share—despite their very un-traditionalist take on these matters—what Peters and Hirst take to be a traditionalist concern with knowledge and pedagogy, and who seem not at all sympathetic to any progressive view that education should be concerned with mental health or self-expression.

Thus, even on the basis of what has been said so far, we have fairly clear grounds for distinguishing between at least three strands or traditions of unconventional or non-traditional educational thought. In this regard, we might perhaps first distinguish between progressives and radicals, identify-ing radicals—as Darling largely does—with such modern 'de-schoolers' as Ivan Illich, Everett Reimer, John Holt, John Tayor Gatto, and Paul Good-man. That done, we might then distinguish two fairly clearly defined but contrasting traditions or schools of commonly designated 'progressive' educational thought and practice. The first, earlier considered, is usually associated with A. S. Neill—though we have also noticed Neill's work was greatly anticipated by Homer Lane and continued (at least in spirit) by many followers of Neill. This progressive or non-traditional approach draws heavily on psychological—specifically psychoanalytical—theory and seems mainly concerned with the promotion of certain psychotherapeutic goals of personal fulfilment and happiness. Advocates of this approach show almost no interest in development of curriculum or pedagogy—Neill's *Summerhill* was at one stage criticised by HM Inspectorate for its outdated ('chalk and talk') educational methods—and their main goal seems to be freedom from indoctrination and repression. By contrast, a second progressive approach—which we can associate with the work of John Dewey, W. H. Kilpatrick, and their countless North American followers—would be profoundly suspicious of such therapy, but is immensely interested in questions of the development of distinctive and innovative forms of curriculum and pedagogy. To be sure, it is to the influence of Dewey and Kilpatrick that modern attempts—in the United Kingdom as well as North America—to develop non-subject-based thematic curricula and non-didactic teaching methods may be traced.

On this score, it might be said that some progressives would appear—with regard to their interest in curriculum and pedagogy—to be a closer to (at least some) traditionalists than to other so-called progressives. But is it now appropriate to regard traditionalists as constituting one unified or homogenous position? On the contrary, though traditionalists might well be said to share significant commitment to a culture-transmission view of education, they have clearly been divided on a number of substantial educational issues. One such major issue concerns the social or political distribution of educational goods or benefits. Thus, according to a school of thought (used here in the loosest sense) going back to Plato, the brute facts of human inequality of intelligence, aptitude, or interest dictate that it is not appropriate to provide the same educational opportunities to all young people in the context of state schooling. Notoriously, in the modern British context, such thinking led to the educational apartheid of the 1944 Education Act whereby children were assigned—following success or failure in the so-called 11+ examination—to different kinds of academic or vocational schooling by dint of their allegedly diverse individual needs. But it seems that such thinking was developed throughout the twentieth century by a distinguished group of British writers, cultural critics, and educational theorists—arguably including D. H. Lawrence, T. S. Eliot, F. R. Leavis, and G. H. Bantock (as well as various sociopolitically prominent contributors to the infamous *Black Papers* of the 1960s and 1970s)—into a fairly distinctive school of elitist or anti-egalitarian educational thought. To be sure, such thinkers disagreed on particular issues—regarding, for example, the relative importance of class and heredity for such selection—but they were nevertheless reasonably at one in the view that the same kind of education and/or schooling is not suited to all.

However, a position that seems to contrast strikingly with such elitism was developed by the new British analytical philosophers of education in the 1960s and beyond. Indeed, as the leaders of this new philosophical movement, Richard Peters and Paul Hirst developed a conception of education predicated on the entitlement of all to broad initiation into a range of forms of knowledge and understanding allegedly required for the full development of human rationality. The emphasis here on common initiation into culturally established knowledge is clearly in line with traditionalist educational perspectives, though equally strong emphasis on the importance of developing critical enquiry also marks it out as a 'liberal' (rather than 'conservative') species of traditionalism. But the influence of such liberal traditionalism on British egalitarian educational developments of the 1970s could hardly be overstated: thus, for example, the new 'Standard Grade' curriculum—which was specifically developed in the context of Scottish 'comprehensive' reforms to replace the differentiated academic and vocational curricula of former segregated senior and secondary schooling—drew almost to the letter on Hirstian curriculum thinking (Scottish Education Department 1977). Again, John White, another leading light of liberal traditionalism, was (along with many others of the day) a prominent advocate of the comprehensive ideal, and one of his key papers in defence of this ideal (White 1973) was contrastingly placed—in a widely used text on curriculum theory of the period—alongside a major statement by Bantock of his anti-egalitarian stance (Bantock 1973).

Interestingly, White argues in this article that we should view the place of ability in education as a 'goal' rather than as a 'given'. His point is presumably that too many past educationalists—from Plato onwards—have used natural ability (if not social advantage) to determine the future progress of children without giving them opportunity to show what they might do with the right sort of educational support. The educational goal is to enable children, so far as possible, to learn what it is in their interests to learn, and the task of teachers is to assist them by all possible means to do this. The fact that that children are, from the outset, not good at history is no reason for them to give up history, but (perhaps) a reason for learning more, better-taught history. To be sure, it seems to be the standard elitist argument that some children are just not cut out, by virtue of intelligence or ability, to master academic subjects. However, it would seem to be a key liberal-traditionalist point here that this fails to distinguish between intelligence and rationality, which are not at all the same thing—since, of course, one may be clever without being rational or rational without being especially clever. The liberal point is that it is the sacred (moral) duty of educationalists and teachers to equip learners as far as possible—within the limits of their abilities—with the forms of knowledge apt for civilised rational thought and agency. This can and should be done for young citizens within a fairly wide spectrum of ability excluding severe learning difficulties or mental handicap. Thus, while we should not deny that not all young people will have the interest to pursue history to any great depth, we should nevertheless recognise that some basic acquaintance with past traditions and events is one aspect of their common educational due.

That said, there are also arguably types of educational traditionalism, broadly conceived, to which both the elite (or conservative) and liberal forms would seem opposed. To see this, we may begin by noting the well-known liberal emphasis on the 'intrinsic' value of education—whereby, for liberals, education should be regarded as an end in itself rather than as a means to this or that social, economic, or other end. In this regard, liberal traditionalists are prone to a fairly sharp distinction between the *intrinsic* worth of education and the *extrinsic* value of vocational training. However, while elitists are prone to advocate vocational training for the masses, most if not all of them would also insist on the intrinsic educational value of academic initiation for the gifted few—and, indeed, it would appear that some (such as, for example, Lawrence and Bantock) are also inclined to emphasise the intrinsic value of the vocational 'handwork' they otherwise distinguish from 'mind-work' (see Lawrence 1973). At all events, Matthew Arnold—the most famous modern advocate of a culture-transmission view of educational traditionalism— was prompted to defend the intrinsic worth of educational initiation into such forms of understanding as history and poetry against those inclined to dismiss such pursuits as practically (socially or economically) redundant or useless. Moreover, Arnold variously castigated those who regarded the acquisition of knowledge merely as a means to further social or economic benefits as (amongst other things) 'philistine', 'instrumentalist', or 'utilitarian'.

The term 'utilitarian', of course, suffers from the familiar philosophical trouble that it is prone to diverse, broader and narrower, construal. Moreover, this term is a little sensitive in the present context, since Robin Barrow's educational philosophy is widely associated with utilitarianism. That said, there is arguably no tight connection between utilitarianism as a moral theory and the kind of educational instrumentalism that Arnold criticised—and, indeed, Barrow (2008) has explicitly denied any such connection between his own interest in ethical utilitarianism and his educational views. However, it may be that on a less reflective moral consequentialism—whereby actions and policies are judged right or wrong on the basis of their predictable beneficial outcomes—the processes and institutions of public education have often been construed as means to such benefits. In this light, politicians will assert that the country's material prosperity depends on the growth of scientific and technological knowledge, and educational policymakers accordingly leap to demanding more science teachers or teaching in schools. But much of such thinking probably also rests on some failure to distinguish—as Barrow has always rightly insisted that we should—between education and *schooling*. Thus, whereas the processes and institutions of schooling may well be the means to the production of various (often other-than educational) social and economic benefits, education is primarily concerned to promote goods of human personal growth—of intellectual and moral development, aesthetic appreciation, and general civilised sensibility—that are clearly not instrumental in this (or any) sense at all. That said, it might also be that such educational consequentialism has been the default norm or view of much if not most past and present educational policymaking.

TOWARDS A TAXONOMY OF SCHOOLS OF THOUGHT

At all events, on the basis of discussion to date, it is arguable that we are already in a position to distinguish several significantly contrasting traditions or schools of educational thought, namely:

Platonic or Elitist Traditionalism: which advocates different or 'alternative' curricula for children of different ability, social background (or class), and/or even interests. Generally, such positions distinguish a more academic curriculum of intrinsically worthwhile forms of knowledge and understanding—considered fit for the intellectual elite—from a practical or vocational curriculum for the masses. That said, while some such positions regard the former as superior to the latter, others appear to consider them as of equal (but different) value, and some even suggest that the latter may be of superior value to the former.

Liberal Egalitarian Traditionalism: which favours something like a 'common' curriculum, in the name of a more egalitarian approach to educational opportunity. In post-war Britain and elsewhere, philosophers such as R. S. Peters, Paul Hirst, and R. F. Dearden regarded the knowledge and understanding associated with liberal education as of intrinsic worth and as of benefit to all. As seen, John White (1973) argued that it is more the job of educationalists to create abilities and interests in young people than to regard them as 'given'. Such liberal egalitarianism clearly influenced the development of comprehensive educational curricula in Britain and elsewhere.

'Utilitarian' or Instrumentalist Traditionalism: which is arguably the default position of much if not most latter-day educational policymaking. Such thinking, robustly opposed by the nineteenth-century founding father of modern liberal educational thought, Matthew Arnold, regards education as effectively a means to externally conceived individual, social or economic ends or purposes and seems often blind to the 'intrinsic' value or satisfaction of the content and processes of education as such. As previously indicated, there may be some confusion (or reduction) of education to schooling on this view.

Psychological (Psychoanalytic) Progressivism: which regards personal happiness, largely construed as psychological well-being, as the main educational goal. Such well-being would appear to be accorded intrinsic value, although this may be variously realised given the nature of individual differences. Influenced by Freud and psychoanalysis, educational theorists and practitioners such as Homer Lane and A. S. Neill (and their many followers) developed a form of progressivism focused on the promotion of individual freedom in an educational climate free from undue authoritarianism, coercion, or restraint.

Pragmatist (Instrumental) Progressivism: which is the product mainly of the pragmatist and constructivist epistemology of John Dewey and his many followers. Dewey's 'instrumentalism' shows typical progressive distrust of received conceptions of knowledge and enquiry and traditional methods of instruction; but (unlike psychological progressivism) it is more concerned with social (democratic) progress than individual mental health and with the development of innovative (integrated) curricula and pedagogy. It may therefore be also both more utilitarian and egalitarian than its psychoanalytic counterpart.

Educational Radicalism or 'De-schooling': which rejects the very idea of institutionalised state educational provision. Insofar, the position(s) of such 'radicals' as Illich, Reimer, and Goodman are not easily characterised as either traditional or progressive. For present purposes, however, such radicalism might be counted as a more progressive position—since there is a strong emphasis on rejection of traditional modes of socialisation (construed as indoctrination and/or social control) in the name of personal liberation or 'emancipation'. That said, radicalism is also probably a predominantly 'instrumentalist' perspective—since it emphasises the value of the practically useful over the 'useless' academic. It also seems to be politically egalitarian, albeit reconciled to individual differences.

It should be clear, however, that the educational perspectives identified above are far from exhausting all possibilities and that other reasonably distinctive traditions or schools of educational thought might be added to this list. One might, for example, want to include some more distinctively 'ideological' perspectives—of the kind considered by Barrow in his *Sage* essay on schools of thought—such as Catholic (perhaps more specifically Thomist) and Marxist approaches to education.

Clearly, this is also a game that we can all 'play at home': the present pressing question, I suppose, is whether it is worth playing it—for any useful theoretical or practical purposes—at all. It is my view that it may indeed offer a potentially illuminating point of entry to the often rather boring study of educational theories and ideas, and be of some real use to student teachers and others bent on an educational career. The present author has in fact taught college courses on educational theory structured on something like this 'schools-of-thought' basis that do seem to have helped students see interesting connections between individual thinkers (or thinkers often presented as 'individual') and the broader educational themes and concerns in which their thought is implicated. That said, I also appreciate that such arguments may not impress an educational thinker of such rugged individuality as Robin Barrow. Indeed, some of Barrow's arguments against schools-of-thought thinking—that, for example, to think in such terms is also to risk blurring no less important differences between individuals (such as Peters and Hirst, or Neill and Lane, or Dewey and Kilpatrick)—are well taken. But given familiar difficulties of exploring all such fine differences in the short time available in typical education college courses, the schools-of-thought option might nevertheless be proposed as at least a heuristic possibility.

REFERENCES

Bailey, R., R. Barrow, D. Carr, and C. McCarthy (eds.) (2010) *Sage Handbook of Philosophy of Education*, London and New York: Sage Publications.

Bantock, G. H. (1973) 'Towards a Theory of Popular Education', in *The Curriculum: Context, Design and Development*, ed. R. Hooper, London: Oliver & Boyd.

Barrow, R. (1975) *Plato, Utilitarianism and Education*, London, Routledge & Kegan Paul.

———. (1978) *Radical Education*, London: Routledge.

———. (2008) 'Or What's Heaven For?, in *Leaders in Philosophy of Education: Intellectual Self-Portraits*, ed. L. Waks, Amsterdam: Sense Publishers.

Bennett, N. (1976) *Teaching Styles and Pupil Progress*, London: Open Books.

Carr, D. (1985) 'On Understanding Educational Theory', *Educational Philosophy and Theory* 17(1) pp. 19–28.

———. (1995) Review of 'Child-Centred Education and its Critics', by John Darling, *Cambridge Journal of Education* 25, pp. 237–238.

———. (1998) 'Traditionalism and Progressivism: A Perennial Problematic of Educational Theory', *Westminster Studies in Education* 21, pp. 47–55.

———. (2003) *Making Sense of Education: An Introduction to the Philosophy and Theory of Education and Teaching*, London: Routledge.

Darling, J. (1978) 'Progressive, Traditional and Radical: A Re-alignment', *Journal of Philosophy of Education* 12, pp. 157–166.

———. (1994) *Child-Centred Education and Iits Critics*, London: Paul Chapman.

Gribble, J. (ed.) (1967) *Matthew Arnold*, London: Collier-Macmillan, Educational Thinkers Series.

Hirst, P. H. and R. S. Peters (1970) *The Logic of Education*, London: Routledge & Kegan Paul.

Lane, H. (1928) *Talks to Parents and Teachers*, London: Allen & Unwin.

Lawrence, D. H. (1973) 'Education of the People', in *Lawrence on Education*, ed. R. Williams and J. Williams, Harmondsworth: Penguin.

Neill, A. S. (1968) *Summerhill*, Harmondsworth: Penguin.

Peters, R. S. (1959) *Authority, Responsibility and Education*, London: Allen & Unwin.

Scottish Education Department (1977) *The Structure of the School Curriculum in the Third and Fourth Years of the Secondary School* (The Munn Report), Edinburgh: HMSO.

White, J. P. (1973) 'The Curriculum Mongers', in *The Curriculum: Context, Design and Development*, ed. R. Hooper, London: Oliver & Boyd.

Wilson, P. S. (1971) *Interest and Discipline in Education*, London: Routledge & Kegan Paul.

6 Robin Barrow on the Aims of Education

Harvey Siegel

Robin Barrow is an analytic philosopher of education in the grand old style. Strongly influenced by R. S. Peters in particular and the development of analytic philosophy of education at the University of London's Institute of Education more generally, his work is very much in 'the ordinary language' tradition and is known for its precision, clarity, and wit. In some ways Barrow is the last of a dying breed, inasmuch as these days most practicing analytic philosophers are less wedded to ordinary language analysis. (Though this is controversial; Barrow himself has devoted considerable effort to characterizing his brand of analysis, on which more below.) It is an honor and a pleasure to participate in this effort to pay tribute to Barrow's contributions.

Barrow has published extensively on many topics in and adjacent to philosophy of education: Plato, ethics, aesthetics, mind, intelligence, philosophical analysis, etc. His positive views generally accord high value to reasons and reasoning, truth, respect for persons, beauty, equality, knowledge, honesty, love, and many other items valorized by the Western tradition; he has devoted considerable effort to both characterizing them—that is, offering analyses of them—and defending them from what he takes to be misguided criticisms. Without committing myself to every detail, I have considerable sympathy for this impressive body of work. In what follows I focus on Barrow's treatment of the aims of education. Here too I in large part agree with Barrow's views about these aims, although, as is inevitable in this sort of effort, I will raise a critical question or two about the way he arrives at them in what follows.[1]

BARROW ON THE AIMS OF EDUCATION

On Barrow's view, 'the question of what our educational aims should be' (p. 15)[2] is of fundamental importance. His reason for thinking so is that it is the only way we can reasonably and responsibly guide practice:

> No matter how much of our view of life will in fact be inescapably governed by time and place, and no matter what the difficulties in

establishing ultimate value claims, we can do no other (short of revert-
ing to complete nihilism) than assume that there are more and less
plausible conceptions of education and seek to ground our practice in
the most plausible account of the ideal. (pp. 15–16)

The most plausible account of the ideal will be given by pursuing

> Peters' succinct recognition that the aims of education are intrinsic
> to it. . . . While we might have extrinsic reasons for educating people
> (such as to serve the economy), the fact remains that the normative
> force of the word is the consequence of its inherent valued objectives or
> aims. To argue about the aims of education is to argue about what it is
> to be educated. (p. 16)

What is 'education'—either the word or the concept; Barrow mentions both
in the cited passages immediately above and below—such that the aims of
the practice are 'intrinsic' to it and 'inherent' in it?

> The Western tradition to which I and most of those reading this are
> heirs . . . in fact provides us with a very consistent concept of education
> defined in terms of understanding. Shifts in views of education over the
> centuries arise not from any rejection of this fundamental criterion,
> but from shifts in views about the nature of knowledge and under-
> standing. It therefore seems not unreasonable to argue that the essence
> of education today is the provision of understanding of the dominant
> traditions of thought and inquiry in the Western tradition, including of
> course, recognition of the limits of the appropriateness of a given type
> of understanding in respect of what kinds of issue it can deal with, and
> recognition of what is taken to be problematic within the field. (p. 17)

This concept (or is it 'conception'?[3]) of education is filled out in terms of
an educated person's understanding of science and scientific inquiry, and
of aesthetic, moral, religious, mathematical, historical, and literary understanding, all of which 'speak most directly to attempting to understand
what it is to be human' (p. 18). So: the essence of education is 'the provision
of understanding of the dominant traditions of thought and inquiry in the
Western tradition' (p. 17).[4] Barrow is emphatic on the point:

> There is a very straightforward difference, in any age and whatever
> the prevailing epistemological views, between giving people received
> answers to specific questions (or giving them nothing), and giving peo-
> ple access to understanding the ways in which we have heretofore tried
> to make sense of our world. It is the latter that I maintain as a matter
> of historical fact has always been the essence of the Western view of
> education: development of an understanding of how we try to make

sense of our world. Not only is this what education has meant, it is also an ideal to strive for regardless of what we call it. (p. 18)

It is, he notes, 'a variant . . . of a conception that has remained constant since the time of Plato' (p. 18), and so, importantly for Barrow, has important historical credentials.[5] It also 'carries with it a commitment to the ideal of autonomy, for the point of providing understanding is to give the individual the opportunity to see things for themselves, to make their own sense of the world' (p. 18).

Barrow laments the failure to pursue inquiry concerning the aims of education in general, and Peters's recognition of their intrinsic character in particular, in memorable terms:

> What this [i.e., the failure] means in practice is that, since the ends of education are largely ignored or treated as unproblematic, but in either event not emphasised and argued for, what actually goes on in school is increasingly driven by the extrinsic aims of, for example, industry, ideology, and the implicit assumptions of research methodology. In other words, because there is not widespread contemplation of what we take education to be, what we are necessarily aiming at if we are sincerely concerned to educate people rather than train them, socialise or indoctrinate them, there is correspondingly no widespread ability to argue against the assumption that the success of the educational system is to be judged in terms of such things as whether school leavers are well placed to find employment or whether they are politically correct, ecologically sensitive, caring individuals. (p. 17)

There is much to applaud in Barrow's lamentation. Let us grant his main point: if we don't actively engage the question 'What should our aims of education be?', we leave our educational activities vulnerable to hijacking by 'extrinsic' aims furnished by things like 'industry, ideology, and the implicit assumptions of research methodology', or as he also remarks, 'the demands of industry, government, religious pressure groups and the like' (p. 20). That is, if we fail to engage the question of aims, 'extrinsic' aims furnished by interests other than educational will likely, perhaps inevitably, take over and drive those activities.

Even granting—indeed, insisting upon—this very important point that Barrow effectively makes, however, worries arise. In particular: (1) Is Peters's intrinsic/extrinsic distinction and his claim that educational aims are 'inherent' in the word/concept the best way to think about such matters? (2) Are the aims of education rightly thought to be delivered by our understanding of what education is or what it is to be educated? That is, are the questions 'What are the aims of education?' and 'What should the aims of education be?' equivalent to the questions 'What is it to be educated?', 'What do we take education to be?', 'What aims are intrinsic to the concept of education?', or 'What aims are part of the meaning of 'education'?'? In the next sections I take up these two concerns.

'INTRINSIC' AND 'INHERENT' VALUES AND AIMS:
THE MEANING OR ESSENCE OF 'EDUCATION' AND
THE POWER OF ORDINARY LANGUAGE ANALYSIS

Barrow is clear that his method, like Peters's, is that of conceptual analysis.[6] On Barrow's view, conceptual analysis is 'an attempt to articulate what we understand' (p. 15) by the word or concept being analyzed. The aim of the analytical exercise is the articulation of the meanings of words or concepts as they are ordinarily used by competent speakers/conceivers. Analyses are 'arrived at by reasoning according to certain rules, and by reference, where appropriate, to facts that are themselves defined as facts in accordance with certain rules of evidence and reasoning' (p. 19); they are in a certain sense ideal, but not for that reason arbitrary (pp. 19–21); they are 'governed by rules to which we are as a matter of fact committed and which we neither have reason to reject nor can intelligibly do so' (pp. 19–20). Importantly, successful analysis reveals 'the values that are presupposed' (p. 20) by the relevant practice, and thus provides 'criteria against which to determine and judge our practice' (p. 20). So, when we subject 'education' to conceptual analysis, we are endeavoring to understand both the concept and the associated practice. On this understanding of analysis, what is the meaning of 'education' (either the word or the concept), such that getting clear on that will tell us everything we need to know about the concept 'education', the nature of education, the aims of education, and the criteria in accordance with which we should evaluate the practice of education?

It is worth noting a couple of brief critical points that count against this conception of conceptual analysis as a methodological touchstone for philosophical work concerning education. First, it presupposes that we all understand the same thing by the analyzed concept, in this case 'education.' This presupposition has been subjected to withering criticism in the post-Peters philosophical literature.[7]

Second, it ignores an equally long-standing conception of analysis in analytic philosophy of education, championed by Israel Scheffler, that acknowledges the importance of linguistic analysis but also notes its limitations and urges as well 'the rigorous, logical analysis of key concepts related to the practice of education.' Scheffler understands 'logical analysis' to involve not just the analysis of meanings in ordinary language, but also careful attention to and sophistication concerning 'language, and the interpenetration of language and inquiry.' He urges philosophers of education 'to follow the modern example of the sciences in empirical spirit, in rigor, in attention to detail, in respect for alternatives, and in objectivity of method'; to strive for argumentative rigor; and to make full 'use of techniques of symbolic logic brought to full development only in the last fifty years' where relevant and appropriate. This emphasis on symbolic logic and the demands of inquiry and theory differentiates Scheffler's brand of analytic philosophy from Peters's and Barrow's, which is essentially limited to the analysis of 'ordinary language.' While Scheffler's analyses always took full notice of ordinary meanings and usages, he did not hesitate to utilize logical and other techniques to supersede ordinary language when philosophical understanding and theory could benefit from such utilization.[8]

Finally, consider the character of Barrow's analysis of 'education'. There is no denying that his analysis of the word/concept is very rich and detailed. Indeed, it is so rich that it is hard to believe that all that insight can be got from the ordinary meaning of the word or the analysis of the concept. Consider: on Barrow's view, the concept is historically consistent (pp. 17–19), even 'constant' (p. 18); the content intrinsic to the concept includes, and so education must involve, understanding of (making sense of) the world (p. 18), 'the provision of understanding of the dominant traditions of thought and inquiry in the Western tradition' (p. 17), that is, understanding our traditions of understanding (p. 18), the valorizing of autonomy (p. 18), the development of mind (p. 20), and must have 'something to do with the business of acquiring knowledge' (p. 21). Is all this really intrinsic to the concept? Are we really entitled to infer that it is because 'it is a fact that that is broadly what the term means in the English language' (p. 21)? This seems an awful lot to get from conceptual analysis, especially in light of the by now generally conceded point that the meanings of such contested concepts as 'education' are variable, changing, and contextual. Is there a single thing that is 'the nature of education' (p. 18), such that its 'essence' (p. 18) can be discerned from the analysis of its meaning? If so, does it follow that when interested parties disagree about its nature and its inherent aims, at least one of them is simply misunderstanding the word or the concept? It is hard to see how this implication can be avoided; if it cannot it comes very close to a *reductio*, since intelligible disagreement would be rendered impossible, whereas it seems rather that such disagreement is not only possible but rife.

I do not want to make too much of this last critical point. After all, Barrow insists that alternative conceptions of education (or 'education') can be rationally evaluated (p. 19), and he himself urges that we engage in sustained inquiry concerning Peters's succinct recognition and that such analytical inquiry can 'increase our understanding of the nature of the enterprise we are concerned with' (p. 20). I want to suggest simply that it is implausible that Barrow's account of education and its aims, which in considerable part I endorse, can rightly be got from analysis of the word/concept. I want also to endorse Scheffler's alternative, and to my mind richer and more productive, conception of the sort of analysis in which philosophers of education ought to engage.[9]

ARE THE QUESTIONS EQUIVALENT?

Barrow is clear, indeed insistent, that the question 'What should the aims of education be?' is to be answered by getting clear on the concept 'education': 'The importance of emphasising the need for inquiry into the aims of education, *which I take to be another way of referring to the need to examine the concept of education*, cannot therefore be dismissed as an inherently subjective or relativistic activity' (p. 22, emphasis added). I agree with Barrow about the subjectivity and relativism. But are these matters really equivalent? In fact Barrow suggests several such equivalences, which I here articulate in the form of questions:

    i. What should the aims of education be? (p. 15)
    ii. What is it to be educated? (p. 16)
    iii. What does 'education', the English word, mean? (p. 16, p. 21)
    iv. What does 'education', the concept, involve or entail? (p. 22)
    v. What do we take education, the practice, to be? (p. 17, p. 22)

That these questions come apart, and so are not equivalent, is evident upon brief reflection. For example, we might recommend that our educational aims include that of fostering caring, as Nel Noddings (1984) does, without thinking that 'caring' is part of the meaning of the word or the content of the concept, thus separating the first question from the third and fourth. We can take the practice of education to be in various ways deficient or inadequate, thus separating the fifth question from the first, third, and fourth, and possibly the second as well. We can think of being educated in (for example, British upper) class terms, thus separating the second question from the others. The point here is not deep: the several questions are distinct, and treating them as if they are not is bound to lead us down the primrose path, at least from the point of view of a theoretically adequate account of education's aims.[10]

AIMS AS CRITERIA BY WHICH TO GUIDE
AND EVALUATE PRACTICE

Barrow makes clear that his 'main concern in [Barrow 1999] . . . is not to argue for this conception of education, but to argue for the vital importance of considering the nature of education—of articulating and arguing for specifically educational aims' (pp. 18–19). He effectively makes the crucially important point that guiding and evaluating educational practice depends upon a clear view of its aims: 'An analysis of the concept of education or an attempt to articulate its intrinsic aims serves, or should serve, as a statement of the criteria against which to judge our relative success or lack of it in seeking to educate people in practice' (p. 19). As he also puts it, the articulation of educational aims reveals 'the values that are presupposed' by the practice, and thus provides 'criteria against which to determine and judge our practice' (p. 20; see also p. 16).

I have already noted my doubts concerning the equivalence of 'an analysis of the concept of education' and 'an attempt to articulate its intrinsic aims'; I won't repeat those doubts here. Nevertheless, once we set aside this alleged equivalence, Barrow's key point, that aims provide criteria by which we can intelligently guide and evaluate practice, remains unscathed. This is a terrifically important point.[11] As Barrow also puts it: 'Without an [articulated] educational ideal, we have no argument to support . . . specifically educational demands' (p. 20). If this is right, philosophers of education cannot but endeavor to investigate the aims of education. Even if Barrow is wrong about the proper procedure—i.e., conceptual analysis—for investigating and establishing those aims, he is surely and importantly right about the importance of the endeavor, both for philosophy of education and for the establishment of sound educational policy and practice.

However, I must explicitly acknowledge a problem I now face. On Barrow's view, the procedure to be followed is clear: 'In the world as we understand it, constituted as we are, we have to determine our educational practice, and judge our degree of success in that practice, primarily by reference to our understanding of the nature of the enterprise (of the concept)' (p. 22). I have already rejected the idea that the nature of the enterprise, the aims that rightly guide it, and the criteria in accordance with which we rightly evaluate it are determined by the character or content of the concept. Have I thus boxed myself in by rejecting the only procedure on the table we might follow in order to establish the aims we seek to articulate and establish? I want to endorse at least a considerable portion of Barrow's account of aims, but I have forsworn his own preferred justification of that account. That is, I cannot say, as Barrow does, that these are the aims of education, and that they are justified in virtue of their being intrinsic to the word/concept 'education' and their inhering in either the concept or the practice of education. Is there another way of justifying aims?

JUSTIFYING EDUCATIONAL AIMS AND IDEALS: AN ALTERNATIVE PATH

On Barrow's view, as we have seen, one argues about educational aims and ideals by examining the word or concept 'education' to see what ideals are 'inherent' in the concept: 'the normative force of the word is the consequence of its inherent valued objectives or aims' (p. 16).

There is another way to think about justifying educational aims/ideals, one that does not rest on conceptual analysis: namely, giving reasons in support of candidate aims/ideals. This is, as Scheffler has done, what I have tried to do with respect to my own preferred aim, that of fostering the abilities and dispositions constitutive of critical thinking (Siegel 1988, 1997, 2003). This other way tries to justify them not by analyzing the meaning of the word or the concept, but rather by offering reasons that, if successful, support or count in favor of the proposed ideal. In my case, while I offer several such reasons, the most important is the idea that educators (like all of us) are obliged to treat their students (and everyone else) with respect as persons, and that so treating them requires that their education endeavor to foster their critical thinking (Siegel 1988, Ch. 3).[12]

There are two points to note. First, my preferred aim is (I think) completely compatible with Barrow's; I doubt that we have any substantive disagreement about the content of the aim. This is because (to use some of Barrow's characterizations) fostering critical thinking also involves and contributes to the development of mind, the valuing of autonomy, the enhancement of understanding, etc. But second, my justification of the ideal does not depend upon reflecting on the meaning of the word or the analysis of the concept 'education.' Rather, it offers a reason—namely, that educators (like everyone else) are obliged by the ethical principle (usually associated with Kant) of respect for persons to treat their students with such respect, and that so treating them requires endeavoring to enhance their capacities for and inclinations to engage in critical thinking—for thinking that the fostering of critical thinking is a fundamental aim and guiding ideal of education. I have obviously not attempted to justify this claim here. I use it only to show that there is another way to try to justify purported educational aims and ideals besides Barrow's and Peters's proposed 'intrinsic' one. If by 'intrinsic' is meant something like 'internal to the concept' or 'inherent in the meaning of the word', then critical thinking seems not to be so 'internal' or 'inherent.' And of course respect for persons is not itself part of the meaning of the word or inherent in the concept 'education'. Nevertheless, if I am right, respect for persons offers a powerful 'external' (to the concept) reason for regarding critical thinking as a fundamental educational ideal and the fostering of it as a basic educational aim. Of course I might be wrong; my arguments for so regarding critical thinking might fail. But that is a topic for another place. Here, the point is rather that aims and ideals need not be either found or supported 'intrinsically'. If this is right, then Barrow/Peters-style conceptual analysis is not the only way in which educational aims and ideals might be justified.

CONCLUSION

Despite the various critical points made above, I hope it is clear that those critical points are minor in the scheme of things, and that Barrow's most important claims about the aims of education are in my view more or less entirely correct: It is vital that philosophers of education (and everyone else concerned with the quality and future of education) seriously and explicitly engage with inquiry concerning the central aims and overarching ideals of education, that educational practice be guided and evaluated by reference to those aims and ideals, and that it is a terrible mistake, with enormous consequences, to let that practice be guided by 'external' interests that are either irrelevant or contrary to the furthering of education's legitimate aims and ideals. On these points I am content to follow Barrow's lead, and to express again my admiration for the insight, erudition, and wit his work consistently manifests.[13]

NOTES

1. If Barrow and I have a substantial disagreement—other than that concerning the power of 'ordinary language analysis' discussed below—it concerns the nature of philosophy of education itself. Barrow follows the 'London School' in regarding philosophy of education as (if I may put it thus) a part of the broad area of educational studies, and as being responsible, first and foremost, to efforts to improve educational practice. I rather think of philosophy of education as first and foremost a part of, and responsible to, *philosophy*. Of course this must be seen as a difference of degree; philosophy of education, at least on my view, must look both to the parent discipline and to educational practice. But it gives short shrift to the former only at great peril. I regret that I cannot pursue this matter here. For a brief articulation and defense of my view, see Siegel 2007 and the 'Introduction' to Siegel 2009. For Barrow's doubts, see his review of that volume, Barrow 2009b.
2. All untethered page references are to Barrow 1999.
3. Barrow discusses not only the *word* or *term* (e.g., p. 16, p. 18, p. 21), but also both the *concept* (e.g., p. 17, p. 19, p. 22) and the *conception* (e.g., p. 16, p. 18, p. 19, p. 20) of 'education'. But he does not explicitly distinguish these. Cf. Rawls's influential articulation of the concept/conception distinction in the first section of *A Theory of Justice*, which is developed in terms of the concept versus alternative conceptions of justice. (Rawls 1971, pp. 5–10). (Rawls credits H. L. A. Hart (ibid., p. 5, note 1), whose discussion he says he is following.) I should note that Barrow does distinguish word and concept elsewhere, e.g., Barrow 2009a, pp. 13ff.
4. As will be obvious to the *cognoscenti*, these traditions are more or less those enshrined in Hirst's highly influential 'forms of knowledge' thesis (Hirst 1965).
5. It is perhaps worth noting that, as Israel Scheffler has reminded me, from an anthropological or historical point of view many societies have engaged in practices they regarded as 'educational' but that are quite at odds with ours; moreover, philosophers have offered accounts of education very different from one another (e.g., Plato thought of education as suitable for individuals dependent on the class they belonged to, while Dewey advocated education for democracy). These uncontroversial facts seem to call into question both the 'constancy' Barrow here points to and the idea that educational aims are rightly thought of as intrinsic to the concept. My thanks to Scheffler for his instructive comments and suggestions.
6. Barrow offers a sustained and subtle analysis and defense of Peters's philosophical methodology in his (2009a); see also his (2010).
7. For an entertaining and effective discussion, see Harris (1999).
8. The quoted passages in this paragraph are from Scheffler 1973, p. 9; the paragraph is adapted from Siegel 2001. For a broad, historically informed

account of analytic philosophy of education and the place of ordinary language analysis within it, see Curren, Robertson, and Hager (2003). For a more general account of philosophical analysis and its vicissitudes in the last century, see Soames (2003).

9. For a fine recent collection of papers concerning Peters's brand of conceptual analysis, see Cuypers and Martin (2009).

10. Interestingly, Peters himself seems, at least toward the end of his career, to agree (Peters 1983, p. 37). See Barrow's heroic attempt to defend Peters's earlier thesis that the aims of education are intrinsic to it from his (i.e., Peters's) later rejection of that thesis (Barrow 2009a, pp. 17–18).

11. Scheffler makes it too (cf., e.g., his 1973), as have I (e.g., Siegel 1988).

12. I hasten to point out that, like most everything I have argued for over the years, this too is taken from Scheffler. Cf. Scheffler 1973, esp. Chs. 5, 6, and 11.

13. Thanks to Robin Barrow, John Gingell, and Israel Scheffler for helpful comments on a previous draft.

REFERENCES

Barrow, R. (1999) '"Or What's a Heaven For?": The Importance of Aims in Education', in *The Aims of Education*, ed. R. Marples, London: Routledge, pp. 14–22.

———. (2009a) 'Was Peters Nearly Right about Education?', *Journal of Philosophy of Education* 43, Supplement, October, pp. 9–25.

———. (2009b) 'Review of H. Siegel (ed.), *The Oxford Handbook of Philosophy of Education*', *Teachers College Record*, published 22 December 2009, http://www.tcrecord.org ID Number: 15881, retrieved 29 May 2012.

———. (2010) 'Schools of Thought in Philosophy of Education', in *The Sage Handbook of Philosophy of Education*, ed. R. Bailey, R. Barrow, D. Carr, and C. McCarthy, London: Sage, pp. 21–35.

Curren, R., E. Robertson, and P. Hager (2003) 'The Analytical Movement', in *A Companion to the Philosophy of Education*, ed. R. Curren, Malden: Blackwell, pp. 176–191.

Cuypers, S. E. and C. Martin (eds.) (2009) 'Reading R. S. Peters Today: Analysis, Ethics and the Aims of Education', *Journal of Philosophy of Education* 43 Supplement October.

Harris, K. (1999) 'Aims! Whose Aims?', in *The Aims of Education*, ed. R. Marples, London: Routledge, pp. 1–13.

Hirst, P. (1965) 'Liberal Education and the Nature of Knowledge', in *Philosophical Analysis and Education*, ed. R. D. Archambault, London: Routledge.

Noddings, N. (1984) *Caring: A Feminine Approach to Ethics and Moral Education*, Berkeley: University of California Press.

Peters, R. S. (1983) 'Philosophy of Education', in *Educational Theory and its Foundation Disciplines*, ed. P. H. Hirst, London: Routledge & Kegan Paul, pp. 30–61.

Rawls, J. (1971) *A Theory of Justice*, Cambridge, MA: Harvard University Press.

Scheffler, I. (1954) 'Toward an Analytic Philosophy of Education', *Harvard Educational Review* 24, pp. 223–230. Reprinted in Scheffler (1973).

———. (1973) *Reason and Teaching*, Indianapolis: Bobbs-Merrill.

Siegel, H. (1988) *Educating Reason: Rationality, Critical Thinking, and Education*, London: Routledge.

———. (1997) *Rationality Redeemed? Further Dialogues on an Educational Ideal*, New York: Routledge.

————. (2001) 'Israel Scheffler', in *Fifty Modern Thinkers on Education: From Piaget to the Present*, ed. J. A. Palmer. London: Routledge, pp. 142–148.

————. (2003) 'Cultivating Reason', in *A Companion to the Philosophy of Education*, ed. R. Curren, Oxford: Blackwell, pp. 305–317.

————. (2007) 'The Philosophy of Education', in *Encyclopaedia Britannica Online*, http://search.eb.com/eb/article-9108550, retrieved 29 May 2012.

————. (ed.) (2009) *The Oxford Handbook of Philosophy of Education*, New York: Oxford University Press.

Soames, S. (2003) *Philosophical Analysis in the Twentieth Century*, vols. 1 & 2, Princeton, NJ: Princeton University Press.

7 Is Barrow Nearly Right About Philosophy of Education?

Ruth Jonathan

When a professional qualification became mandatory for graduates wishing to teach in Britain some forty years ago, I signed up for a postgraduate certificate in education, after a decade teaching adults, secondary pupils, and prison inmates in Finland, Kenya, and the UK. That varied experience, of learners, their aspirations, and social contexts, made the pressing questions for me, not *how* to teach but what and why. To my surprise, the course component I had assumed would be irrelevant was the one I found not just useful but exciting and enlightening. Indeed Philosophy of Education, as taught by Robin Barrow and Ron Woods, not only addressed directly the pressing questions of what education was for and why it matters to the development of every individual: their approach also exemplified challenging and engaging teaching. Over the intervening decades, first as Masters' student of those two demanding and entertaining teachers, then as protégé and, after a short while, long-distance colleague and friend of Robin Barrow, I too have given over my working life to philosophy of education. Over that time, we have argued at length about what should be the most pressing questions for our analyses, but those differences of focus are built on agreement about an intellectual bedrock from which I have never wished to diverge.

That bedrock is Robin Barrow's insistence that philosophy has 'huge practical value' (Barrow and Woods 1974 (foreword to 1987, 3rd edition, xvii)), but that 'in order to be able to make telling comments on the world. . . . one needs to develop an armoury of specific as opposed to general concepts' (Barrow and Woods 1974 (foreword to 1982, 2nd edition, xi)) with the purpose of this conceptual rigour being to 'explore and iron out obscurities, contradictions, confusions, absurdities and so forth that may be involved in people's hazy grasp of the ideas in question' (Barrow and Woods 1974 (foreword to 1987, 3rd edition, xvii)). On the same page he also notes that '. . . . philosophers should be applying themselves more than they sometimes have in the past to the practices and assumptions of those around them' (Barrow and Woods 1974 (foreword to 1987, 3rd edition, xvii)). These two concerns— conceptual clarity and practical application—must be at the heart of any philosopher's work, for unless, *pace* Wittgenstein, that work is not intended to make some difference in the world, to devote one's professional life to it would be like a form of intellectual flower-arranging. However, since the first concern is a necessary condition for any value in the second, the preoccupation with conceptual clarity is primary. Barrow has indeed given attention to the practices and assumptions of educational theory and policy and has repeatedly exposed the 'emperor's new clothes' of changing fashion, and he has done this with insistence on that clarity of thought which is the hallmark of his prodigious published output (17 books, 109 articles).[1] In all of these writings, Barrow's stance is plainly that of a teacher, urging and enabling those directly involved in education to think carefully about what they are doing and why, a task that in my view he has consistently carried out in a way matched by few of our contemporaries. The divergence between us is that I would claim that the task he has undertaken may be too modest and circumscribed a role for philosophy of education.

To say this is not to detract from the primacy of the analytic row that Barrow has hoed. And with an output of Barrow's quantity and quality, it seems churlish to chide him for what he has not additionally done, but that is what I intend to do in this chapter. I am making a plea for philosophy of education to become more 'engaged'. By that I do not mean that we should all become activists or polemicists in the field of educational policy, or even that our analyses should primarily address policymakers and politicians more urgently than education professionals. Addressing policymakers is now on the agenda of some philosophers of education, and this is a useful but limited task.[2] It is limited because the education policy audience is not captive, like students, nor predisposed, like colleagues. Moreover, experience teaches us that only in times of conscious social renewal does rational enquiry into complex social practices gain purchase on the policy process. When theoretical argument is not pushing at a social door that is at least ajar, it falls on deaf ears—and even where it is taken into consideration, a host of externalities may overtake it.[3] So for me the jury is out on matters of audience. The most worthwhile 'normal science' focus for the philosopher may well be to address primarily those now directly involved in education (teachers and local administrators) so that they will be equipped to see and say that the emperor is naked when the mood of the times becomes more receptive—often through the evident failure of past fashions. Barrow has determinedly pursued this path through many changes of fashion, not just in education but in philosophy of education.

I therefore mean more by 'engagement' than involvement in the educational policy process and more by 'contextualising' our work than a simple taking account of the current environment in which teachers teach and learners learn. I would like to argue, too briefly, that philosophers of education should be engaged in two far more complex philosophical tasks which philosophers centrally concerned with the social practice of education should be particularly well placed to advance. The first is to explore how far full acceptance of the fact that this practice is irredeemably social must impact on our analyses of aims and practices for the education of the individual. The second, which should be prompted by that acceptance, is to bring the contradictions and impasses of liberal philosophy of education to bear on current debates about tenable forms of liberalism itself. Only by so doing can we extend Barrow's advice that philosophers of education should pay more attention 'to the practices and assumptions of those around them' and give adequate scrutiny to our own assumptions. This is a plea that we should go beyond explicating the 'normal science' of the education of individuals in a liberal society and use the insights of public education's persistent failure to redeem its promises—of personal emancipation and concomitant social progress—to understand and possibly advance the intellectual paradigm in which we work.

Indeed glimpses of the need for those two philosophical tasks can be seen as early as 1978 in Barrow's own work. In his critical analysis of the deschooling/freeschooling fad of the time (Barrow 1978), after demolishing its advocates' case in terms of clarity and logic, he sums up with a more fatal, but incomplete, substantive objection, namely that 'the most serious problem facing the radicals is the contradiction between their ideas and their proposals' (Barrow 1978, p. 176). This is not quite correct, as we can see from Barrow's next sentence: 'To varying degrees they are politically minded: they want and hope to produce a more just, equal and democratic society. But by temperament they are individualists. Even in the most congenial circumstances individualism does not rest easily with those ideals' (1978, p. 176). The contradiction he picks out is in fact more deep-rooted than he suggests, since it lies within the *nexus of ideals* which the 'radicals'—avowedly progressive liberals, try to hold in tension. For a 'political' mindset is not limited to those who have an explicit agenda for change in the social world. All of us operate with implicit assumptions which animate our taken-for-granted understanding of the world and hence of our dealings with it. Insofar as anyone, traditional or 'progressive' liberal educator as much as 1970s 'radical' educator, is an individualist who also values a 'just, equal and democratic society', conflicts of interest await in relation to the social practice of education as much as they do in respect of arrangements for progressive taxation,[4] if less obviously. These can only be obscured by a belief at the heart of liberal education policy, practice—and philosophy. Namely that the education of the individual (at best of all individuals) will itself powerfully contribute to building the desired society. In affluent western democracies, governments have been pursuing this Holy Grail for well over a century now, with policies constantly revised to delay, disguise, or mitigate the unwelcome fact that not only does the separate good of each not sum empirically to the good of all, however much we fine-tune procedures, but that it logically cannot.

With few exceptions,[5] philosophers of education do not grapple seriously enough with the implications of this uncomfortable dilemma. Many simply ignore it. Those who do at least acknowledge it, from Dewey to

Barrow, balance with one foot on each of its horns thanks to assumptions at the heart of classical liberalism which should have been called into question by the extension of public education over the past two centuries, more than by any other social development—and which one would think, therefore, should attract the attention of philosophers concerned with education even more than of social and political philosophers in general. With isolated exceptions, this has not happened. Rather, the standard procedure, by philosophers of education as well as by policymakers and public, is to assume that the dilemma would be resolved if 'good education' were better conceptualised, constituted, and distributed and if its relation to the surrounding society were better understood and mediated. Thus when Barrow turns his attention to the relation between the education of the individual and the values of the surrounding society, he rightly states that the 'radical educators' cannot rely on the teaching of 'society' or 'the community' for the education of the next generation unless that environment is itself 'educative'. This problem cannot not be resolved, he maintains, 'until we have properly educated a complete generation. At the same time, one cannot properly educate a generation by the means proposed by the radicals, since they are the means that depend on an educative environment' (Barrow 1978, p. 179). He is right, of course, to expose a circularity which is glaringly obvious in the proposals under critique, since they advocate simply delegating the teaching of values, culture, etc. to 'society'. But unless we suppose that a liberal education in formal schooling is immune to the values and culture of the social environment—which Barrow does not—we would require some other assumption to vindicate his underlying belief that when 'we have properly educated a complete generation', we will have an 'educative community'. Without some implicit assumption to support the belief that the education of an entire generation of individuals, as conceived by Barrow in common with traditionalist Anglophone philosophers of education, would result in the constitution of a particular kind of society, we would have no reason to suppose that a focus on the education of individuals, properly constituted and distributed, will bring in its wake a just and equitable society, such as he frequently alludes to.

We are given an unqualified statement of this sanguine belief in a quote on the flyleaf of Barrow's *Philosophy of Schooling* (1981) in which Dewey declares that, provided the school imbues each child with worthy surrounding social values and the capacity to exercise autonomy, 'we shall have the deepest and best guarantee of a larger society which is worthy, lovely and harmonious.' I am suggesting that, although Barrow nowhere makes such a bald claim explicitly, nonetheless implicit reliance on classical liberalism's virtuous spiral in which individual emancipation through education would bring social progress towards a just and equitable society, with each process, once underway, sustaining and making potent the other, is required to underpin his work, just as it is required to underpin most traditional work in philosophy of education, from R. S. Peters's *Ethics and Education*

(1966) onwards. For like Peters, Hirst, and many who have come after them, Barrow sees liberal education as a matter of inducting the rising generation into worthwhile forms of knowledge/modes of thought, in a manner which enables individuals to develop the cognitive attributes necessary for the eventual exercise of rational autonomy. Moral education, scrupulously avoiding indoctrination, such that the young are taught not what to think about moral matters, but how to think clearly, rationally, and without confusion or prejudice, is part of this education whose overall aim is to develop rationally and morally autonomous individuals. Now whilst Barrow is right to say that the methodological hallmark of this tradition—philosophical/conceptual analysis—'makes no a priori assumptions about reality, appearance or anything else' (Barrow 2010a, p. 21) this does not mean that the precepts it offers for the conduct of education require no scaffolding of supporting beliefs about the individual, about (contingent) social structure—and about the recursive relation of individual and society, irrespective of historical contingencies.

It seems odd for Barrow to charge, in his recent revalidation of R. S. Peters's educational vision (Barrow 2010a, p. 21) that just now, in a social context where skills and utility are thought to be at a premium, ' . . . educational theory and practice have ended up with a false view of what it is to be human, and hence a false view of education . . . partly because we have failed to do the conceptual work' (Barrow 2010a, p. 23), without then going on to acknowledge that to put a premium on 'developing the mind and human reason for its own sake' (Barrow 2010a, p. 23), must also rest on a particular view of 'what it is to be human', similarly requiring conceptual work. Without that, we too risk 'a false view of education', its aims and practices. It is hard to see how anyone can confidently 'trenchantly assert the plausibility of Peters' conception of education', viz. 'developing the kind of understanding one admires' (Barrow 2010a, p. 23), with reference only to aims and content, without an explicit view of 'what it is to be human'.[6] And since the one non-contingent thing we are sure of is that humans are necessarily social creatures, that must require a view of the individual's relation to society and hence of the significance of the individual's social embeddedness and social construction for the aims and content of education.

Now Barrow cannot be accused of ignoring the social. Indeed in his *Philosophy of Schooling* (Barrow 1982, p. 1) he set out to give particular attention it, endorsing in his preface 'the need to look into the question of the relationship between school and society'. However, he goes on immediately to state: 'I do not mean how they do relate, but how they ought to relate. . . .' (Barrow 1982, p. 1). He rejects that first question on the grounds that, being empirical, it is outside the philosopher's remit. (That hasty rejection is rather odd from a philosopher who has rightly castigated much empirical research in the social sciences in general and in education in particular for neglecting conceptual and logical questions.[7]) The grounds for this rejection are that 'no empirical enquiry as such is philosophical', as 'the business of philosophising is exclusively a business of reasoning' (Barrow 1981, p. 4). Of course, it is no business of philosophy to study the empirical empirically, but to tease out the *assumptions* underlying a state of affairs, to question whether a social policy could *logically* bring about its expressed aims, or to make judgements about the *relative merit* of alternative proposals is clearly the business of reasoning. Despite this and therefore restricting himself to the second matter—how schools ought to relate to society, Barrow considers only the contingent (local and historically temporary) questions of how schools might facilitate social demands, for example, for greater equality by 'bussing' or anti-sex-stereotyping measures (Barrow 1981, p. 49) or what should be the social source of curriculum prescription, on the sound grounds that 'what we do in schools depends on what sort of society, ideally, we would like' (Barrow 1981, p. 79).

All of this, of course, is fine as far as it goes, but it does not go nearly as far as it should. It principally concerns ways in which schooling should respond to the social status quo either to accommodate it or to mitigate its perceived shortcomings (provided those concessions to social demands are carefully limited). For the avoidance of doubt, I am not here accusing Barrow of endorsing social conservatism. Indeed we see in his *Injustice, Inequality and Ethics* (Barrow 1982) that he is concerned with a range of questions relating to social justice, from affirmative action to income inequality, and that he rightly understands 'equality of opportunity' as 'an equal opportunity to become unequal' (Barrow 1982, p. 106). But I am accusing him of holding fast to a conception of education in which that social practice, though perforce it must take account of the social environment, should hold as true as possible to its neutralist liberal aim of developing rational and moral autonomy in individuals, on the underlying assumption that this course will eventually lead to a fairer and more desirable social world. It should be stressed here that Barrow is not guilty of any socially unconcerned version of this thesis: when he states that 'One error we have made is to look at schools primarily to be social reorganisers. . . . why should schools be organised with a view to bringing about greater social equality?' (Barrow 1982, p. 194), that is clearly not because he is indifferent to unfairness. Rather it is because he regards social justice, social structure, and social inequality as requiring attention, to be sure, but by extra-educational means. The assumption here must be that whilst these matters of social justice are important in themselves, they are not only discrete from the social practice of education but also, from the philosopher of education's point of view, are primarily salient as obstacles to realising the social aim of liberal education whereby its equitable distribution across the citizenry would bring closer that virtuous spiral of individual emancipation and social progress towards 'a more just, equal and democratic society' (Barrow 1978, p. 179), provided the social factors which contingently frustrate the operation of that virtuous spiral were mitigated or removed.

What that position entirely leaves out is that even if, as Barrow reasonably advocates, education were not looked to to solve problems of social structure, and even if there were political will and democratic support for programmes of social reform to iron out or at least reduce inequalities in income, health, housing, etc. (in relation to which education tends to be a 'dominant good' (Walzer 1981)), nonetheless, inequalities in power, social esteem, and scope for the exercise of personal autonomy would persist. They would do so *not in spite of education*, however scrupulously conceptualised, *but because of it*. For however constituted and however carefully distributed, public education is arguably the modern world's most powerful engine of inequality, both at the level of individuals within a polity and that of power relations between polities. It is not good enough for philosophers of education to note that education brings both intrinsic and extrinsic rewards (with the latter beyond the purview of educators or theorists of education). Nor is it good enough to suggest, as Barrow does, that schools would be better able to focus on the intrinsic value of education in a world where its extrinsic rewards did not lead to differential earnings or life-chances. (Barrow 1982, p. 127). That standard position, in which the aims of liberal education are seen as separate from social realities but liable to frustration by them, such that those contingencies require separate social attention, fails to acknowledge that unless 'extrinsic' rewards are very narrowly conceived ('earnings') or vacuously glossed over ('life-chances'), the standard distinction between those two types of benefit that education is traditionally declared to confer on the individual begins to look much less secure. This is because 'social realities' are not restricted to contingencies of particular social arrangements but also encompass the logically inescapable social construction of the individual.

The oversimplification which understands the intrinsic and extrinsic benefits of education to individuals as discrete is mirrored by a second, related, oversimplification in traditional liberalism, and fatally in liberal theorising about education, namely that the 'goods' of the world can be neatly divided into those which are public and those which are private. Both of these dichotomies benefit from closer scrutiny, and the social practice of education is particularly well suited for exposing problems with them both. For reasons of space, little time will be given here to the inadequacy of liberal theory's convention of dividing the 'goods' of the world into the public and the private, exhaustively. That neat division cannot reflect the complexity and interdependence of our social world: in particular it cannot do justice to the social practice of education. Among policymakers and the public, arguments about whether education should be treated as a public good, provided and regulated by the state, or as a private good, provided by the market and regulated by the choices of individual consumers, have generated much heat in recent years ('magnet schools', 'academies', fee-paying schools, or the proper funding of higher education). Philosophers of education on the other hand have recognised that education is a good both public *and* private: public because of its crucial role in relation to societal well-being, due to the part it plays not only in realising society's aspirations but, importantly, in forming them. However, although all citizens in a democracy benefit from the existence of public education and all share its indirect benefits, all do not—and cannot—share its direct benefits equally, however much opportunities are equalised. We are each affected by the education, or lack of it, of others: this we experience collectively. But we are also each powerfully—and differentially—affected by our own education, or lack of it: this we experience privately.

Now although philosophers of education traditionally recognise this, noting that education is 'a positional good', as reflected in Barrow's remark that equality of opportunity amounts to 'an equal opportunity to become unequal' (Barrow 1982, p. 106), I am claiming that they tend not to take account of the ramifications of that insight in their justification of the aims of liberal education. For if the social practice of education is not simply unable to bring about a fairer social world without concomitant reform of structural conditions, but is in fact a prime driver of inequality, with an inescapable tendency to frustrate the intended outcomes of any such reforms, where does that leave the pious belief in liberalism's virtuous spiral whereby the spread of public education, properly constituted and distributed, would bring about an 'educative community' (Barrow 1978, p. 179) or 'a more just, equal and democratic society' (Barrow 1982, p. 194)?

Instead of revisiting the assumptions on which that pious hope is based, assumptions about 'what it is to be human', philosophers of education tend to focus their analyses of the complexity of education's value on the purportedly individual dimension of the distinction between intrinsic and extrinsic value, with the latter being outside the purview of the aims and content of education. I would claim, though, that a recognition that education is irredeemably social in all its aspects makes this procedure of more limited value than is usually acknowledged. For as I have argued more fully elsewhere (Jonathan 1997, Ch. 3), even education's intrinsic goods, though personal, are not purely private, since they have an inescapable social dimension and social parameters. What counts as my learning, to me as well as to others, depends not merely on what I know, but also on what others know; my learning has an opportunity-cost which affects what others come to know; and the value of my learning to me, intrinsically as well as extrinsically, depends to varying degrees on social and material conditions developed and inhabited by others. Similarly, what counts as a talent in me depends on the skills, abilities, and valuations of others; the development of any talent has an opportunity-cost borne by others as well as the talented; and my exercise and enjoyment of my talent, as well as its development, depends to varying degrees on the skills, abilities, and valuations of others who share, admire, or merely tolerate its exercise. These considerations suggest that even the intrinsic value of education to the individual has a social dimension in a finite world of interdependent social actors and therefore also has a 'positional' aspect, if less obviously so than education's extrinsic rewards. Finally and perhaps most importantly, we could only suppose that my rational autonomy, responsibly exercised, did not risk restricting or encroaching on the similar autonomy of others if we believed that the talents, inclinations, and preferences of each would harmonise and sum to a collective reality which equally permitted their expression—or if we supposed instead that the talents and preferences of some were inherently restricted.

The former of these possibilities was the pious hope of nineteenth-century liberalism, persisting in liberal philosophy of education still: the latter is the implicit counsel of despair of that crass neo-liberalism which latterly deems all goods which are not unproblematically public as therefore private and best competed for in a market of individual choice. I do not intend here to focus on the damaging social consequences of the latter version of (paleo)-liberalism, or on its disingenuous conflation of the good of each with the good of all, or even on its problematic consequences for the constitution of the education even of favoured individuals (see, e.g., Jonathan (1997) (2001)). (This being the case because the distribution of a 'good' which is neither public nor private, but social, changes the constitution of that 'good' in ways which are not subject to rational steering, since all future developments resulting from an aggregation of the uncoordinated preferences and choices of separate individuals are necessarily emergent properties rather than stable conditions.) For the purpose of this reconsideration of philosophy of education's research agenda, I am instead simply seeking to draw attention to the fact that at the heart of liberal theory, and most obviously at the heart of traditional theorising about liberal education, we find that on closer scrutiny much that is standardly relied on in the analyses of philosophers of education, such as a distinction between education's intrinsic and extrinsic value to the individual, or a corresponding distinction between the private (individual) and public (social) benefits of the social practice of education, though superficially plausible—and useful for the avoidance of very obviously sloppy thinking—do not stand up to a closer, *philosophical,* examination of 'the relationship between school and society', not in the only sense that Barrow allows, of how education and society 'ought to relate' but in the more basic question of 'how they do relate', which he rejects as no business of the philosopher (Barrow 1981, p. 1). That rejected focus of analysis for the philosopher of education in fact opens up two important fields of enquiry.

The first of these falls within the 'normal science' of the philosopher of liberal education. It may involve acceptance of the fact that whereas, as Barrow asserts, conventional liberal philosophy of education undoubtedly has 'huge practical value' insofar as its conceptual rigour is a necessary tool to 'explore and iron out obscurities, contradictions, confusions, absurdities and so forth that may be involved in people's hazy grasp of the ideas in question' (Barrow and Woods 1974 (foreword to 1987, 3rd edition, xvii))—a vital task; its substantive arguments for the aims and content of education rest on shakier ground when these set out to go beyond the exposure of evident nonsense. If, as Barrow acknowledges, the liberal educational aim of 'developing the mind and human reason for its own sake' depends upon a supporting view of 'what it is to be human' (Barrow 2010a, p. 23), then a re-examination of that view, which takes sufficient account of the social construction of individuality, the social framing of intrinsic value, and the social parameters and implications of the exercise of individual autonomy, must have relevance to our aims for the education of individuals, for on the standard principle that 'ought implies can', any justification couched primarily in the rational autonomy of the individual requires further supporting assumptions.

To make this claim may seem at odds with my opening declaration in this chapter, that the task Robin Barrow has so well discharged may be too modest and circumscribed a role for philosophy of education. I would argue that it is not at odds with that assertion, however, for the second and more important focus which I wish to urge for philosophy of education's future research agenda goes beyond its 'normal science' framework, which is set firmly within the classical, neutralist liberal paradigm. That paradigm has been subject to questioning by social and political philosophers for a quarter of a century now. I maintain that the limited contribution of philosophers of education to that questioning is more than regrettable, since they are especially well placed to contribute to such a re-examination, given that there is no social practice in which the dubious beliefs of nineteenth-century liberals have been so controverted by events as in the practice of universal public education in the developed democracies over the past century, and no area of theorising where core analyses are more dependent on implicit confidence in those beliefs than in Anglophone philosophy of education as it has been centrally conducted since its revitalisation in the mid-twentieth century by R. S. Peters and P. H. Hirst.

It seems doubly odd that so few philosophers of education have ventured to take part in this debate when over the past twenty years there has clearly been an impetus within their field to look to new frameworks for research and teaching. In North America this has brought what Barrow refers to as the teaching of 'isms'—pragmatism, idealism, existentialism, etc. in order to draw out their educational implications, whereas in Britain there has been a vogue for 'postmodernism'—a cherry-picking of the (translated) work of diverse Continental philosophers who would not themselves recognise membership of a common school of thought. Barrow has suggested these moves to be a regrettable shift away from the rigorous analysis of concepts, argumentation, and hidden premises (Barrow 2010b), and with that I concur. But I am more dubious about the suggested motivation, that this is primarily a search for novelty and academic respectability. It seems very possible that these philosophical tangents are partly pursued because expert practitioners such as Barrow have taken work *within* the neutralist liberal paradigm as far as it can go without coming up against the philosophical brick wall of that paradigm's boundaries. Those boundaries, I would argue, may be less confining than those of other conceptual frameworks, in the same way that representative democracy is the least bad way we have yet discovered of organising ourselves politically, but they are confining nonetheless and should be subject to re-examination just as we still look for ways of better recasting representative democracy. Barrow has long insisted that once an individual thinker has 'adopted a particular philosophical stance', say Marxism, existentialism, or utilitarianism, ' . . . true philosophy ceases; indeed the need to think practically ceases . . . ' (Barrow 2010b, p. 3), and whilst this may be overstating the case, the extent to which it is true must also be true for the stance of the neutralist liberal.

Readers scarcely need reminding of the fact that liberal social projects throughout modernity are rooted in the Enlightenment project and early European and North American democratisation, whose central tenets relied on an assumed connection between increased knowledge, sound reasoning, and right judgement. This is explicit in nineteenth-century justifications for the three-pronged modernising social project which was to be realised through the free exchange of goods and ideas, the spread of education, and the extension of the franchise. And this lies at the heart of liberal democratic theories of education which have seen learning as the road to both individual emancipation (from the constraints of prevailing ideas and circumstance) and to social progress. The twinning of those two aims, throughout that history of optimism about education's transformative power, relied on the earlier Enlightenment belief that gaining knowledge and understanding—achieving rational autonomy—would lead to sound judgement (in the moral sphere as elsewhere) and that such judgements, multiplied across society, would gradually build a better world for all—a world fairer as well as more prosperous. Throughout that long history, all good things were thus to be delivered by education, and progressively to everyone. Part of the power of those long-held beliefs, as so often, lies in the fact that they are undeniably half-true. Whilst personal empowerment is not necessarily accompanied by a social commitment to the well-being of one's fellows, it is true that unless individuals are empowered—in the modern world effectively by education—their opportunities to turn that commitment to good effect are restricted. And whilst education is not necessarily the royal road to social progress, in terms of equity as well as prosperity, substantial material preconditions are not possible without it. Stating the obvious like this should alert us to the need to go further and ask what it is about education which keeps alive our optimism in its socially transformative power and provides *some* of the preconditions for a socially transformative project, yet which also pulls in the opposite direction: towards an ethos of social competition and the reproduction of a hierarchy of relative social advantage, despite improvements in absolute well-being.

Some of these conundra have been alluded to in this chapter but not fully pursued. That is not merely for reasons of space but because we may have to admit that they cannot be resolved within a philosophical paradigm which has generated them. It is my contention that if philosophers of education are securely to ground, for example, the intrinsic value of certain kinds of knowledge and understanding, or the overarching aim of agnostically promoting rational and moral autonomy in individuals, whilst *at the same time* maintaining the belief that, spread throughout the population, these individual attributes will sum to a better world for all in which all are equally empowered, they must bring their understanding of these impasses for philosophy of education to bear on the wider philosophical enquiry of today, namely the search within a revitalised political and liberal philosophy for a more tenable theory of liberalism than that of the social optimists of the nineteenth century. If they wish to avoid the dog-eats-dog counsel of despair of recent neo-liberalism, which in embracing atomistic individualism and a consequent wholesale discounting of human interdependence is clearly even more theoretically untenable than liberal neutralism (as well as resulting in catastrophic policies for various social practices, and notably public education, ratcheting up and embracing social competition to the eventual disbenefit of all), there seems only one broad direction in which to go.

Philosophers of education of note, such as Barrow, whose work has provided much of the grounding for that of many others, including this writer, are aware that educational theory as well as practice exists in a nexus of values, realities, and frameworks of interpretation in continuous interaction. In this dynamic, our prevailing social theory and our established social practices each reflect and underpin the other in periods of stable consensus, and each challenges and highlights points of weakness in the other in periods of contestation such as the present. Uncomfortable though they are, it is thus through such periods of contestation that developments in our understanding, as well as modifications in our circumstance, take place. Therefore it is not enough for philosophers of education simply to expose fallacies and absurdities in, for example, recent trends to the marketisation of educational opportunity or the concomitant commodification of knowledge, useful though that work is. For such work only addresses the symptoms and damaging consequences of the course on which social change now seems set, and has little to say about, and no effect on, the underlying engine of that course. If it is thought that this task should be left to social and political philosophy, we should remind ourselves both of the power of theory and practice to modify each other and of the fact that public education is the only social practice which both reflects and modifies social realities through the formation of persons.

So at a time when the central tenets of liberalism are the subject of debate, it would be strange if philosophers whose primary object of interest is education had no part to play in re-examining those tenets. In disputes over whether the self is or is not prior to its ends, over whether autonomy is to be considered as an individual value or as a social good, over where the boundaries lie between the public and private domains, over whether the state (and the educational institutions it provides and regulates) can or should stand neutral between competing ideas of the good, etc., the connection between these questions and any justifying theory for the *aims, content, and processes* of education is undeniable. Similarly, on matters such as the legitimate scope of the state, on whether individuals 'own' their talents and attributes, on how far individual choices in a social context should be considered self-regarding, etc., then any justifying theory for the appropriate *distribution* of education is of crucial relevance.

It is evident—and unsurprising—that the contemporary watershed in social philosophy is mirrored by an equivalent watershed in the conduct and direction of our most fundamental social practice. It therefore seems urgent for philosophers of education to move beyond their 'normal science', conducted within the long-unchallenged paradigm of a neutralist liberalism—the framework of sociopolitical theory to which liberal philosophy of education pervasively makes implicit reference—and to bring the insights of their field of study to the work of social and political philosophers who currently seek to address that now-creaking paradigm's shortcomings and build it on firmer foundations for the future than are afforded by the pious optimism of the past. Throughout all of Robin Barrow's teaching and published work, his constant theme is the duty of the philosopher of education to persist in the analysis of concepts, the scrutiny of argument for rigour, consistency, and clarity and the search for explicating the value and purposes of education. The research agenda proposed in the latter part of this paper is entirely consistent with those commitments. So to return to the question of this chapter's title: 'Is Barrow Nearly Right about Philosophy of Education?', the answer in this writer's view has to be largely yes, in terms of its role in the critique and clarification of proposals and justifications for the education of individuals within a long-standing liberal paradigm. But an acknowledgement of the constraints and limitations of that paradigm needs also to be a focus of analysis for philosophers of education who are mindful of the wider social project whose furtherance has long underpinned the democratic extension of that education to all.

NOTES

1. See e.g., R. Barrow (1976) (1978) (1984) (1990) (2006a) (2006b) plus papers and articles too numerous to list.
2. See e.g., (2006b) The *Impact Papers* regularly produced by the Philosophy Society of Great Britain on aspects of educational policy.
3. My own research and publication, aimed at underpinning the thinking of policymakers (since the mid-1990s primarily in South Africa), even though it was by the invitation of statutory bodies and ministries, has met a very varied and uncertain fate.

4. On the latter, see the face-plausibility of analyses found in, e.g., R. Nozick (1974).
5. M. Hollis (1982) or (1990), R. Jonathan (1997) or (2001).
6. Barrow has indeed touched on this question in recent work but not pursued it to the degree I am suggesting would be necessary.
7. See, e.g., R. Barrow (with L. Foreman-Peck; 2006b).

REFERENCES

Barrow, R. (1976) *Common Sense and the Curriculum*, London: Allen & Unwin.
———. (1978) *Radical Education*, Oxford: Martin Robertson.
———. (1981) *Philosophy of Schooling*, Sussex: Wheatsheaf.
———. (1982) *Injustice Inequality and Ethics*, Sussex: Harvester
———. (1984) *Giving Teaching Back to Teachers*, Sussex: Wheatsheaf.
———. (1990) 'Understanding Skills', *Thinking, Feeling, and Caring*, London: Falmer Press.
———. (2006a) *Academic Ethics*, London: Ashgate.
——— and L. Foreman-Peck (2006b) *What Use is Educational Research? A Debate*, London: Impact, imprint of PESGB.
———. (2010a) 'Was Peters Nearly Right About Education?', *Journal of Philosophy of Education* 43(1).
———. (2010b) 'Reflections on Philosophy of Education, Classics, Literature and Universities', talk delivered to Philosophy for Educational Renewal group, Conway Hall, London, April 2010.
Barrow, R. and R. G. Woods (1974) *An Introduction to Philosophy of Education*, London. Methuen.
Hollis, M. (1982) 'Education as a Positional Good', *Journal of Philosophy of Education* 16(2).
———. (1990) 'Market Equality and Social Freedom', *Journal of Applied Philosophy* 7(1).
Jonathan, R. (1997) *Illusory Freedoms: Liberalism, Education and the Market*, Oxford: Blackwell.
———. (2001) 'Higher Education Transformation and the Public Good', *Kagisano*, imprint of the Council on Higher Education, South Africa.
Nozick, R. (1974) *Anarchy, State and Utopia*, New York: Basic Books.
Peters, R. S. (1966) *Ethics and Education*, London: Allen & Unwin.
Walzer, M. (1981) *Spheres of Justice*, New York: Basic Books.

8 Some Reflections Arising from Jonathan on Barrow

Ian Gregory

Ruth Jonathan rightly pays tribute to Robin Barrow's contribution over the last forty years to the philosophy of education. His many books and articles over that time have all been distinguished by an unrelenting determination to get and be clear about the issue or set of issues being pursued. The clarity of his writing never allows for any doubts as to where he stands on the problem at hand. And what shines through is his sense that philosophy is important and (whether it is allowed to or not) *ought* to make a difference. The term 'analytical philosophy' so often used to characterise what is most typical of Anglo-American academic philosophy is not altogether without its ambiguities. However characterised, Barrow's contribution to the philosophy of education is exemplary of the very best writing within that tradition. Like Ruth Jonathan, I have known Robin Barrow over a long period of time. At a personal level what has always most impressed me is that the commitment to banishing obscurity, exposing shoddy argument, drawing the right conclusions, and insisting that philosophy matters is not simply a matter for the academy but something that should be carried through into our individual lives. Anyone who has late into the night and (often) not-so-early morning argued and drunk wine with Barrow, while listening to the forbidden pleasures of country music, will testify to the intellectual stimulation to be gained from conversation with this devotee of reason. All conducted, it must be said, with rare good humour.

Jonathan clearly agrees with Barrow in seeing philosophy as having a key role to play in the shaping of practice. Indeed in terms she says that, *pace* Wittgenstein, unless it embraces such a role, philosophy becomes nothing more than a kind of intellectual parlour game. There is little sympathy for the Wittgensteinian sentiment that philosophy leaves everything as it is. Whether this lack of sympathy towards Wittgensteinian quietism is more general, or simply addressed to philosophising about education, is unclear. There can be no doubt however that she and Barrow are as one over the practical implications of philosophical debate for educational practice. Given the importance she attaches to its possibilities, it is perhaps a little surprising that the primary audience to whom philosophers of education are encouraged to carry their message is not those who most shape our educational institutions—the politicians and policymakers more generally—but rather those more immediately and directly involved in education—the teachers and administrators. Jonathan gloomily, but probably rightly, thinks that those who make policy are unreceptive to the kind of rational enquiry represented by philosophical activity until it is clear their preferred policies are failing. And that teachers and administrators equipped with a measure of insight garnered from the philosophers of education will see, as she puts it, 'that the emperor is naked when the mood of the times becomes more receptive'. Speculation about which audience would best reward the efforts of philosophers hoping to influence education practice throws up no issues of philosophical interest. My own sense is that giving up on trying to engage the interest of politicians and policymakers is a mistake. They are, after all, the ones who make and shape policy. If they characteristically pay no attention to those who purport to offer them rationally grounded insights into the practice of education, there seems little reason to be sanguine about them listening to teachers and local administrators bent upon getting them to see things differently even at times of crisis. The story of educational policymaking since the end of World War II, after all, has always been one that largely and quite deliberately has disregarded the teaching voice.

Turning to more philosophical matters, Jonathan and Barrow both believe that the outcome of philosophical reflection about education can be better, because more rationally based, practice. If individuals engaged in a practice simply have no very clear idea of what they are doing, if they are ostensibly pursuing some end about which they are conceptually confused, if they are bad at drawing appropriate inferences, it seems the merest good sense to suppose what they do will cast little light on their notional concerns. Barrow in his discussion of provision for 'gifted children' (for instance) (Barrow 1990, Ch. 3) parades at some length the ways in which any provision for, and research into, 'giftedness' can go wrong. This writer finds it all persuasive. The scope for misinterpretation and misunderstanding of the outcomes of research into gifted children on the part of those who are so confused is considerable. Wittgenstein famously reminds us that in psychology there is empirical method and conceptual confusion. And the clarificatory role associated with analytical philosophy of education into the language and concepts of education carries the same warning message for those whose task it is to determine the aims and purposes of education and to devise programmes of learning that will deliver on those aims and purposes.

But Ruth Jonathan, while embracing the pursuit of clarity, the elimination of obscurity, and greater rigour in educational argument, all the desiderata the analytical philosophy prides itself on, is not satisfied. She wants a proper marking of the irredeemably social dimension of educational practice along with recognition of how that must impact upon the analyses of the aims and practices in respect of the education of individuals. And she also has the conviction that what she calls 'liberal philosophy of education' can help cast light upon 'tenable' forms of liberalism. Fuelling this desire to extend the ambitions of what she thinks of as liberal philosophy of education is the task of trying to build upon our understanding of the 'persistent' failure of public education to deliver on the grand ambitions of personal advancement and emancipation along with social progress. It is asserted that lying at the heart of liberal education, policy, practice, and philosophy is the belief that the education of the individual will conduce to building the desired society. The provision of good education will importantly shape the moral betterment of society. Putting it briefly, if the ambitions of liberal theorists are realised, the outcome of a good education for all will be a just and equitable society. It's unclear whether Jonathan thinks the efforts so far to deliver on such a society have been a total failure, or just not been as successful as it might have been hoped. What is clear is that as she presently conceives the model of liberalism informing liberal theorising about education and its practices, it (logically) cannot fully deliver. Nothing can, as she puts it, ' . . . mitigate the unwelcome fact that not only does the separate good of each not sum empirically to the good of all, however much we fine-tune procedures but that logically it cannot.' Any adequate statement of the ends, aims, and purposes of education must take on board fully the implications of the fact that we humans pass our lives in society and are social creatures importantly touched and shaped by the experience of social living. Putting it negatively, any attempt to make provision for education rooted in a conception of humans quite divorced from their 'social embedded-ness' must fail them—certainly if the ambition is to see education as the motor to a more just, equal, and democratic society. Education itself, whatever its impact on the individual, is one of the great determinants of inequality within our society. As Jonathan puts it: 'For however constituted and distributed, public education is arguably the modern world's most powerful engine of inequality, both at the level of individuals within a polity and that of power relations between polities.'

What to make of all this? And what to make of Jonathan's plea that 'we bring the contradictions and impasses of liberal philosophy of education to bear on current debates about tenable forms of liberalism'? I am very unclear about all of this and within my very brief compass cannot do justice to issues of this very great complexity. Informing Jonathan's take on the matters of her paper is the final belief that public education premised on a liberal theory of education has conspicuously failed. The failure of public education at the individual level is not the main issue. It is the apparent failure at the societal level that is particularly the focus of concern. She is clearly unimpressed by how far we have advanced towards the just, equitable, democratic society which it is claimed is the promise of liberal education, and which is the sanguine sentiment underlying liberal-neutralist philosophy of education. It's worth commenting on the difficulties associated with making any overall judgement about whether moral progress has occurred over time. What is the currency of debate? What are the key criteria to be brought to bear on any such judgement? Even if we can give clear meaning to the idea of moral progress, isn't it possible that advances have been made in areas of moral concern while regression has occurred in others? And how does one measure the weight to be given to those advances as against the losses? And lurking behind all such judgements surely lays the suspicion that the claim of lack of moral progress is simply a moral judgement giving expression to disagreement with the moral direction of society? This latter anxiety being particularly pertinent within the context of liberal theorising as what informs Jonathan's stance looks like some distinct preference that the cause of equality should be more served, as against those who would see our society as giving proper emphasis upon freedom as the cardinal good to be served by liberalism. Even if there is agreement that the promises of liberal education have not yet been adequately realised, it is always possible to claim that the failure is a consequence of not having successfully delivered on a best education for the individuals living within our society.

It seems to me that the most compelling reason for giving up on this variant of a liberal theory of education is not the palpable failure to deliver but rather the difficulty of making coherent sense of the ambition. The claim is made that the dominant mode of liberal philosophy of education reflects the thought that the enlightenment good education will bring, in its wake, if successfully delivered, not only individual transformation but also social transformation. For Jonathan this social transformation is to be identified with a more just, equitable, and democratic society. To say this is to say everything but also to say nothing. What needs to be fleshed out is just what the distinguishing features of such a society might be. I imagine it would be a society characterised by those values typically associated with the liberal outlook. Among the fundamental values found in the socially transformed society would be a large measure of tolerance; celebration of autonomy; the freedom for people to live their lives as they see fit, subject to the constraint of the harm principle; and recognition of the equal dignity and worth of each individual. Translated into more specific features of such a society, it would mean the reduction of sexism and racism, freedom of association and speech, freedom to practice one's religion, the celebration of cultural diversity, democratic structures of government, equality of opportunity, a high premium of human rights, and so on. Presumably the *gravamen* of Jonathan's sense of a failure to deliver on the part of public education is that there is too little evidence of such values and achievements to be found as a consequence of the provision of public education in societies actuated by the nineteenth-century liberalism she associates with the paradigm dominating liberal philosophy of education. The name of Mill looms large here. Fairly undeniably, Mill did associate the spread of educational opportunities with moral progress as an outcome at both the individual and social levels. If we accept the pessimistic assessment of Jonathan as to the outcome of public investment in education, the implications are clear, When reflecting upon the possibilities of liberalism and liberal theory for education, we should bear in mind both the failures of liberal education to deliver on its ambitions, and be accepting of the fact that the separate good of each cannot usher in the good of all. I don't detect on Jonathan's part a sense that liberalism is a busted flush. Rather we need to put it on surer foundations and create a liberal philosophy of education that speaks better to the possibilities of education. Talk of the aims and purposes of education will in this context reflect a more realistic sense of education's possibilities, rooted in its individual and inescapably social dimensions. And perhaps encourage a more clear-sighted pursuit of some of those ambitions arising from the concern with the exercise of responsible autonomy and social transformation. We may at the same time come to terms with the fact that in pursuing the good of each, we cannot realise the good of all.

Liberalism comes in many guises. That is to say, while recognising that disparate thinkers share enough in common in outlooks, attitudes, and values to be called liberals, there is plenty of evidence that the grounds invoked to justify the liberal-neutral outlook are varied. Furthermore, just what is involved in the neutrality, so often seen as the hallmark of the liberal outlook, can generate issues of its own. Whether all those who in the last forty to fifty years have engaged in the philosophy of education under the influence of Peters and Hirst would recognise themselves as Millian liberals I simply don't know. Whether indeed Barrow does I am unclear. He can speak for himself. It might be worth noticing that in his more recent writings on moral education, he certainly countenances the possibility that someone who is morally educated might nevertheless fall far short in terms of their moral conduct. There is no guarantee that one possessed of the wherewithal to make appropriate kinds of judgements, confronted by a moral issue will necessarily act as moral reasoning might indicate.

The challenge Jonathan poses is to come up with a more fruitful conception of the liberal outlook brought to bear upon educational concerns. Such a conception has to turn its back on the pious belief that the personal emancipation good education might bring about in individual lives will result in moral progress throughout society. However the (more?) just, equitable, and democratic society is to be achieved, it will not be achieved simply by attention to education of individuals, partly because of the differential impact of educational provision upon individual lives as it affects others. If the neutral stance associated with liberalism is to be sustained we need to be clearer about what such a stance involves and how that might impinge upon educational practice and provision. The espousal of liberal neutrality, and what it means in practice, seems likely to be much affected by the justificatory grounds informing why neutrality is to be valued. To embrace a policy of liberal neutrality is to take a moral stance on the how and why of the distribution of goods throughout society. And of great importance among those goods is education. Indeed, it seems the plainest good sense to accord to education the highest priority among the goods that go to make individual lives productive and fulfilling. Whatever human wellbeing consists in and demands, a mind developed as the result of education is the very precondition of the possibility of a life in which the significant exercise of choice and the exercise of autonomy is possible. It is in this context one gives substance to the overriding inspiration informing the liberal outlook: that each autonomous individual comes to enjoy the good life according to their own deliberations. At bottom, liberalism represents a celebration of the individual and of the individual creating the life he or she wishes to lead because it is the life the individual has chosen. The commitment to neutrality has to be given substance. The liberal cannot of course be neutral in respect of neutrality itself, and there has to be recognition that decisions have to be made as to what in any given situation the liberal has to be neutral towards, and the particular manner in which neutrality is manifested. It is in this connection that the grounds justifying the importance of neutrality carry significance. A Millian belief in the possibility of moral progress as against (say) highlighting the cardinal importance of autonomy within the individual life, or emphasising the overriding value of equality as a fundamental value, or an acceptance of cultural diversity and value pluralism may all be invoked in justifying why neutrality matters in the distribution of human goods. There is no *a priori* reason to suppose, however, that neutrality pursued in the name of those different justifications will result in coinciding policy recommendation. Indeed in the light of experience, every reason to suppose that disagreements over issues of policy can be traced to just those fundamental differences in justification. How we interpret neutrality will be a function of our underlying justifying grounds. From those underlying justifying grounds different policy recommendations may flow.

We have noted the variety of grounds that inform the stance of liberal neutrality. The suggestion has been made that those differences in grounds might well find expression in differing policy recommendations. There is an issue about just what being neutral means for the liberal. And there is certainly an issue on how neutrality finds expression in the shaping of policy. Within the domain of education and its provision, it is easy to envisage situations in which liberal neutrality is infringed. Policy decisions might be taken which deliberately favour one religious group within a society as against other religious persuasions or of a secular outlook. It might take the form of closing all other schools of religious persuasion and pouring great sums of money into schools of the preferred religious outlook. Or again policy might be passed which it is suspected will have the result of advancing the standard of well-being of a religious faction as against others while not being the intent of educational policy. Liberals might object on one or other ground to such policies in the name of neutrality. Different liberal theorists take differing attitudes towards the importance of intent as against outcome as holding the key to what amounts to a proper characterisation of neutrality. For my own part, the doubts I earlier raised about how we might measure in any very coherent way what counts as moral progress seem equally applicable to the making of judgements about how policy bears overall on life within a community. Easier to countenance is the idea that policymakers should have the intent to be impartial towards the preferred lifestyles, values, or fundamental beliefs of those likely to be touched by policy. In terms of the secular as against the religious, the Catholic as opposed to the Protestant, the Jew, or the Muslim, educational policy, if true to its liberal credentials, must not invoke any consideration that favours one party over the other: this while recognising that the impact upon one group may/is likely to be greater than upon the other. The reasons for policies, however, owe nothing to wanting to favour some group rather than another. A policy implemented to deliberately reduce funding for Catholic schools because they are Catholic is different from a policy implemented that has the same effect but which is passed for reasons to do with putting the public finances on sounder footing. It just happens that the funding of Catholic schools is differentially affected. There are all kinds of murky issues lurking here demanding much fuller consideration. Considerations of space spare me the need to pursue them more fully.

Where do the previous rather hasty and inconclusive musings leave us? Anyone who counts themselves as a liberal, whatever the most fundamental beliefs informing their liberalism, is inspired by the idea that individuals have the capacity to enjoy a meaningful life that gains its meaning in important part from that life reflecting their choices, their beliefs, their interests, their values, that is, those things to which they attach most significance. Using terminology familiar from the liberal lexicon, individuals have the potential to enjoy what for them constitutes the good life. At its richest, the idea of the good life embraces the idea of a measure of reflection entering into the deliberations of individuals as they live their lives. Choices are significant and satisfactions are pursued and enjoyed because the agent sees that for them (anyway) personal fulfilment resides in those ends that reflection recommends to them. The liberal is comfortable with the possibility that people will create for themselves good lives quite different from those of other people and that there may be there are as many good lives as there are individuals. Neutrality is exercised by not seeking to impose any particular and determinate conception of the good life upon others. It is surely trite wisdom to insist that education predominantly opens up to individuals many of those riches that can be incorporated as part of the good life, both for their own sake and as instrumental in determining the good life. For my own part, I think that the main contours of Peters' analysis of education are correct. Its emphasis upon the enlargement of understanding by initiating individuals into various worthwhile activities is difficult to gainsay. The great achievements of the human mind manifest in the various domains of knowledge and understanding—intellectual, moral, aesthetic, technological—if mastered and practiced, represent rationality at work, the power of reason in human lives. It is the exercise of reason that makes possible the idea of a good life that is more than just a reaction to states of affairs. Education at its best celebrates the notions of reason, critical intelligence, deliberation, the capacity for reflective thought, all of which we humans can bring to bear on our situation so as to bring about lives over which we have a greater measure of control. At the individual level, anyway, it conduces to life going better than it might otherwise for the individual. It is right to be sceptical whether it necessitates life going better for all (whatever that might mean). It is not so much the subject matters of educational programmes that is so crucial to giving substance to the notion of the good life as the wherewithal it affords to make more informed choices. Through the pleasures to be found in the intellectual life, the life of the mind is for many a very important feature of what for them is the good life. A good education is surely emancipatory. Informed judgements across the range of goods, pleasures, and key decisions to be made out of which good lives are constituted, makes the exercise of freedom that much more significant.

Liberal educators cannot be neutral about the importance of education. They cannot be neutral about the desirability of enlarging the mind and cultivating reason and emotional intelligence. They cannot be indifferent to the provision of educational programmes, and their distribution, which they believe fall short of the best that are realistically available. Neutrality finds expression in making available the best educational opportunities, not deliberately conniving at advantaging some over others in terms of the quality of education provided and then leaving to individuals how they receive and what they do with those opportunities. As is often pointed out, equality of opportunity must live with the possibility of subsequent inequalities fuelled by the provision of relevant opportunities. The contingencies of living offer no guarantees that as some individual lives go better, other lives won't go worse. It is not part of the liberal-neutral take on things to take final responsibility for how things transpire—at least not if what has been done is the best in the circumstances that could be done. The last caveat might be thought to be important. Given the commitment to individuals living the good life according to their own light—by which is meant that the life consists of goods, commitments, preferences, satisfactions freely chosen—what is the liberal to do when confronted by cultural outlooks and practices that only too evidently impact upon the potential access individuals could enjoy of possibilities that might enter into a conception of the good life? Put briefly, what should the liberal do if it is palpable that there are cultural practices and outlooks that are coercive and oppressive? It would be common ground on the part of all liberals—no matter what the leading principles and values are informing their liberal perspective—to condemn sexism, racism, and the like. Whatever liberal neutrality enjoins, it is intolerant of cultural practices that interfere with or severely limit the possibility of ever forging a conception of the good life representing choices rooted in an appreciation of what is on offer to be enjoyed. Liberalism's enemy is illiberal ideology and practice. Given curricula and educational programmes will always be forged within particular social contexts. Different conceptions of how to deliver on a concept of education inspired by the thinking of R. S. Peters (say) will emerge as a response to how, with this group of individuals, located in this social context, substance is given to the ideals of education. Too often it is imagined that liberal theory is the creature of moral scepticism. Precisely the reverse is, I think, true. What is marked in the writings of the great contemporary liberal theorists is the acceptance of the objectivity of the moral sphere. Neutrality is itself a moral ideal. If moral sentiment were simply a matter of feelings—to put it too crudely—little would be left by way of making a case for the importance of neutrality. There is, of course, division within liberal circles between those who see the various moral values and ideals as in some manner commensurable and those who, while insisting upon the objectivity of moral values and ideals, claim incommensurability as an ineradicable feature of the moral sphere. Sometimes, that is to say, choices have to be made in full recognition that violence is done to another moral value. Be that as it may, the emphasis upon living the good life is common currency, even if there is a debate about the significance of the choices made in living the good life.

A key issue is how, confronted by the evils of sexism and racism (say), liberal-neutral educators should conduct themselves. The answer seems to be they should try and ensure that in the name of the good life, or autonomy, or equality, or value pluralism, or (again) moral progress, that at the very least attention should be drawn to the limiting and stereotyping nature of such outlooks. But in order to preserve the distinction between persuasion through reason and coercion, practice has to be sensitive. The liberal educator will be disappointed if after all the effort gone through to alleviate illiberal cultural practices individuals embrace that culture which is the object of such attention. The liberal educator will be disappointed if, despite all the best intentions, the judgement is made that the spread of more enlightened ways of living, visions of the good life pursued, and the enjoyment of freedom seem not much more evident. Peters once said that in education we travel in hope. Liberal educators will heed that sentiment. Perhaps the liberal outlook more than any other stance on the human condition grants to individuals the final responsibility for the life they lead. The purpose of liberal education is to equip individuals to bear that burden.

The largest ambition in Ruth Jonathan's comments on Robin Barrow is to exhort liberal philosophers of education to help shape tenable forms of liberal theory. There is a motif running through her comments that liberal theory is at a watershed and is in a state of crisis from which it needs to be rescued. And where liberal philosophy of education is concerned, the clearest assertion that Millian liberalism has exhausted its possibilities. The dramatic image of a now-creaking paradigm's shortcomings is paraded before us. What is certainly true is that liberal theory is a many-headed creature. But where some might see evidence of crisis, others might see a fruitful and rewarding exchange of ideas, a ferment of rewarding debate. And the contemporary state of affairs seems to this writer to be precisely evidence of such a very healthy state of affairs. Liberal political philosophy has never before excited such debate. Or been so interesting! Where it will all lead is most unclear. The implications for the philosophy of education seem equally unclear. The philosophy of education seems always to have been stimulated by activity going on in 'mainstream' philosophising. I see no reason to suppose that liberal philosophers of education will not as before be consumers of one or other of the variants of liberal theory on offer. The ideals informing liberal theory stand little chance of realisation unless educational policies are pursued that are inspired by those ideals. As Ruth Jonathan reminds us, education is the major vehicle, potentially touching everyone, that puts in place the preconditions that must be satisfied if there is to be any chance of a world instantiating such ideals, But there are no guarantees. Some obstacles to the presence of greater equality, larger autonomy, enlivening cultural diversity, and healthy cultural pluralism are susceptible to influence from education. Many others are not. Liberal educators should go about their task, doing what they can. The ushering in a better world lies beyond their gift. All the liberal philosophers of education can do is do what they do best. They must continue subjecting to philosophical analysis the ambitions and pretensions of educational practice and policy, seeking out conceptual confusion, shoddy reasoning, bringing to light and subjecting to examination the presuppositions informing practice and policy. If they want exemplars, they could do no better than follow the examples of Ruth Jonathan and Robin Barrow, who over an extended period of time have consistently produced work of the most challenging, splendidly intelligent, and relevant kind.

REFERENCES

Barrow, R. (1990) *Understanding Skills*, London, ON: Althouse Press.

9   Robin Barrow's Account of Skills

Paul Hager

During a long career Robin Barrow has made significant contributions to philosophy of education over an impressive range of topics. These include his work on liberal education, on the aims of education, and on the nature of educational activities, as well as a searching and detailed examination of the moral aspects of education. Much of this influential work has been underpinned by a deep and insightful appreciation of Plato. This chapter will focus on Barrow's work concerning the nature of skills, which was mainly published in the late 1980s and the 1990s. During this period Barrow wrote searchingly on several issues surrounding skills. His contributions to some of these issues have remained influential since then. First, Barrow produced an enduring critique of the concept of generic skills (Barrow 1987, p. 192–194; 1990, 1999). Second Barrow offered a distinctive account of the notion of skill, an account which served to stimulate and crystallise wider debate on this topic amongst writers on education. Third, though perhaps less widely recognised, the first half of his seminal 1987 paper on skills provided some searching but less-noticed insights that question, and even suggest alternatives to, his espoused position on the concept of skill. This chapter will outline and discuss these developments. It will be argued that the first two sections of Barrow's 1987 paper delineate important principles on the nature skills, insights which, with the benefit of hindsight, can be seen to anticipate later important work by others. It is clear that this work, added to his critique of generic skills, amounts to a major contribution by Barrow to our understanding of skills.

This chapter begins by outlining Barrow's insights on skills that open his 1987 paper. Then his influential critique of the concept of generic skills will be discussed. Finally his distinctive account of the notion of skill will be considered critically. This will flow into a discussion of later developments in understanding skills. This in turn will lead to an assessment of Barrow's overall contribution to this important topic.

KEY CONCEPTUAL POINTS ABOUT SKILLS
IN BARROW'S EARLY ACCOUNT

Barrow opens his seminal 1987 paper with a series of insightful observations about skills and skill talk (1987, pp. 188–189). Its first major section begins with a wide-ranging account of the many dimensions of skills that emphasise their sheer multiplicity and variety. Eventually, this will lead him to question the value of the term 'skill' as it is typically employed. His account identifies at least five distinct dimensions that underlie the somewhat bewildering multiplicity and variety of items commonly designated as 'skills'. First, he points to the diversity of *types* of thing that can fall under the rubric 'skill'. He instances, amongst others, physical skills, motor skills, intellectual skills, social skills, personal skills, perceptual skills, and creative skills. Since many of these evidently fit into very different types of categories, Barrow worries that the term 'skill' serves to blur important differences.

Second, Barrow notes wide differences in the degree of determination of skills. Skills range from fairly discrete items (such as 'the skills of a good oarsman') to more complex, less clearly definable items (such as 'the skills of the historian') (1987, p. 188). Barrow adds that, as these examples illustrate, some skills are more perceptible than others. As well, he suggests, skills vary in the degree to which 'their precise constitution and boundaries can be determined' (1987, p. 188).

Third, he points out that skills need to be developed, learned, or acquired. An automatic reflex, such as eye blinking, is clearly not a skill. But he emphasises the fact that there is wide diversity in the ease of acquisition of skills. Some develop more or less inevitably, such as the human capacity to grasp objects. However some skills that are learned fairly readily, such as acquiring a language, seem to require a specifically human environment in order to develop. But many (most?) skills are less widely distributed across the human population and the conditions that enable their development vary enormously. Some skills require significant resources for their development (e.g., becoming a trapeze artist); others demand very few resources (e.g., juggling). Some skills may be learnt in isolation; others require other people (e.g., team sports). These considerations lead Barrow on to his fourth dimension for characterising the multiplicity and variety of skills, namely the wide differences in the means by which they are learned or acquired. Some can be self-taught, especially where rules or norms are clearly laid down. Hence in some cases of skill development self-teaching will be easy, but in others it will be more difficult, depending on the particular skill involved and the learner's aptitude. Some skills can be acquired readily by trial and error or experience; others require some form of teaching, such as imitation or direct instruction.

Fifth, Barrow points to yet another dimension of supposed skills that serves to underline their wide diversity. This is that many skills seem to involve multiple human attributes or qualities that go well beyond the physical. His worry is that deployment of the blanket term 'skill' serves to mask 'the extent to which such things as understanding, disposition, values and emotional maturity are involved in the acquisition of all but the simplest physical skills' (Barrow 1987, p. 189).

That some so-called skills are complex in this sense, whilst others seem to be more straightforwardly physical only emphasises further the conclusion that skills are not all of a similar kind. As well, this dimension of diversity amongst so-called skills is further underlined by the fact that in some cases it is difficult to specify the extent to which these non-physical human aspects are implicated. Thus some skills may be ' . . . partly physical and partly intellectual, for instance; distinctions may often be a matter of degree, and some skills may simply be hard to classify' (Barrow 1987, p. 190).

Taken together, these five different dimensions help to explain the bewildering multiplicity and variety of items that are commonly called 'skills'. It is this seemingly promiscuous deployment of the term 'skill' that worries Barrow. This loose usage of the term is evident, according to Barrow, from the fact that 'skill' is often used as a synonym for ability. He proposes to remedy this undesirable situation by arguing that skill is but a subclass of ability. This is a main driver of his regimented definition of skill that will be considered in detail in the sections following the next one. As we will find, later writers, such as Winch, have concurred with Barrow that skills are but a subclass of abilities, but have drawn different conclusions from this vital point.

Overall, Barrow's insightful 1987 discussion of general features of skill talk points to important but often overlooked matters, such as the complexity and holistic features of many so-called skills. As will be shown later, Barrow's 1987 discussion foreshadows a number of key principles about the complexity and holistic aspects of skills that are prominent in contemporary understandings of this topic.

BARROW'S CRITIQUE OF THE CONCEPT OF GENERIC SKILLS

Following his detailed discussion of general features of skill talk in his 1987 paper, Barrow went on to attack

> . . . the most insidious use of the word 'skill'—namely, to pick out alleged generic intellectual abilities, as in reference to critical thinking skills, problem-solving skills, creativity skills or values clarification skills. (Barrow 1987, p. 192)

Barrow's major argument against the notion of supposed generic skills such as critical thinking or problem solving is that these activities are actually domain-specific rather than general (see, e.g., Barrow 1987, pp. 192ff.). This is so because it is a necessary condition for being (say) a critical thinker within a given domain that one has significant understanding and knowledge of that domain. In short, critical thinking is context dependent. From the fact that somebody is a critical thinker in some given domain or discipline, it does not follow that they will be a critical thinker in other unrelated domains or disciplines. Yet, Barrow maintains, proponents of generic skills, such as critical thinking or problem solving, often naively assume that these are stand-alone sets of skills that can be taught as such and, once acquired, can then be applied readily across all domains and disciplines. It seems that this kind of uncritical assumption is what has served, at least in some cases, to make the notion of generic skills appear attractive to policymakers.

Barrow (1990) takes his context-dependence argument further to question some common practices in educational institutions—whether, for example, it makes sense to describe children generically as 'gifted' or 'talented', or whether it is even coherent to identify supposed generic classroom activities such as 'brainstorming'. This context-dependence argument by Barrow (and others, notably McPeck 1981) has gained wide acceptance and continues to be influential (see, e.g., the contributions by Hager, Winch, Hinchliffe, and Beckett and Mulcahy to Hager and Holland 2006). Because of his zeal in attacking naïve understandings of generic skills, Barrow sometimes appears to be denying that there is anything generic about critical thinking, problem solving or, even, teaching. But careful reading of his work serves to correct this superficial impression (see, e.g., Barrow 1987, p. 192). He concedes that (say) a generic critical thinking course can develop some useful inclinations and understandings, but insists that such inclinations and understandings will not enable critical thinking within a particular domain or discipline unless one first has significant knowledge and understanding of the concepts and structures that comprise that domain or discipline. Likewise, Barrow vigorously rejects the notion that the preparation of teachers can usefully focus on generic teaching skills independently of the context in which the teaching take place, specifically the 'nature of particular subject matters and the particular natures of different students and teachers' (1987, p. 188).

Having outlined Barrow's major influential argument against generic skills, we now turn to his account of the nature of specific skills.

BARROW'S CRYSTALLISED ACCOUNT OF SPECIFIC SKILLS

As was outlined earlier, Barrow was worried by the bewildering multiplicity and variety of common uses of the term 'skills'. Having identified and discussed five different dimensions that help to explain this multiplicity of uses, Barrow's response, in his 1987 and subsequent work, to what he regarded as this unhealthy and illogical conceptual inflation involved in typical 'skill talk', was to adopt and recommend a much different and very limited conception of skill. Claiming support from *Webster's Dictionary*, Barrow proposed that the term 'skill' be restricted to abilities or behaviours ' . . . that are essentially physical, perfected by practice, relatively context free . . . and involve minimal understanding (Barrow 1987, p. 191).

Paradigm examples of skills according to this very narrow conception are 'the ability to dribble a ball, the ability to plane a piece of wood, or the sleight of hand of the conjuror' (Barrow 1987, p. 190). Further examples discussed in later work include: 'standing on your head' (1990), 'wiggling one's ears', and 'palming a card' (1999).

By 1999, Barrow's characterisation of skills restricted them to only those abilities that 'are discrete, specific, physical and trainable' (Barrow 1999, p. 133). This is still basically the same as the 1987 definition where 'discrete' corresponds to the earlier 'relatively context free'; 'specific' seems to correspond to the earlier 'involving minimal understanding'; 'physical' corresponds to the earlier 'essentially physical'; and 'trainable' corresponds to the earlier 'perfected by practice'.

It is interesting to consider Barrow's proposal to restrict severely in this way the concept of skill in the light of the five dimensions that he earlier identified as underpinning the multiplicity of common uses of the term. It is apparent that his proposed definition effectively eliminates the first, second, and fifth of the five dimensions. He drastically prunes the range of *types* of thing that can count as skills. Such candidates as intellectual skills, social skills, personal skills, and creative skills are ruled out by his definition. Likewise, by defining skills as being discrete and relatively context free Barrow effectively eliminates the wide differences in the degree of determination of skills. In order to fit his definition skills must have relatively determinate boundaries. Finally, by insisting that skills are limited to essentially physical activities, Barrow's proposal minimises the involvement of such things as understanding, dispositions, values, and emotions. For him activities featuring these sorts of complexity are abilities rather than skills.

However, Barrow's narrow definition of skills does not eliminate the third and fourth dimensions that account for the multiplicity of common uses of the term. It seems clear that his paradigm examples of skills (listed three paragraphs above) will vary widely in their ease of acquisition. Some will be more easily developed; others will be more difficult to acquire. While most people can probably learn to plane a piece of wood, 'wiggling one's ears' or even 'standing on your head' might elude many. Likewise there is obvious diversity in the best means of acquiring Barrow's paradigm examples of skills. Some will be able to be acquired by trial and error; others will likely require some form of teaching.

Thus, though Barrow's proposal does not eliminate all of the factors that account for the multiplicity of uses of the term 'skill', it is sufficient, apparently, to satisfy his desire to combat the 'appalling error' of 'calling everything indiscriminately a "skill"' thereby seeing 'everything on the model of a specific, discrete, physical, trainable behaviour' (Barrow 1999, p. 133). However, is the remedy worse than the illness it seeks to cure?

HOW CONVINCING IS BARROW'S CRYSTALLISED ACCOUNT OF SPECIFIC SKILLS?

The key argument against Barrow's narrow account of skills is that uncontroversial examples of skilled performances typically involve wider holistic understandings and dispositions as well as facility, deftness, or dexterity. As will be demonstrated in the next section, this has been the basis both of direct criticism of Barrow's proposal and of later developed accounts of skill. In this section, the arguments put forward by Barrow to support his narrow position are scrutinised. The crucial argument in the 1987 paper (p. 190) relies on one dictionary definition (*Webster's Dictionary*). Webster, as quoted by him, states that skill is:

> (1) a great ability or proficiency, expertness that comes from training or practice, or (2a) an art, craft or science, especially one involving the use of hand or body, and (2b) ability in such an art, craft or science.

Barrow adds that Webster mentions that the more general definition of a skill (namely, '(3) knowledge, understanding or judgement') is now obsolete.

What is immediately apparent is that in reading this dictionary definition as supporting his narrow characterisation of skills as 'closely tied up with notions of physicality, training and perfection through practice, and minimally involved with understanding' (Barrow 1987, p. 190), he is, arguably, making some questionable assumptions. First, Barrow obviously reads clause (1) as implying that only a relatively small subset of abilities can be properly thought of as skills. But it seems to me that a more accurate reading of (1) is that it characterises a skill as any ability that has reached a high level of performance as a result of training or practice. On this alternative reading of the dictionary definition, the field of skills remains very large indeed, certainly much larger than Barrow depicts it. It includes, for instance, the skills of concert violinists and test match cricketers. Webster's specific mention of an art, craft, or science definitely supports this wider reading. Against this, Barrow's preferred examples (dribbling a ball, planing a piece of wood, a conjurer's sleight of hand) look to be decidedly more narrow cases of skills.

Second, from the fact, noted by the Webster entry, that skill in its general sense is no longer applied to largely mind-centred activities such as knowledge, understanding, or judgement, Barrow infers that skills in general only minimally, if at all, involve understanding and the like. But this is a misreading. The dictionary definition does not claim this, and the multiple references to art, craft, or science only serve to reinforce this conclusion. Likewise, when *Webster's Dictionary* states that the skilled art, craft, or science often involves the use of hand or body, Barrow takes this to mean that the skill is virtually all physical. Again, the dictionary definition does not make this strong claim. It merely states that the art, craft, or science frequently involves the use of hand or body, that is, the use of hand or body is but one aspect of the skill. In fact, as will be shown in the next subsection, knowledge, understanding and judgement are crucial components of typical skilled performances, including those of concert violinists and test match cricketers.

In short, the conclusion is that Barrow reads a lot more than is actually there into the *Webster's Dictionary* definition that he quotes. Thus his argument that Webster supports his unusually narrow understanding of skill is less than cogent.

In fact by consulting several dictionaries a more nuanced account of skill becomes evident, one that incorporates both wider and narrower understandings. For a start, several dictionaries distinguish between the 'uncountable' and 'countable' senses of the term skill. The former represents a wider, more holistic understanding of skill and is presented as the primary sense. The latter sense covers specific skills. It includes the narrow cases of skills that Barrow recognises, but also includes particular skills that are wider than those circumscribed by his criteria. For example, the Oxford Advanced American Dictionary defines skill in the uncountable sense as 'the ability to do something well', whilst skill in the countable sense refers to 'a particular ability or type of ability'. Instances of the uncountable sense are 'The job requires skill and an eye for detail' and 'what made him remarkable as a photographer was his skill in capturing the moment'. Instances of the countable sense are 'we need people with carpentry skills' and 'she shows good management skills'.

In addition, other dictionaries agree with *Webster's* that training or practice is an important part of skill attainment. For instance, the *Cambridge Online Dictionary* defines skill as 'an ability to do an activity or job well, especially because you have practised it'. Once again, while this definition does cover Barrow's narrow examples of skills, such as dribbling a ball or planing a piece of wood, by mentioning 'job' it also appears to cover wider life activities, such as being a skilled carpenter or a skilled manager.

A further significant and telling point is that various dictionary entries specifically contrast skill, as a richer concept, with its narrower relatives: dexterity and adroitness. Certainly dexterity and adroitness seem to be close to some of Barrow's supposedly paradigm examples of skills such as dribbling a ball, planing a piece of wood, or palming a card. Yet, in contrasting skill with dexterity and adroitness, these dictionary entries imply that skill involves something in addition to mere dexterity and adroitness of performance. The multiple references to art, craft, or science suggest what this something extra might be. As *Webster's Revised Unabridged Dictionary 1913* aptly puts it:

> Skill is more intelligent, denoting familiar knowledge united to readiness of performance. Dexterity, when applied to the body, is more mechanical, and refers to habitual ease of execution. Adroitness involves the same image with dexterity, and differs from it as implying a general facility of movement (especially in avoidance of danger or in escaping from a difficulty).

PARADIGMATIC CASES OF SKILLS ARE MORE
HOLISTIC THAN BARROW MAINTAINS

Early critics of Barrow's crystallised account of specific skills maintained that it served to exclude far too much from the proper domain of skills. Morwenna Griffiths called it 'an unnecessarily narrow view of skills' (Griffiths 1987, p. 208). She drew upon Ryle's work to attack Barrow's propensity to associate skill with mindlessness. Richard Smith (1987, p. 197) argued that Barrow's characterisation of skills amounted to 'a denigration of skills-based activities as inevitably lowly, mechanical and beneath educational notice'. As against this, Smith wanted to insist upon

> . . . the intrinsic value of skills, properly conceived: not just in the obvious sense that they help us to earn our living and fashion things to our liking, but also in that they are an important dimension of a well-constituted relationship between human beings and their world. (Smith 1987, p. 197)

Both Griffiths and Smith shared Barrow's concern with the careless and misleading ways that the term 'skills' was being deployed in much educational discourse, for example, '. . . . a worrying number of people trying to reduce complex practical activities to a checklist of relatively simple and mindless ones (Griffiths 1987, p. 208).
However both Griffiths and Smith concurred that the educational implications of Barrow's proposal were alarming.

Accounts of skills subsequent to Barrow's narrow proposal have tended to take a more holistic view of the matter. The importance of a degree of holism in any convincing account of skills can be appreciated by examining a mundane example. Consider the skills involved in driving a motor vehicle. These can easily be analysed into a set of myriad discrete skills (starting the ignition, activating the right turn blinker, applying the foot brake, etc.). Each of these fits Barrow's proposal in being discrete, specific, physical, and trainable. Supposing we set out to identify a complete list of motor vehicle driving skills and came up with (say) eighty of them. Suppose further that someone demonstrated that they could perform each of these eighty discrete skills. Would that allow us to conclude that they were a skilled driver? Obviously not, because skilful driving is more than being adept at each of these discrete skills. There is no contradiction in the notion of someone being adept at each of these discrete skills, yet still being a very poor driver. This is because skilful driving consists in a holistic performance tailored to the particular road and traffic conditions and many other circumstances that obtain at a particular time. So the skill of driving resides not so much in the discrete skills as in the capacity to put them all together in effective combinations that are appropriate to current conditions. This immediately points us towards a more holistic notion of skill centring around, as well as technique, the exercise of things such as perceptual discrimination, persistence, attention to detail, planning ahead, judgement, habits, etc.

This example also suggests that the uncountable sense of skill is the primary one since skilful driving is an uncountable skill in the sense of 'the ability to do something well'. By contrast, the eighty or so discrete driving skills are clear examples of skills in the countable sense. My claim that the uncountable sense of skill is the primary one is supported by considering paradigm cases of application of the terms 'skilled' or 'highly skilled'. A professional orchestral violinist is clearly someone who is highly skilled as violinist. This involves numerous countable skills relating to the mechanics of violin playing, reading music, etc. But overlying this is the uncountable sense of skill and musicality by which a holistic performance is fashioned and delivered that takes into account and responds to multiple factors such as the particular preferences of the conductor, the playing of the violin section as a whole, the role of the violins in the overall orchestral fabric of the particular work, the audience, the vagaries of the venue, and so on. Similarly, the superior skills of a test match cricketer consist primarily of skill in the uncountable sense. For example, numerous discrete physical and mechanical skills can be attributed to a batsman who scores a test match century. But the real skill that we admire lies in the way these are subsumed into an overall performance that perfectly suits the prevailing circumstances and conditions. To take but one instance, a cover drive for four by the centurion is not just the mechanical reproduction of the stroke as portrayed in a coaching manual. It is the stroke adapted to suit and allow for many factors including the prevailing pitch conditions, the wind (including its changes), the condition of the ball (e.g., whether reverse swing has started), etc. So the performance of the successful cover drive is not just a discrete, isolated physical skill. Rather significant understanding and know-how are needed to shape the actual instances of executing this and a myriad of other skills employed in the overall highly skilled innings. These two examples also exemplify the point that while skilled performance often involves significant physical skills, it also usually involves much more. In this respect, they reflect the numerous dictionary entries that list the arts, crafts, and sciences as typical sites of skilled performances.

These holistic considerations are reflected in more recent accounts of skill (e.g., Winch 2010; Beckett and Mulcahy 2006; Hager and Halliday 2006, pp. 124–125). Let us consider Winch's account in some detail. According to Winch, 'to act skilfully is not to perform a type of act, but to act in a certain (praiseworthy) way' (2010, p. 43). This feature of being subject to normative appraisal is taken by Winch to be a defining feature of skills. He agrees with Barrow that skills are a subset of abilities. But for Winch, what defines this subset is this normativity feature of its members: 'The concept of a *skill* seems to be the ability concept which opens up the vista of normative appraisal in terms of the *degree* to which an activity can be performed well or badly' (Winch 2010, p. 41).

As noted previously, the *Cambridge Online Dictionary* defines skill as 'an ability to do an activity or job well, especially because you have practised it'. Since there usually are degrees of how well an activity or job is done, this definition carries with it the notion of normative evaluation of the skilled performance. It is also significant that the uncountable sense of skill aligns naturally with the idea of normative appraisal, whereas the countable sense fits less well. This is so because countable skills that are discrete, specific, and physical in Barrow's sense are often less open to normative appraisal in that one can either perform them or one cannot. There are no *degrees* of how well they can be done. Taken together, these ideas support the conclusion that the uncountable sense of skill is the primary one.

Winch's account of skills accepts that they involve the use of method or technique, however he adds that 'it is plausible to suggest that skill involves more than this' (Winch 2010, p. 43). What is this something more that characterises a skill? According to Winch (2010, pp. 43–44) skills are typically complex, involving most or all of the following components:

> Physical capacities
> Technique
> Moral qualities (such as persistence and attention to detail)
> Habits (such as taking care of one's equipment)
> Refined perceptual discrimination
> Knowledge (which is often displayed enactively rather than verbally)
> Judgement

Thus, Winch's conclusion is that 'to possess a skill is to possess something complex, with different integrated and interrelated aspects' (Winch 2010, p. 44). This is certainly true of the three instances of holistic skills already described in this section (driving a motor vehicle, professional orchestral playing, or test match cricketing). In each case, physical capacities need to be guided by and integrated with such things as persistence, attention to detail, habits, refined perceptual discrimination, and judgement.

Winch rightly observes that this complexity is missed if discussions of skills are focused just on descriptions of the *tasks* to be performed. Confusing tasks with skills effectively strips away key attributes of the skills leaving behind a thinner, limited version of what is a much richer concept. Winch calls this error 'conceptual deflation' (Winch 2010, p. 45). In fact, over recent decades many attempts to implement competency-based training have foundered on just this error. (Recall Griffiths's earlier worry about reducing 'complex practical activities to a checklist of relatively simple and mindless ones').

In fact, there is a deeper reason for the widespread occurrence of this error. It lies in the fact that task descriptions can be readily and minutely detailed and specified to fit a given purpose, whereas specifying the nature of the human attributes needed to carry out the task well is much more elusive and contested. Winch's list of skill components (two paragraphs above) illustrates the challenge involved in specifying clearly and unequivocally the details of this side of skilled performance. Thus, too often, versions of competency-based training concentrate on what is supposedly objective (task descriptions), and ignore what is less tangible (the human attributes that underpin skilled performance). The inevitable result is inferior training and skill development (see Hager 2004).

Early in this chapter we saw that Barrow identified five dimensions that underlie the bewildering multiplicity and variety of items that are commonly called 'skills'. This lay behind his reforming proposal for a relatively narrow definition of skills. How do these dimensions relate to Winch's more holistic understanding of skills? By limiting the concept to essentially physical skills, Barrow first reduced the range of *types* of thing that can count as skills. His definition excluded such candidates as intellectual skills, social skills, and personal skills. In fact there is not a great deal of difference between Barrow and Winch on this issue. Winch outlines and discusses what he terms moderate and immoderate conceptual inflation (Winch 2010, pp. 50–54). Moderate conceptual inflation relates to talk of so-called intellectual or mental skills and transferable skills. Winch argues that such talk is 'essentially benign' in that it does not lead to conceptual incoherence. For his holistic account there are no either purely physical or purely mental skills. All skills involve elements of both, so the difference between supposedly mental and supposedly physical skills is a matter of degree. He is also comfortable with such 'transferable' skills as literacy and numeracy so long as it is recognised that to

> ... say that a skill is transferable is not to imply that it is necessarily unproblematically transferable. (Winch 2010, p. 51)

For Winch immoderate conceptual inflation of the term skills 'is confused and the consequences are misleading and lead to incoherence' (Winch 2010, p. 50). He provides detailed argument as to why the concepts of 'general transferable skills' and of 'social skills' are prime examples of immoderate conceptual inflation. So Winch is in broad agreement with Barrow's position on the first dimension. He also agrees fully with Barrow's rejection of generic skills. The main difference between them is that *contra* Barrow, Winch maintains that virtually all skills are complex and have significant mental as well as physical components. But is this difference a large one? Early in the chapter in Barrow's detailed discussion of skills issues, we noted his view that some skills may be

> ... partly physical and partly intellectual, for instance; distinctions may often be a matter of degree, and some skills may simply be hard to classify'. (Barrow 1987, p. 190)

Winch's claim is that all skills feature these dual characteristics. It is certainly plausible to maintain that even relatively self-contained skills such as Barrow's preferred examples (dribbling a ball, planing a piece of wood, and a conjurer's sleight of hand) are complex in that, besides their obvious physical aspects, they also include non-physical elements of the kind discussed by Winch.

The second dimension brings out a major difference between Barrow and Winch. Barrow defines skills as being discrete and relatively context free, whereas for Winch they are complex and need to be adapted to variations in context. All of this is part of the holism that their adequate understanding requires according to Winch.

As was argued earlier, Barrow's narrow definition of skills does not eliminate the third and fourth dimensions. So there appear to be no important differences between Barrow and Winch regarding the ease of acquisition of skills or the best means of acquiring them. Barrow's account nullified the influence of the fifth dimension by limiting the term 'skills' to essentially physical activities. In making this move, Barrow sought to minimise the involvement of such items as understanding, dispositions, values, and emotions. Winch's more holistic account denies that this is desirable, or even possible, if any nuanced understanding of these matters is to be attained.

As noted earlier, both Barrow and Winch view ability as a much wider notion than skill. Both argue that skill is a subset of ability. And, further, Winch suggests that there are important abilities, such as planning, communicating, coordinating, controlling, and evaluating that can be usefully distinguished from skills by being viewed as higher order abilities. In recent work (Winch in press), he calls these higher order abilities 'second order traversal abilities' and regards them as 'central to work'. Winch explains:

> It is a characteristic of the exercise of such second order transversal abilities that, although they presuppose the exercise of skill, they are not to be identified with skills. Thus, for example, the ability to plan, although it may involve, (but need not) the ability to draw diagrams or to write a sequence of instructions, it is not to be identified with such skills, since it is evident that an individual can do these things without actually planning. This is an important point since there is a prevalent reductive discourse of referring to planning as 'planning skills', communicating as 'communicating skills' and so on. What makes, for example, planning, something more than the exercise of planning skills is the seriousness of intent and attention that is brought to bear on the activity, not just the exercise of skills but in orientation to what it is intended should be achieved.

Winch notes further that these second order transversal abilities 'are very often social activities, involving the active participation of others'. Whether or not this account suffices to distinguish adequately skills from non-skill abilities remains to be seen. However, the notion of orders or levels within abilities does look to be a useful one for capturing some of the complexity and holism that this chapter has argued surround the notions of ability and skill. After all, even uncountable skills seem to be of a higher level or order than do countable skills.

Winch's mention of the social aspects of second order transversal abilities serves to remind us that there are other approaches to the understanding of skills evident in recent literature. The salient point is that 'knowledge and skills reside in *shared practices* as much as in individuals' (Beckett and Mulcahy 2006, p. 243). In the growing literature centred on the concept of practice

> . . . the focus has shifted from knowledge and skills as something people possess to something they do as part of practice. (Beckett and Mulcahy 2006, p. 243)

This practice literature shares the theme, prominent in this chapter, that skills and abilities need to be understood as complex and holistic. This is not the place to pursue this further, but these issues are taken up substantially in Hager, Lee, and Reich (2012).

CONCLUSION

Not the least of Robin Barrow's many significant contributions to the philosophy of education is his wide-ranging work on skills. A quarter of a century after his critique of generic skills was first published, it remains cogent and widely influential. As well, his 1987 analysis of issues surrounding general features of skills and skills talk has proved to be very insightful. It drew attention to important but often overlooked matters, such as the multifaceted diversity across supposed skills. It thereby foreshadowed various key principles about skills, such as their complexity and holism, which are prominent in contemporary understandings of these matters. Though Barrow's own particular proposal for limiting the usage of the concept of skill has not attracted wide support, his overall contribution to this cluster of topics is still influential today. When his many other contributions to philosophy of education are taken into account, his standing as a major figure in this discipline is beyond question.

REFERENCES

Barrow, R. (1987) 'Skill Talk', *Journal of Philosophy of Education* 21(2), pp. 187–195.
———. (1990) *Understanding Skills: Thinking, Feeling and Caring*, London, ON: Althouse Press.

———. (1999) 'The Higher Nonsense: Some Persistent Errors in Educational Thinking', *Journal of Curriculum Studies* 31(2), pp. 131–142.

Beckett D. and D. Mulcahy (2006) 'Constructing Professionals' Employabilities: Conditions for Accomplishment', in P. Hager and S. Holland (eds.) *Graduate Attributes, Learning and Employability* (Lifelong Learning Book Series, Vol. 6), Dordrecht: Springer, pp. 243–265.

Griffiths M. (1987) 'The Teaching of Skills and the Skills of Teaching: A Reply to Robin Barrow', *Journal of Philosophy of Education* 21(2), pp. 203–214.

Hager, P. (2004) 'The Competence Affair, or Why Vocational Education and Training Urgently Needs a New Understanding of Learning', *Journal of Vocational Education & Training* 56(3), pp. 409–433.

Hager, P. and J. Halliday (2006) *Recovering Informal Learning: Wisdom, Judgement and Community* (Lifelong Learning Book Series, Vol. 7), Dordrecht: Springer.

Hager P. and S. Holland (eds.) (2006) *Graduate Attributes, Learning and Employability* (Lifelong Learning Book Series, Vol. 6), Dordrecht: Springer.

Hager P., A. Lee, and A. Reich (eds.) (2012) *Practice, Learning and Change: Practice-Theory Perspectives on Professional Learning* (Professional and Practice-based Learning Book Series, Vol. 8), Dordrecht: Springer.

McPeck, J. E. (1981) *Critical Thinking and Education*, New York: St. Martin's Press.

Smith R. (1987) 'Skills: The Middle Way', *Journal of Philosophy of Education* 21(2), pp. 197–201.

Winch C. (2010) *Dimensions of Expertise: A Conceptual Exploration of Vocational Knowledge*, London & New York: Continuum.

———. (forthcoming) 'Learning at Work and in the Workplace: Reflections on Paul Hager's Advocacy of Work-based Learning', *Educational Philosophy and Theory*.

10 Barrow on Liberal Education and Schooling

Christopher Winch

Robin Barrow has committed himself, over the years, to an explanation and defence of a particular vision of liberal education which owes much to the earlier writings on education of R. S. Peters. Central to this defence has been a sharp distinction between education and schooling. However, just as Peters was, in his later work, concerned to situate liberal education within a broader field of legitimate educational concern, so it should be possible to do the same with Barrow's work on liberal education by questioning the impermeability of the Education/Schooling distinction, thus opening up a broader conception of liberal education that at the same time remains largely true to Barrow's vision.

A CATEGORIAL CONCEPT OF EDUCATION

R. S. Peters was primarily concerned to develop a *categorial* account of education, that is, an account of education as a human institution irrespective of any particular instantiation in a specific time or place. In his earlier writings on this subject he maintained that such an account would be fairly detailed ('thick' in the jargon), but gradually realized that any attempt to make it too detailed would lead to a partial or complete assimilation of the categorial concept to a particular interpretation and to the filling out of that concept specific to a time and place rather than to a context-free account. The assimilation of the concept of education to particular conceptions of it would, while providing detail, also vitiate the possibility of providing a philosophically credible universal account of a fundamental human institution. This must be an ever present danger for anyone attempting such an exercise, as every philosopher stands within a particular education tradition from which it is difficult to completely detach oneself, even when attempting comprehensive philosophical detachment.

In his considered later view, such a categorial conception involved preparing young people for life; it had to involve learning and/or some form of upbringing or development and the preparation had to be for something regarded as worthwhile (Peters 1981). I agree with Peters's late account of the categorial concept except for one crucial point that he leaves out, although arguably it is implicit in what he says about the contestability of educational concepts. The omission is that the preparation has to be regarded as worthwhile *for someone by someone*. When the someone in question is not the same, then the possibility can arise that what is regarded as worthwhile by *Someone A* for themselves is not regarded as worthwhile by *Someone A* for *Someone B*. It may thus be the case that A thinks that B (and his like) should have an education which is substantially *different* than the one offered to A (and his like). As a corollary, a B-type education would not be worthwhile for an A-type person. This is one important way in which one could have a bad (inappropriate) education. Such views about different educational experiences for different types of people might arise for a number of reasons:

1] B is a slave and A is a member of the ruling slave-owning group.
2] As above, but B is a helot or member of the working or peasant class and A is a landowner or capitalist.
3] B has been found, by some accepted procedure, to be incapable of benefiting from certain kinds of education that requires a particular kind and degree of 'intelligence'. A, on the other hand, can benefit from these kinds of education.
4] B belongs to an inferior racial or sexual grouping to A and so to give him and his like an A-type education would be disruptive to the good ordering of society.
5] B has different interests, abilities, and talents to A and would person- ally benefit from an education different in kind to that of A.

Finally, there is also the not insignificant case whereby the members of A's group cannot themselves agree *either* on what is a worthwhile life for A-type people *or* what is a worthwhile preparation for a life for A-type people, or maybe they disagree about both.

The list of possibilities is not exhaustive. An important point worth not- ing is that both the believers in one or more of 1—5 and those who believe that 1—5 provide no grounds for providing a distinct type of education for A and B may believe that their views are universal, applying to all kinds of human situations, rather than just the particular society in which the debate about kinds of education is taking place. But the fact that A regards his views as universally true does not mean that those views are universally true. In fact, anyone attempting to set out even a moderately detailed cat- egorial account of education needs to take particular care to ensure that they do not claim universality for features of education present in their own societies that they find especially attractive, without ensuring that they are indeed universal features.

It is not at all difficult to see how a categorial concept of education may be instantiated in different (often mutually incompatible) *conceptions*. A *conception* of education is a particular interpretation of the categorial concept. Contestation about different conceptions arises primarily because different groups have different interpretations about what is worthwhile for themselves and secondarily because some groups may consider a certain form of education suitable for another group and that group might disagree with that view.

VALUES, AIMS, AND EDUCATION

In order to get clearer about this, we need to look more closely at the idea of preparation for a worthwhile life. Most obviously, perhaps, a worthwhile life (for a society, for a group, or for an individual) is underpinned by *values*. Values are the fundamental ethical commitments of individuals, societies, and groups. They are, for example, beliefs about rights, equality, and justice, together with religious beliefs on which the former often depend. Linked to values are empirical, quasi-empirical, and metaphysical beliefs about the way the world is ordered, about human ability and its distribution, and about the way in which society should be ordered (Haldane 1989). It seems indubitably to be the case that people do not all espouse the same values concerning justice, equality, and so on, let alone about these broader religious, empirical, and metaphysical issues which underpin the way in which education is undertaken.

That being the case, and if education is both an expression of values held and an attempt to perpetuate those values, together with the other beliefs that support and are supported by those values, it is inevitable that different conceptions of education will arise. Very often these different conceptions will take the form of emphasis or weighting of different aspects of education: liberal, vocational, or civic. They need not, however, be mutually exclusive.

But they may also take the form of recommendations of rigid separation of different kinds of education for different kinds of people, as in Plato's *Republic*, for example.

> Therefore inasmuch as you are all related to one another, although all your children will generally resemble their parents, yet sometimes a golden parent will produce a silver child, and a silver parent a golden child, and so on, each producing any. (Plato 1950, p. 114)

It does not follow either that an individual child will respond to the type of education that is appropriate for him or her. Careful selection and rigorous monitoring in different streams of education will be necessary to ensure that the right type of child receives the right type of education for their preferred station in life (preferred that is, by the Guardians of the *polis*).

In some cases the values are underpinned by a speculative moral psychology that dictates a clear curricular and pedagogic route to the desired end of a worthwhile life. The moral psychology that lies behind Rousseau's *Emile* (1762) is a good case in point. The goal of a society governed as a direct democracy by individuals who regard themselves as free, equal, and un-dominated by anyone else, is thought to be only obtainable by educating people in such a way that they are never exposed to explicit normative pressure (Dent 1988; Winch 1996). One may well hold to Rousseau's political values but not subscribe to his moral psychology and hence to his curricular and pedagogic prescriptions, on the grounds that the latter are not empirically sustainable but are nothing more than speculations. Later followers of Rousseau, most notably perhaps, Piaget and his followers, have sought to provide some empirical justification for his views, albeit working within a metaphysics of human development that Rousseau first set out. Indeed, one of the main criticisms of Piagetian developmentalism is that it attempts to universalize data gathered in very specific circumstances (Vygotsky 1962; Donaldson 1978). Incidentally Rousseau's speculative moral psychology led him to the view (in contrast to Plato's in the *Republic*) that women should have radically different educations to those enjoyed by men, a view which he held to be universally valid, but one which would, in our society, be taken to be universally *invalid*.

What is the logical relationship between values on the one hand and associated beliefs about types of people and their educability on the other? One interesting consequence of recognizing a categorial concept of education is that it implies that education is an intentional activity, even if not always an explicitly intentional activity. A preparation for life involves having an end in mind (a worthwhile life) and a viable strategy for preparing to achieve it (an educational process). To institute the latter, the former must be rendered in some form which makes a viable strategy possible. This need not be explicit, it may be conceived of as an implicit goal shared by all who are concerned with the enterprise of education, without ever having to be articulated or debated. At the other extreme it may be very explicit and emerge after wide-ranging debate. Values embodied in goals which are susceptible to strategic implementation are the *aims* of education, whether they be explicit or implicit, lacking in generality or detailed.

Furthermore, it is evident that, if aims express values and if those values are subject to intra- or inter- societal variation then they themselves will vary. The very possibility of such variation leads to the *contestability* of educational aims and the fact that they are frequently subject to debate and disagreement leads to the fact of their actually being *contested*. One might argue that there is no serious dispute about values—that we all share the same basic ideals about justice, rights, human worth, and dignity, etc. and that therefore there is no serious dispute about educational aims (cf. Carr 2010).[1] However, such a move only gains purchase by a covert shift from consideration of education as a universal phenomenon to a consideration of its instantiation in the here and now. Considered from a universal perspective it is evident that there has been and continues to be enormous variation in the values that societies hold concerning such issues as the nature of justice, of rights, and of what constitutes a worthwhile life and for whom. One might reply that something like the reaction of the Good Samaritan to the injured traveler exhibits a universal reaction to human distress and thus an exemplification of a universal human code (Pinzauti 2012). Even if this philosophically controversial thesis were admitted, it would not alter the fact that societies have always and continue to organize themselves in ways which exhibit massive diversity in value orientation. The fact that there is often some convergence due to the successful political activity of disadvantaged groups that have succeeded in getting some of their own values implemented does not count against this point (cf. Vico 1968 for an account of class struggle in antiquity that leads to this kind of outcome).

Even when morality is based on a universalist approach, such as within the natural law tradition followed by Hobbes, or through its development via the categorical imperative of Kant, it is far from clear that there is going to be convergence on what such a high level principle actually means in terms of moral conduct and legislation, and hence for education. For example, Hobbes thought that the derivatives of the moral law should be taught by rote to ensure right conduct, and he also thought that proselytization was against the Law of God. The implications of this position for religious education are pretty obvious. Notoriously as well, Kant's attempts to derive maxims from the categorical imperative have met with considerable scepticism (see Ward 1974, for example).

The final point worth making about the reality of contestability concerns class conflict. Although we usually associate the idea that class conflict is the motor of history with Marx, the idea was already well developed in the work of Giambattista Vico in the early eighteenth century (Vico 1968), who traces the effects on our culture of class conflict from the dawn of civilization. Class stratification has obvious and conflicting effects on our views as to what kind of education is good for whom and from whose point of view. Successful class conflict by the subordinate classes can change the ways in which education is implemented. Even those who advocate for educational provision in favour of the subordinate classes may have different views as to what benefits them most. Thus it is arguable that part of the popularity of Italian fascism amongst the working class in the early 1920s may have rested on their advocacy of technical education (Murphy 2002, pp. 69–70), while their left-wing opponents were adamant in their demand for a classical education for the proletariat, and in their view that vocational education for the masses was a means of keeping them in a subordinate position (Gramsci 1975).

AIMS AND THE CURRICULUM

However, contestability goes beyond this. The categorial concept of education allows the derivation of categorial subconcepts. We have already noted the logical dependency of educational aims on values (among other kinds of beliefs), but we can go further. Any rational attempt to put a set of educational aims into effect will require a more detailed instantiation in terms of content (Barrow (1976) helpfully defines the curriculum as prescribed content) and hence as a cumulative programme of knowledge, know-how, character formation, and understanding that is to be developed in order to realize educational aims. What though, given the logical subordination of the curriculum to aims, should be the place of accumulated systematic knowledge (disciplines), grouped for pedagogical purposes, otherwise known as *subjects* into which the curriculum has, in the centuries of formal schooling, been organized. One view is that the subjects provide an indispensable resource for any curriculum and must be, in some form and in some degree, incorporated into it. Another view, to be found in the work of John White, is that an aims-led curriculum means that there can be no preconception in favour of subjects, and that their adoption must be contingent on whether or not they best satisfy the educational aims that a society or group has decided upon (cf. White 2007). There seem to be at least two important issues in play in this dispute. The first is a practical one concerning the usefulness of the subjects as curricular resources and whether it is worthwhile or even practicable to reorganize knowledge to suit specific aims. The second is a philosophical issue and concerns whether or not acceptance of the general principle of the priority of aims entails that the position of subjects is entirely subordinate to aims-fulfillment. This cannot be assumed, I would argue, without a view as to whether it is wise to dispense with the resources offered by the accumulated wisdom represented by the subjects. So on this view, an aims-led curriculum does not directly entail the subordination of subjects, but the subjects themselves represent a side constraint on curriculum design.

There is however, a third issue of contestation worth mentioning. When advocates of an aims-led curriculum do, as White often does, make specific curricular recommendations that imply a subordinate or truncated role for certain subjects, then one is entitled to ask whether or not the general logical point about the relationship between aims and curriculum has been subtly transformed into an argument from the adoption of aims in general to the adoption of certain specific aims (such as autonomy) in certain presumed social conditions (e.g., for White, the impending omnipresence of a leisured society in the developed world (White 1997)) and hence to highly specific curricular decisions concerning the role of the subjects. While there is nothing philosophically suspect about presenting an argument from philosophical premises concerning particular aims to philosophical conclusions about prescribed content, there is something philosophically suspect about confusing a categorial point about the logical structure of the conceptual field of education with specific advocacy of a contestable view about particular aims and their relationship with the subjects.

PEDAGOGY

A different kind of confusion occurs in relation to pedagogy. Carr, for example, acknowledges that there is wide. ranging and profound disagreement on ethically valid pedagogies (e.g., op. cit. 2010, p. 101) but denies that their existence amounts to contestability in the sense described above. Observing, quite rightly, that on many occasions such conflicts about rival pedagogies are resolved in terms of a practical solution which commands at least the conditional assent of all parties, he concludes, wrongly, that this fact invalidates the contestability thesis (ibid., p. 102). Even allowing for the case (favourable to his point of view) that such conflicts are nearly always resolvable, the fact that they are does not necessarily involve convergence on value orientation (although, in some cases it may) but rather a compromise on the extent to which the implementation of conflicting value stances may be resolvable in a pedagogically and ethically viable *modus vivendi*. It is unlikely, for example, that a Rousseauvian who holds that any overt imposition of an adult will on a child is corrupting can be brought to acknowledge any alignment of values on pedagogical matters with a traditionalist who believes that pedagogy necessitates overt introduction of a child into a normative order in which an authoritative teacher is the prime pedagogical mover. A *modus vivendi* concerning the implementation of values is not a convergence on the values themselves, but a convergence on the extent to which and manner in which practices can be constructed which represent partial implementations of those conflicting values in ways acceptable to the parties that find themselves in disagreement. Indeed, we cannot expect that any significant compromise can be obtained on values that constitute important elements of a person's stance towards the world and even of their personal identity in a broad sense of that term.

LIBERAL EDUCATION IN A BROAD SENSE AND ITS RELATIONSHIP TO VOCATIONAL EDUCATION

How do these considerations bear on the question of whether liberal education occupies a privileged place in the educational pantheon, or indeed, whether it is (categorially speaking) the only practice that is worthy of the appellation 'education'? A positive answer to this question, held by Barrow, Carr, and the earlier and middle Peters, still commands considerable although by no means universal consent. A common approach by those who take this view is to separate some worthwhile experiences of preparation for life which do not satisfy liberal aims from those that do and call the former 'schooling' rather than 'educational' practices (e.g., Barrow 1981). It is, however, implicit in what has been said before that practices that involve learning, instruction, etc. as preparation for a worthwhile life, fall squarely within the categorial educational concept, rather than under any contingent contestable conception (cf. Gingell 2010). That being so, it can be asked first, in what sense are non-liberal forms of education actually educational and second, to what extent are liberal forms of education compatible with other forms, such as vocational education?

Here it is possible to give a quite detailed and positive answer. Many countries which do attempt to articulate aims for their public education systems try to do so in a way that takes account of at least some of the main dimensions of a worthwhile life in the kinds of societies that we live in. Broadly speaking, countries like France and Germany (but not the UK) distinguish between preparation that develops a person as a unique individual, that develops a person as an economically productive member of society, and that develops a person as a citizen. Individual, vocational and civic dimensions are not, of course, exhaustive of the dimensions of a worthwhile human life. Many would, for example, emphasize the domestic and the religious dimensions of life and lament the fact that they do not receive sufficient attention in modern public education systems. But given that these three dimensions are recognized in the aims of such systems, the question (with both conceptual and practical dimensions) arises as to what extent can they be jointly pursued, and in such a way that they are educational.

My strategy for exploring this question will be to take a broad liberal conception of education as a point of reference and to ask to what extent the programme of such a conception has strong analogues in the other conceptions, particularly in that of vocational education. I hope, in this way, to dispel the idea that one has to change the terms of the debate in order to gain a foothold of understanding for vocational conceptions of education. In fact, what one encounters in developed forms of liberal education has very clear analogues in developed forms of vocational education, and this allows us to appreciate their close similarities. These similarities arise because the values and aims that underpin both vocational and liberal education in modern European societies are not that dissimilar, and therefore compromises concerning values in the implementation of either are not too drastic. This is possible because, although such societies do have quite clear class stratification, they do not have the near impermeable kind of class structure that is to be found in more traditional societies, nor indeed the more informal but nevertheless deep-seated and quasi-antagonistic kind of class relationships to be found in England.

There are two aspects to traditional liberal education which should be distinguished, even when they are closely related to each other. The first, perhaps most emphasized by writers like Peters, Hirst, and, indeed, Barrow, is that of inculcation into the high culture of the civilization which the young person being educated has inherited. And, as Gingell and Brandon (2001) pointed out, this does not necessarily have elitist implications, nor does it imply that all and only what has traditionally been thought to belong to high culture should belong to it. The key point is whether or not the selection that comprises the curriculum is 'the best that has been thought and said'. Liberal academic education in itself does not presuppose the kind of division between high culture and an ersatz popular culture for those of more feeble educational potential of the kind proposed by, for example, G. H. Bantock (1968), who in effect adopts view 3 above as a selection principle for different kinds of education for different kinds of people.

The second element is the development of character—not just in the sense of moral education but also as the development of an ability to exercise independent thought and judgement. It is also now commonplace for many writers in the tradition of liberal education to emphasize the development of *autonomy* or the ability to chart a course in life as the primary educational aim for individuals. Not necessarily because the exercise of autonomy is always and everywhere the only valuable state of an adult human, but because, in the kinds of societies in which we live (and these include both liberal market and more socialist arrangements) we are expected to and cannot avoid exercising autonomy (Raz 1986, Ch. 14).

A point often overlooked, but well worth dwelling on, concerns the fact that, unlike the time when liberal education was first developed in classical Greece and even later in the work of such enlightenment thinkers as Rousseau, in contemporary times the great majority of the population subject to mass compulsory education is destined to work for a living, and this includes women as well as men, as the 'living wage' which would support a family practically no longer exists except for the most wealthy. Thus the autonomous person is, perforce, one who very likely will spend most of his or her adult life either employed or self-employed. Few will enjoy the privileged life of a *rentier*.

This has had consequences which philosophers of education have not devoted enough time and attention to. Even those enjoying a 'classical' liberal education will expect to have to work for their living. The 'character' side of education will unavoidably concern itself with virtues aligned with those of a society in which most members will be involved in paid employment. This alters the terms of debate for those exploring the relationship between liberal and vocational education and affects the kind of liberal education that is on offer.[2]

One important way in which this socioeconomic 'elephant in the room' has an impact on what we understand by liberal education is first that both the cultural and character elements of such an education become oriented, whether deliberately or not, to preparation for a world in which paid employment is a central part of the educatee's future life. The growing role of higher education as the final phase in liberal education (as well as in professional education of various kinds) means that the subject or subjects in which one becomes a relative expert at tertiary level become critical for one's employment prospects.

This happens in two ways. First, through the fact that university education acts as a kind of filter on the labour market: The subject that one studies is regarded either as a marker of intellect or character. The institution and class of degree that one has obtained is also regarded as such a marker. In both these cases one's certificated education acts as a *positional filter* in the labour market, whether or not one's education has prepared one for a specific role in employment. The second way is connected with the fact that, to a greater or lesser degree, the subject that one studies at university is part of the technical knowledge that one needs to carry out a particular role in employment. In practice these are often difficult elements to disentangle from one another, but taken together they provide a powerful alignment of liberal education with the exigencies of employment. In many cases the connection with the labour market is made through further postgraduate professional education which allows the individual to tailor his subject expertise to the needs of particular employment roles.

LIBERAL AND VOCATIONAL EDUCATION

These considerations provide good reason to suppose that the aims of vocational and liberal education in our kind of society need not be as distinct as is commonly supposed. But in order to establish this point more securely it is important to lay to rest one particular canard that has been allowed to fly for far too long. This is the misidentification of vocational education with vocational training, a misidentification which R. S. Peters had already drawn attention to thirty years ago (Peters 1982, Ch. 3). Training, the inculcation of the ability to perform confident and accurate routines associated with a task, plays a necessary role in all forms of education (see Wittgenstein (1951) and Ryle (1949) for an account of the importance of training in learning). And although there is such a thing as vocational training, it is not to be identified with vocational education. Vocational training involves inculcation of the ability to perform tasks connected with employment. Vocational education is concerned with preparing an individual to operate within a certain employment context, such as a profession or other kind of occupation, and although it will undoubtedly involve episodes of training, will by no means be exhausted by them any more than liberal education is exhausted by learning times tables or the alphabet.

It is, of course, unreasonable for employers to expect that an educated person present themselves at their place of work ready to do a job without further preparation. But is it unreasonable for an employer to expect that educated people acquire some of the personal and social characteristics necessary to be effective employees? One concept that keeps getting in the way in the Anglo-American-Australian context is that of *skill*. Employers complain that university and school graduates lack the skills necessary for employability, while universities and schools retort (with some justice) that it is not their job to provide future workers with the skills necessary for employment. However, there are some personal characteristics and kinds of ability that it is, arguably, the responsibility of liberal educators to develop, at least to a certain degree, and these characteristics and abilities are necessary to becoming an effective and responsible employee as well as an autonomous individual. Robin Barrow has himself argued (Barrow 1987) that the term 'skill' is manifestly inadequate as a label for many kinds of important and valuable kinds of practical ability and should not be used for them.

Unfortunately, English lacks a ready-to-hand term that covers these abilities, and it is therefore regrettable, but perhaps not surprising, that 'skill' gets pressed into all kinds of inappropriate and misleading services. However, we are not bereft of conceptual resources for identifying and describing these kinds of abilities. We owe to Gilbert Ryle (1979, Ch. 1) in particular the concept of an 'adverbial verb' or type of action which does not necessarily have one type of manifestation, but is manifested differently according to different contexts and purposes. A subset of these is particularly important to our enquiry—those that are in the context of German vocational education called '*Fähigkeiten*' (as opposed to '*Fertigkeiten*' or skills). They include such abilities as being able to plan, coordinate, control, communicate, cooperate, negotiate, and evaluate, primarily in the context of work. It is characteristic of these abilities that, although they may depend on the exercise of skills for their realization, they are not to be identified with any particular skill or set of skills. The possession of 'planning skills' such as being able to draw a diagram or describe a putative course of action is not the same ability as the ability to plan, although it may, in certain circumstances, be a necessary component of such an ability. To be able to plan, to cooperate, or to evaluate requires not just the possession of certain skills, but the seriousness, attention, and commitment that results in planning, cooperation, or evaluation actually being capable of taking place, rather than motions of, say, planning just being gone through. In other words, such abilities, to be truly exercised, need to draw on certain personal characteristics and, dare one say it, *virtues*.

Thus in some respects, good quality vocational education is very well equipped to develop one of the prized goods of education, namely character. This is a theme common in the literature of the German-speaking countries: Goethe's Wilhelm Meister and Keller's Heinrich Lee are good examples of *Bildungsroman* characters who develop and discover themselves through sustained occupational engagement as novices struggling to achieve a sense of what is excellent in the occupation and how they measure up to those standards. This is not to say that school-based education is incapable of providing such goods, but the artificial character of schools, lauded by, for example Oakeshott (see Fuller 1976), becomes an obstacle in some respects, as the German vocational educator Kerschensteiner (1930) recognized. If the development of character is taken to be a central aim of education (*Erziehung* rather than *Bildung* in the German tradition), then schools' efforts to do so cannot be dismissed as 'schooling' rather than 'education' unless one has already taken a firm position on the educative nature of some kinds of learning to the detriment of others. It is notable that in this respect Barrow follows the earlier Peters rather than the later, who became much more aware of the possibilities of varieties of education that engaged fully with the practical and even with the vocational spheres of life.

Surely though, a conservative form of liberal education, conceived of as *cultural initiation,* cannot be managed through vocational education, however sophisticated? Vocational education is not preparation for child or adolescent labour; it concerns preparation for adult life, primarily but not exclusively in the medium of employment and must, therefore, make use of the resources of liberal education as a preliminary, building on and even extending the liberally educated capacities of the student by doing so. We have already noted the growing role of specialization within liberal education and the somewhat porous boundaries between an achieved education as a purely personal good, as a positional good, and as an instrumental good in the labour market.

Just as in our society liberal education conceived of as cultural initiation has more than a purely personal aim, but fits individuals for employment and citizenship, so good quality vocational education has significant liberal and civic aspects. Vocational education which aims to prepare young people for technically complex work requiring high levels of independence and coordination cannot but rely on a firm liberal educational footing in which the traditional secondary school subjects figure very strongly. Decent levels of literacy and numeracy will be an absolute prerequisite, and in many occupations a good scientific education will also be important. Many 'high skill' occupations depend on the application of systematic, often scientific, knowledge to practice, not just in the sense of maxims to be applied in the workplace, but as bodies of knowledge that can be interrogated as part of professional judgement. Furthermore the acquisition of a broad 'cultural literacy' (Hirsch 1987) is important to give employees, of whom independence and intelligence of action are expected, a broad conceptual and contextual understanding of their society, in order to make independent professional judgements. Needless to say, employees who are expected to obey orders and to carry out narrow routines will not need such attributes. For such employees, vocational training will be adequate.

I mentioned earlier that although there can be variation in what kind of education is suitable for what kind of person, in societies that are relatively equal and cohesive, that variation can be rendered into conceptions that bear quite a close resemblance to each other. A particularly important issue is that of the extent to which liberal education should continue to be a significant element of vocational education. I have already suggested that, in some respects, the *Erziehung* element in vocational education can relatively easily be realized, perhaps to a greater extent than in some forms of liberal education. But it can be argued that a continuing liberal element in vocational education also has an important liberal as well as vocational role. A good case has been made out that the traditional liberal curriculum embodies 'powerful knowledge' (see some of the contributions in Lauder et al. (2012) and in particular the contribution by Muller). It is not just that the traditional liberal subjects continue to be very prestigious and confer an enhanced social status on those who have a good acquaintance with them; it is also that they are, arguably, necessary for one to have influence in one's own society. Without good numeracy, literacy, a sure grasp of history, geography, and science, not to mention acquaintance with languages and the arts, it is difficult to get a decent grip on the concerns of the dominant sections of society whose thought-world tends to be formed through an intensive version of precisely such an education.

Such an education, extended into one's late adolescence and early adulthood, allows one to develop the kind of informed desires (Winch 2005, Ch. 7) that are an important component of the range of choices for a worthwhile life that an educated person might reasonably be expected to make. This is true for the choices one might make for one's occupation as well as for other aspects of one's life. It also helps to create a firm grounding for continuing personal education. In this respect a continuing subject-based and liberal strand within vocational education is a prerequisite of the Humboldtian conception of *allgemeine Menschenbildung,* or general human education, which provides for the condition of continuing development of individuality, while at the same time allowing an individual to play a part within established social roles (Benner 2003). Last, but not least, it has an important *civic* function. In order to engage with political, social, and economic elites on their own terms, a good acquaintance with the high culture that constitutes their principal medium of thought is important for the sustaining of an informed and active citizenry which aspires to engage with the direction of their own society. This point remains the case whatever explicit provision for civic education is made within vocational education programmes.

It is sometimes argued that the presence of academic subjects in vocational education is not necessary for vocational purposes and that apprentices and students should rather be able to access the knowledge that they need in order to carry out specific vocational projects and tasks. Rather than being introduced to subjects, it is argued, students should be able to access *Lernfelder* or fields of learning which will enable them to glean the knowledge necessary to complete the work that they are undertaking. While *Lernfelder* may indeed be able to do this, it is difficult to maintain at the same time that they will continue to provide the powerful knowledge needed to provide access to civic activity and to their further personal development. It is true that the *Lernfelder* are concerned with the specifically technical knowledge required to practice within an occupation, rather than the broader knowledge associated with civic and personal development. However, the disciplines associated with technical competence, such as mechanics or economics, are also part of the extended liberal education of someone preparing for work, just as they are for the economics graduate wishing to go into banking or the engineering graduate wishing to become an engineer. It is desirable, therefore, that subjects continue to be given an important role in the technical aspects of vocational education.

CONCLUSION

It has been argued against those who argue against the 'contestability' of educational concepts that there is no one preferred form of education. However, in developed Western societies with a broadly classless temper, the provision of different educational routes to individuals with different interests and aspirations need not involve the provision of routes that do not share significant similarities. Indeed, it is argued that the character-developing aspects of European type apprenticeship is a very effective vehicle for achieving some important liberal aims, while the continuation of subject-based academic education is a crucial component of a vocational education worthy of the name. Barrow's vision of liberal education not only survives the promotion of such diverse routes but positively requires a broad education up to and including lower secondary education.

NOTES

1. There is some evidence that Carr, since the publication of Carr (2010), modified his views on this issue and that they are now closer to, if by no means identical with, the ones espoused in this article.
2. R. S. Peters (1981) 'Democratic Values'. White's (1997) *Education and the End of Work* can be seen as an attempt to reinstate the conception of education for a world without work in a contemporary setting.

REFERENCES

Bantock, G. H. (1968) *Culture, Industrialisation and Education*, London: Routledge.
Barrow, R. (1976) *Common Sense and the Curriculum*, London: Allen & Unwin.
———. (1981) *The Philosophy of Schooling*, Brighton: Wheatsheaf.
———. (1987) 'Skill Talk', *Journal of Philosophy of Education* 21(2), pp. 187–196.
Benner, D. (2003) *Wilhelm von Humboldt's Bildungsphilosophie*, Weinheim: Juventa.
Carr, D. (2010) 'Education, Contestation and Confusions of Sense and Concept', *British Journal of Educational Studies* 58(1), pp. 89–104.
Dent, N. (1988) *Rousseau: An Introduction to his Psychological, Social and Political Theory*, Oxford: Blackwell.
Donaldson, M. (1978) *Children's Minds*, London: Fontana.
Fuller, T. (1976) Review of *On Human Conduct*, by Michael Oakeshott, *The Journal of Politics* 38, pp. 184–186.
Gingell, J. (2010) 'Reading Philosophy of Education', in *Philosophy of Education: An Introduction*, ed. R. Bailey, London: Continuum, pp. 147–157.

Gingell, J. and E. Brandon (2001) *In Defence of High Culture*, Oxford: Blackwell.

Gramsci, A. (1975) *Selections from the Prison Notebooks*, London: Lawrence & Wishart.

Haldane, J. (1989) 'Metaphysics in the Philosophy of Education', *Journal of Philosophy of Education* 23(2) pp. 171–183.

Hirsch, E. D. (1987) *Cultural Literacy: What Every American Needs to Know*, Boston: Houghton Mifflin.

Hobbes, T. (1968) *Leviathan*, edited with an introduction by C. B. MacPherson, London: Penguin.

Kerschensteiner, G. (1930) 'Das Problem der Lebensnähe unsere Schulen', in *Ausgewählte Pädagogische Schriften*, Band 2, Paderborn: Schöningh, 1968.

Lauder, H., M. F. D.Young, H. Daniels, M. Blarin, and J. Lowe (eds.) (2012) *Educating for the Knowledge Economy?*, London: Routledge.

Muller, J. (2012) 'Forms of Knowledge and Curriculum Coherence', in Lauder et al., London: Routledge, pp. 114–138.

Murphy, J. (2002) *On Hitler and Mussolini*, London: Athol.

Peters, R. S. (1981) 'Democratic Values and Educational Aims', in *Essays on Educators*, London: Routledge, pp. 32–52.

Pinzauti, P. (2012) 'The Autonomy of Morality from Religion: The End of Religion and of Relativism; Howard Mounce on Peter Winch', *Philosophical Investigations* 35(2), pp. 154–166.

Plato (1950) *The Republic*, trans. J. Llewelyn Davies and D. J. Vaughan, London: MacMillan.

Raz, J. (1986) *The Morality of Freedom*, Oxford: Clarendon Press.

Rousseau, J-J [1762] (1968) 'Émile, ou de l'Éducation', Paris, Flammarion

Ryle, G. (1949) *The Concept of Mind*, London: Hutchinson.

———. (1979) *On Thinking*, London: Hutchinson.

Vico, G. (1968) *The New Science*, trans. T. G. Bergin and M. H. Fisch, Ithaca, NY: Cornell University Press.

Vygotsky (1962) *Thought and Language*, Cambridge, MA, MIT Press.

Ward, K. (1974) *The Development of Kant's Views on Ethics*, Oxford: Blackwell.

White, J. P. (1997) *Education and the End of Work*, London: Bloomsbury.

———. (2007) *What Schools are for and Why*, London: Philosophy of Education Society of Great Britain.

Winch (1996) *Quality and Education*, Oxford: Blackwell.

———. (2005) *Education, Autonomy and Critical Thinking*, London: Routledge.

Wittgenstein, L. (1951) *Philosophical Investigations*, Oxford: Blackwell.

11 Swansong
The Price of Everything . . .

Robin Barrow

OTHER MEN'S FLOWERS

It is strange to think that this is possibly my swansong. After forty-five years of teaching and scribbling away at too many books and articles, I am about to hang up my rock 'n' roll shoes. In some moods, I think not a moment too soon: I am tired of repeating the same old mistakes, tired of hammering away at the same old truths, worried about no longer fitting into the scheme of things, and looking forward to a few years without any professional or academic concerns. In other moods I wonder whether I can really walk away from it all so easily.

Be that as it may, I had originally suggested to the editor that I should forego the pleasure of responding directly to each of the preceding papers, on the grounds that it is impossible to do justice to so many contributions in the space available. But, having read the papers, I feel that given the obvious effort involved, the compliment implied, and the very quality of the contributions, I cannot do other than begin by following convention and making a brief comment on each in turn.

David Carr's characteristically lucid paper explores my suggestion that it is potentially dangerous to think in terms of schools of thought and '-isms', and that there is little to be gained by doing so. Of course, in a way, in writing *Radical Education*, focusing on both deschooling and child-centered education, I was implicitly acknowledging the possible utility of labels in terms of teaching and exposition. One concern I had, however, was that there is generally very little real connection between a philosophical school of thought or 'ism', such as idealism, and any particular educational implications. But David suggests that, while that approach may indeed be of little value, thinking in terms of different *educational* schools of thought, providing that we distinguish them with more subtlety and accuracy than we have in the past, might be a most useful approach to teaching philosophy of education in practical terms, and I acknowledge that I find his argument persuasive on that point. But another of my concerns about thinking in terms of schools of thought is that there is a danger of assuming that one must identify with one or another of them, and then proceeding to think only in terms of that one explanatory framework. This tendency is widespread in educational thought (think of those ideologically tunnel-visioned 'instrumentalist traditionalists' or 'psychoanalytic progressives', as David calls them, as well as all those tediously repetitive wannabe Marxist tracts) and is very much to be avoided.

Reference to such '–isms' as pragmatism and idealism also raises the question of the relative emphasis to be placed on general philosophy and philosophy of education, allowing that we can make some sort of reasonable distinction between the two. This is an issue on which, as Harvey Siegel notes, he and I once nearly came to figurative blows. It is also an issue on which my thinking has changed over the years, primarily for practical reasons. I believe that it is a fact, easily demonstrated, that for the most part 'general' philosophers, when they turn to education, betray their ignorance of the subject and particularly of work in the philosophy of education, and also fail to do justice to their usual standards as thinkers. So, despite having argued in the past for more well-grounded and 'proper' philosophy in education (and indeed worrying about what I see as the increasing lack of it today), I nonetheless now argue for more concentrated focus on real educational problems. Let us have more work on what exactly constitutes 'bullying', for example, and whether it is always, in all forms, or necessarily such a dire threat to the well-being of the young as is commonly supposed, and less on the thought of Derrida and its tenuous connection to anything of educational significance.

Harvey's paper is focused, however, on aims. As with David, so here, there are points of disagreement. The problem in this case is to decide whether they are quibbles or fundamental differences. I don't, for instance, 'presuppose that we all understand the same thing by the analyzed concept', and I question whether it is correct to say that 'we can recommend that our educational aims include that of fostering care . . . without thinking that "caring" is part of the meaning of the word or the content of the concept'. Of course we can argue for fostering caring as a further end or aim of our schooling, but I stand by my view that to argue that education should have the fostering of care as one of its aims is logically to imply that the concept involves fostering of care, which latter claim, in addition, I think to be plainly false.

But the more significant point is surely that we agree on the importance of having clearly articulated and defensible aims; and I accept that giving reasons for adopting one's ideal is one way of analyzing the concept (as distinct from being an alternative course of action), though perhaps I have failed to make that clear in the past. I also accept both that education serves various extrinsic ends indirectly and that schooling has a number of further ends and aims besides the specifically educational. (Caring might be considered an example of either.) One specific and intriguing question that Harvey raises is whether critical thinking is inherent in the concept of education. He thinks not, and he may be right, which would certainly mean that (my) analysis is not the end of the story. But then I don't think that I or anybody else ever claimed that analysis was the end of the story. What we do maintain is that to engage in analysis is a good, a very good, way to begin.

In passing, Harvey makes reference to Rawls and the value of making a distinction between a concept and various particular conceptions, a distinction that Christopher Winch also draws attention to. Chris correctly notes that it can be the case that what is worthwhile for A in A's view is not, in A's view, worthwhile for B (although it is not clear to me whether he would acknowledge that situations may also occur in which such a distinction is illegitimately claimed). From this he goes on to derive the important points that we live in a society in which the need for, the exercise of, and the value of autonomy cannot reasonably be denied, and which also necessitates that more or less all of us have to find employment, which has implications for vocational education. While Chris plays fair in drawing attention to the fact that my distinction between schooling and education serves some of the same purpose as his own account of liberal vocational education, I find his argument a great deal more significant and persuasive than I would have done some years ago, partly as a result of changed circumstances but also partly as a result of a shift in my thinking. (As to changed circumstances, it is interesting to note in passing how very quickly and very recently John White's presumption of 'the impending omnipresence of a leisured society', referenced by Chris, has, temporarily at least, become outdated.) Crucial to the persuasiveness of Chris's argument is his emphasis on the distinction between vocational training and vocational education, and with that I strongly concur.

Chris writes convincingly on skills, as does Paul Hager, whose paper focuses on my work on this topic. The accuracy and neatness of Paul's summary of my position reminds me of one of the dangers of this sort of exercise: the compliment implicit in taking what I have to say seriously, and getting it right, can feed vanity. (With a bit of luck, the critical commentary may induce some humility.) I am pleased that he recognizes, as some do not, that I do not deny that there are some aspects of, say, critical thinking that *are* generic, and that my point is that nonetheless, considered as a whole or in itself, critical thinking is not simply a generic skill or even a set of generic skills. To be sure, one may have a generic *disposition* to think critically, but it remains the case that, in so far as there are individuals such as Leonardo da Vinci who think critically across the board (meaning amongst other things effectively and well), that is a contingent (and rare) occurrence. To be a critical scientist, novelist, historian, or philosopher logically entails being a good scientist, novelist, historian or philosopher, and clearly the good philosopher is not necessarily a good scientist.

Paul picks up on my reference to the entry under 'skill' in Webster's dictionary, and, by saying that in doing so I am 'claiming support' for my proposed relatively limited conception and that my 'crucial argument . . .

relies on one dictionary definition', he may perhaps lead the unwary to imagine that I am confusing a linguistic point with a conceptual one. Readers, having just seen my reaction to a claim in Harvey's paper that also revolves around distinguishing between linguistic and conceptual points, will note that I am a little sensitive on this issue. That is because I have spent a great deal of my professional life pointing out and stressing the difference between the two. So I must stress that I did not intend the reference to Webster to be taken as part of my argument; I was merely being linguistically prescriptive. (The conceptual points are contained within the detailed comments about different types of skill.) So when, for instance Paul later writes that drivers have a 'holistic skill' which is more than the sum of its eighty constituent skill parts, I think that he is saying essentially what I am saying, but he is choosing to retain the word 'skill', whereas I think it would be useful to avoid using the same word to apply to both the eighty constituent parts and the whole that is more than the sum of its parts. I think it would be helpful to limit the use of the word 'skill', because, whatever we call them, there is a difference, straightforwardly acknowledged by Paul, between, say, a physical and specific skill such as juggling and broader non-physical abilities such as some of those of the good historian. In much the same way, on a different topic, I argue that it would be useful if we could confine the use of the word 'brain' to refer to the physical stuff inside the skull and reserve 'mind' for that complex idea of the amalgam of our memories, understanding, and perception. But to make that suggestion is distinct from the argument necessary to establish that there *is* something distinct from the physical brain.

With Richard Pring's overall argument to the effect that virtues conceived of as dispositions should be fundamental to our moral stance I have no quarrel, and I concur in the view that the dispositions must be accompanied by the appropriate emotions. I question how easy it is to draw a distinction between intellectual and moral virtues (isn't truthfulness, for example, both a moral and an intellectual virtue?), but my real surprise and concern with Richard's paper is his apparent skepticism about autonomy and the view that we overstress its value in moral education. (I am not certain whether he means in theory, in practice, or in both). Here is another example of a change of emphasis, if not more, in my thinking. In earlier writings, particularly on Plato, I tended to emphasize the importance of a harmonious society and virtuous behavior, relative to individual freedom and autonomy, as Richard does here. But today, while continuing to maintain that certain virtues and principles are objectively good, I tend to stress that there is enough openness about what in practice we ought to do in various situations to make autonomy an extremely important educational goal (and not only in respect of moral questions).

Ruth Jonathan is also inclined to downplay the importance of autonomy. Her contention is that the clarity and clearing away of confusion that I see philosophy of education as providing is 'too modest and circumscribed' an aim, and that we should be more engaged with political reality and actual evils. She is certainly correct in seeing a tension between the claims of individual freedom and the social or common good in my work, and in arguing that I have not got a clear theoretical way to resolve this tension. And, whether we attribute the shortcomings of our society to our failure to succeed in educating people in my sense of 'educated', or to an inadequate or misguided conception, it is fair to say that well-educated people do not in themselves constitute or necessarily create a good society. (I must say in passing that I have never seen an edition of *The Philosophy of Schooling* that contains the quotation from Dewey that Ruth claims to have seen, on the flyleaf or anywhere else!) Contrary to Ruth's implication, I do have a theory of what it is to be human—essentially an Aristotelian teleological view tied up with understanding and mind, articulated, for instance, in *An Introduction to Philosophy of Education, 4th edition*—but it is true that, generally speaking, I have, if not 'tended to ignore', nonetheless focused on things other than, social and political dimensions, and I do see this as something of a shortcoming.

Nonetheless, I agree with Ian Gregory's contention that Ruth pitches her case too strongly in saying that 'arguably the modern world's most power-ful engine of inequality' is public education and that the ideal of providing a liberal education has proved a failure. As Ian says, it is not clear how we should judge the truth of such a claim, and, in any case, the position of the Millian liberal has not been effectively discredited yet. My problem in considering this issue is that in fact I care a great deal about social justice in Ruth's sense (and very much admire the work, both practical and theo-retical, that she has put into pursuing it), but that I share Ian's view that it is not primarily what education is for or about; and the degree of justice within a society is therefore not the criterion whereby to judge the success or failure of its education system. Furthermore, though I do not think that the attempt to provide a liberal education for all has been a resounding success all-told, I believe that it probably has led to an increased amount of tolerance and critical thought, and I can certainly point to a number of other societies where a marked and obvious lack of liberal education corre-lates with an equally marked and obviously worse situation so far as social justice goes.

In my earlier writings there was quite often explicit reference to the com-mon good, specifically to the general happiness, which in later writings has been to some extent replaced by an emphasis on epistemology and freedom of thought. My interest in Utilitarianism, which was transparent in all my early work, even when not theoretically its focus (as in *Moral Philosophy for Education* or *Injustice, Inequality and Education*), has not in itself waned, but I seldom make explicit reference to it now except when I am specifically explaining what ethical theory I find most convincing or how I actually attempt to set about dealing with particular moral problems. I make little or no reference to it when teaching philosophy of education classes. Nonetheless I am extremely pleased that John Gingell and Mike McNamee both chose to write on this topic, since, as indicated, it remains my personal ethical position.

John's paper, incidentally, opens with the most illuminatingly expressed summary of Peters's views on the concept of education that I have ever read. Once in his stride, he emphasizes the difference between a utilitarian viewpoint, meaning simply a means/end viewpoint in terms of efficacy, generally economic these days, and a Utilitarian viewpoint, meaning one that is tied up with the ethical theory and focused on the common good in terms of general happiness. Absurd as it may seem, and hugely misleading as it may be, the two are too often confused, not least in criticism and commentary on some of my work. More to the immediate point, John seems to me to be absolutely correct in his argument against Gutmann's position, particularly on the issue of freedom. In fact, I think it fair to say that he demolishes Gutmann, in particular her uncomprehending assertion that for Utilitarians happiness has to be subjectively defined for each individual. What his paper also does, gratifyingly, is detect a consistency in my thinking on the topic over a long period, despite the different approaches and attempts to write about it that I have made at different times.

Mike McNamee also gratifies me in focusing, albeit quite critically in many respects, on something that I think very important: namely the importance of reflecting on what an ethical theory *is*, or what it is for. Far too often one comes across objections to a particular theory, such as that it fails to tell you exactly what to do in certain situations, that betray a complete misunderstanding of the nature of ethical theory. But I do not think, as Mike seems to do, that the question 'what is an ethical theory?' is quite the same as the question 'what is the role of the moral philosopher?' Nor do I think that it can reasonably be suggested that we are dealing with a 'straw man' here, when critics routinely argue against the theory of Utilitarianism by producing an ingenious dilemma and pointing out that the Utilitarian would not be able to solve it. (Nor, if it is a genuine dilemma as distinct from a mere problem, would any person or theory be able to solve it. And part of my point is that there are dilemmas in life for which no ethical theory has a solution.) There is also an important distinction, I think, to be drawn between an argument 'advancing' a theory and it refuting some particular objection to the theory.

I suggest that Gaita's 'fine and important distinction between responsibility and blameworthiness' leads to the same practical conclusions as my distinction between 'bad but justifiable' and 'wrong'. More trivially, Mike is mistaken when he writes that I 'revel' in the 'adversarial'. The secret of my public persona can now be revealed: I always try to look as if I am comfortable with confrontation, but actually I am not! But I do like his swashbuckling style of writing, and chuckle quietly at the idea of my '"beautiful soul" averting [its] gaze from the real world', while rejecting the conclusion that my theory is 'impotent'.

Finally, it gave me great pleasure to read Richard Smith's flattering remarks about my style. In the second half of his paper he takes me to task for misreading Lyotard, and on that particular point I stand corrected. He also makes some more general but I think, on reflection, valid points about competing styles of philosophy of which I should be more respectful. Given these and other legitimate criticisms, I am all the more grateful to have my writing so elegantly and cogently commended. Whether the flattery is deserved or not in my own case, I do think that the quality of much writing in academia, including philosophy of education, is very poor—opaque, jargon-ridden, over-referenced, under-argued—and I do believe that there is a symmetry between thought and talk. Leaving aside obvious qualifications and exceptions, if you can't write it, you can't say it, and if you can't say it, you can't think it. And whereof we cannot write clearly, we should not write.

All in all, I have taken great pleasure in reading these kind and thoughtful papers, and I am humbled (not before time) by the generosity of spirit involved.

AND ALL SHALL HAVE PRIZES

I shall frame my remaining remarks around the following question, although I shall not attempt to answer it directly: How is it that our society has reduced itself to the level of Oscar Wilde's cynic, knowing the price of everything and the value of nothing? Why is it that we believe only in the measurable and cannot recognize the worth of much that is immanent and see the need for and importance of judgment?

Personally, I have had a most fortunate life and a more 'successful' career than I deserve. I have no complaints worth mentioning. But I do have serious concerns about current trends and fears for the future both in relation to society generally and academia in particular. In what follows, I shall attempt to summarize what I regard as the good and the bad in the recent past and likely future.

A *festschrift* is, in my case, an unearned accolade for which I am nonetheless extremely grateful. There is no false modesty here. I have had the pleasure of contributing to similar volumes for Richard Peters, Paul Hirst, Israel Scheffler, and John Wilson, each of whom made a significant personal impact on numerous individual students, on the wider world of educational thought, and of course on the development of philosophy of education in particular. I can claim no comparable distinction, although I like to think that I have conducted myself with energy and integrity. I regard this volume therefore, with enormous gratitude, as a tribute to friendship rather than scholarship. But, even if I had truly deserved it, though it seems ungracious to say it, I would have reservations about such an honor.

The truth is that I am against the plethora of rewards, awards, praise, and prizes that now swamp academic life: prizes for teaching, for theses and thesis supervision, for articles, for books, for the acquisition of grants, and of course those old favorites, the generic awards for general contributions to the 'profession' (sometimes confused by those involved in it with the 'world'). They are not awarded in a coherent or rational way; they should not be necessary; and they nurture vanity, the besetting sin of academia.

They are not awarded appropriately partly because we are all too human, and partly because in the nature of things they cannot be. They cannot be awarded in a rational and defensible way because assessing quality in such things as teaching and scholarship is a matter of judgment not measurement. It requires the reflective assessment of those who are immersed in the field in question and who are aware of and committed to the criteria of excellence within that field. Despite absurd attempts, such as that of Charles Murray (2003), to establish 'scientifically' that Beethoven was the greatest Western composer of all time or Aristotle the greatest philosopher, it cannot be done.

Murray proceeds in his bizarre endeavor by, first, selecting (by no clearly explained apposite process) a number of relatively well-known reference books in the field (for example, Bertrand Russell's *History of Western Philosophy*); then, second, by counting the number of pages devoted in these volumes to various individuals (seemingly without recognizing that a reference book might take more space to castigate the pretensions of a poor philosopher than to praise a good one). Finally, the individual most referred to is identified with the 'best'. A more blatant and telling example of allowing the methodology to drive the inquiry could hardly be found. Being talked or written about may be measurable, but it clearly does not necessarily have anything to do with the quality of one's work. Being the best is not to be confused with being thought to be best.

What can be done in the attempt to assess quality in such fields is to articulate clearly the criteria of success, making sure that they are criteria that pertain to the nature and object of the exercise. But at least some of the criteria that pertain to good musical composition or good philosophy are necessarily intangible. Thus it is inevitable that we have to judge, rather than measure, whether Beethoven is a great composer. (And it is, incidentally, certain that while we may be able to assert with confidence that various individuals are good philosophers, others poor, we will never in the nature of things be able to establish anything so specific as that X is the best.)

When it comes to rewarding good teachers and scholars, we grotesquely distort the nature of these activities in order to focus on criteria that we can measure, such as, for example, student ratings of their teachers on a scale of 1 to 5, the number of citations of articles, and the size of grants acquired. We do this without any concern for the obvious points that students are not necessarily or even usually in a position to make qualified judgments, that citations may be many because of the topicality or popularity of the subject matter, or because of the weakness of a paper or the ridicule it invites, and that the value of bringing in a large sum of money for a research project depends upon what the project is, whether it is worth doing and whether it needs that amount of funding.

In any case, these prizes are seldom distributed fairly even when measurable indices are employed. One contingent problem is that many awards (e.g., for teaching excellence) are made by university committees rather than committees consisting solely of specialist peers, so that for example, the quality of a humanities teacher may be being assessed by scientists; but the nature of studying science being very different from the nature of studying philosophy, good teaching has to be assessed by reference to different criteria in either case. Similarly, it is impossible in practice to ensure that none of the prejudices and preferences that are an inevitable part of any human being will play a part in coming to a judgment. Few are those who can distinguish between their dislike of a colleague's approach to teaching and a reasoned argument to establish that it is poor teaching. With the best will in the world it is hard to establish whether one's rejection of some Marxist or postmodern tract as poor is the result of objective reasoning or lack of sympathy with the approach. Sadly, it is also hard to disentangle legitimate objection to a colleague's teaching and envy of their popularity.

Judging the quality of the scholarship (i.e., knowledge, understanding, and thinking) of a department by reference solely or primarily to the amount of funding it brings in, the number of students it attracts, and the number of publications produced is indefensible. There are many diverse reasons why students are attracted to particular programs or departments, ranging from interest, by way of parental influence, peer pressure, and putative degree of challenge, to such mundane considerations as cost, availability, and timetabling. The notion that universities should 'reward' departments for attracting students strikes at the heart of the premise that a university aspires to provide initiation into what is independently judged to be worth studying. This, one might have thought, is all very simple and obvious. Prizes are therefore a little suspect, not least in that many invite one to put oneself forward as a candidate and to sing one's own praises.

And so we come to vanity. Am I alone in thinking that academics are unusually ambitious and particularly prone to vanity? Perhaps it has something to do with our general assumption that our minds are our 'peculiar excellence' as human beings combined with the view that exercise of the mind is our trade, leading to the conclusion that we are superior beings. Perhaps it is because we are forever judging and ranking others. Perhaps it is because we are relatively unsupervised and hence not subject to much critical scrutiny. Perhaps it is because students often, and not always for good reasons, flatter our egos. Perhaps it is simply because we keep giving each other prizes. Whatever the reasons, a great many academics seem to see themselves as sages, while at the same time being obsessed with the more worldly goals of fame and fortune. This seems to me a matter of increasing concern. The extent to which even quite new recruits seem to imagine themselves as being yet unrecognized Platos and Wittgensteins, and the willingness with which they present themselves in the market place as 'public intellectuals', I find rather startling.

Awe, as Plato said, should be the beginning of philosophy: a sense of wonder at the mysteries of the universe, and, by implication, humility. We recall Socrates's realization that, if he is wise, it is because he recognizes his own ignorance, the limits of his understanding. Though there may be something of the actor in a good teacher, the life of scholarship does not, ideally, resemble that of the theatre. No doubt there have always been some vast egos and a deal of conceit among thinkers of all kinds, but it seems that within the span of my career we have moved from a time when there was some respect for and deference towards proven scholars, who did not invariably see themselves as particularly special, to a situation in which there is indifference towards and certainly no respect for senior colleagues who, in their turn, see themselves as possessed of great wisdom (perhaps confusing the pose of the apocryphal guru with the mind of the scholar).

Meanwhile, the university itself has become preoccupied with appearance and image, and a good number of its inmates seem to have taken the PR talk, the vision statements, and the reward system, all of which ought really to be jettisoned, a deal too seriously. No reputable university that I know of has any problem recruiting students, certainly my own doesn't; and yet we spend huge amounts on advertising, all of which consists either of pseudoscientific claims about our ranking among universities or of anodyne statements which, throughout the university world, all amount to variations on one theme: 'we are where it's at.'

The idea that a university might do well to define and defend 'where it is' has not been entertained.

TO SING IN PERFECT HARMONY

We do not expect the degree of clarity, certainty, or consistency in philosophy that we do in, say, mathematics. Some erroneously conclude that philosophers have no substantial shared body of knowledge, and, even more egregiously, as if it follows that one can legitimately hold any view one chooses on philosophical matters. I would therefore like to draw attention to some of many the things that I and the other contributors to this volume have in common.

First and foremost, we agree that in order to know where we are going, in order to make judgments about effectiveness, policy decisions, etc., we need to have a clear understanding of what constitutes success—what we are trying to achieve in the name of education. We may quibble over whether this is best expressed in terms of aims, whether it amounts to the same thing as analyzing the concept of education, or whether there is more than one legitimate conception, and, if so, how many. But we agree that we need to know the end(s).

Second, we are at one in seeing this need to clarify the end(s) or purpose of the enterprise as a sufficient reason for recognizing the enormous practical value of philosophy. It is not simply that it adds definition to the picture, to know where we are headed. It is that it does not make sense to choose this path or that, to propose a particular policy, or to regard this or the other as 'effective', if we do not have a clear statement to make about what ideally well-educated people look like or, more formally, what their defining characteristics are.

Third, more generally, we are agreed on the emphasis on analytic philosophy. There are other kinds of philosophy (e.g., Eastern, Continental), other uses of the word (e.g., my 'philosophy' of life meaning simply my 'view' of life), and other perhaps related but distinct pursuits such as studying the aphorisms of Confucius. And there are various schools of philosophy (e.g., idealism, pragmatism, or, on some views, Marxism) each of which, if accepted, offers a particular way of understanding and explaining the world. But each of these different senses and approaches has in common a commitment, implicit or explicit, to a specific mode of explanation. It is vital that all such monolithic approaches to thought be challenged, vital that we do not simply settle for interpreting the world as Marxists, postmodernists, idealists, or whatever. And for that reason it is vital that there be a powerful and erudite body of analytic work, focused on clarifying key concepts and on making fine discriminations, and challenging any and every particular ideological framework. More specifically we need to keep a strong light shining on the question of what it is to be well educated, alongside continued scrutiny of opaque and unclear concepts such as, for example, giftedness, mind, nature, individual potential, intelligence, and worthwhile knowledge.

Fourth, we all agree that though we necessarily work with, and therefore talk about, words and usage to some degree, ultimately it is not words in which we are interested, but ideas. Our ultimate interest, for example, is not in how we use the word 'happiness' but in what happiness is, what constitutes a clear, coherent, and complete account of the concept that is also consonant or compatible with experience and reality. (Harvey Siegel, it may be recalled, characterizes me as an 'ordinary language' philosopher, in which I think he is mistaken. He would, I am certain, endorse what I say here.)

Fifth, while well aware, perhaps to differing degrees and in different respects, of the many factors that may influence our beliefs, we agree on the value of rationality and on the possibility of objectivity. We recognize the value of science, but fear its unwarranted dominance: not everything, let alone everything that matters, can be scientifically demonstrated. Furthermore, we take a Popperian view of science itself, believing that we are warranted in regarding certain claims as true inasmuch as repeated and rigorous testing has not falsified them, rather than that they have been demonstrated to be true.

So, sixth, and more specifically, and notwithstanding Paul Hager's critique of my work on the subject, we repudiate the framework of mental processes and skills that is the hallmark of so much contemporary educational talk. We do not believe that one can reduce human activity to observable behaviors, either conceptually or for practical purposes of research. We recognize the significance of neurophysiological research, but recognize too that to uncover the neurophysiological functions that are necessary to, say, an act of imagination or kindness is not to have provided an adequate conception of imagination or kindness.

Seventh, we are wary of the fatalism that can be induced by certain views of sociological inquiry, and which is likely to be increased by our increased understanding of genetics. The surely undeniable fact that both our genetic inheritance and our circumstances have a part to play in our development, and hence in particular the beliefs and values we come to hold, must not be confused with the quite unreasonable suggestion that we are in some way inescapably what we are and have no responsibility for our progress and development. Quite apart from the oddity of anybody interested in education (which presupposes belief in our ability to change people's beliefs, attitudes, and understanding) committing themselves to any kind of social determinism, the fact is that neither our genes nor our environment dictate our development. While recognizing sociological and psychological questions as being of the utmost importance in education, we are wary of the social sciences. In particular, we question whether they can truly be sciences without either distorting or missing crucial elements in characteristically human interaction. For instance, we are worried by the tendency of some to think that they can isolate and analyze such factors as enthusiasm and commitment by direct observation.

Finally, as far as this attempt at a list goes, we all agree that there is a vital evaluative, more specifically moral, element to education, and that the contemporary tendency to see education in terms of a business model, to use the language of economics and industry (e.g., 'input' and 'output'), and to concentrate on measures of effectiveness simply misses this element. And that takes us back full circle: we think it matters how we talk about education. If we use business terminology, it will become a business.

'ALL TOGETHER NOW, LET'S FALL APART . . . '

What is wrong with our society? Perhaps most obviously we lack trust. We do not trust bankers or politicians; we see corruption in the police force, in journalism, in football; we are familiar with those responsible for health, for television programming or for food supplies ignoring obligations and walking away from responsibility; we are uncertain about tradesmen who knock on our door and marketing agents who phone us at home; we mistrust advertisements; we fear to walk the streets; we do not trust democracy. We have little faith in professionals such as doctors, lawyers, or indeed academics.

This is not the place to attempt to analyze this phenomenon. Not that it needs much analysis: we do not trust them because there have been too many spectacular cases of untrustworthy behavior, whether by government ministers—in Italy (Berlusconi), Britain (Raison, Huhne), France (Pasqua), or Belgium (Claes)—or rank-and-file MPs fiddling their expenses without shame or remorse, by fraudulent academics, by paedophile priests, or by pharmaceutical companies. But clearly size has something to do with it. A multinational corporation employing thousands if not millions of people throughout the world does not have the personal touch of an old-fashioned local or family firm. The bigger the institution, the more removed it is from the concerns of its members and its clients. In practice, size also leads to a retreat from responsibility. The Francis report that recently castigated the NHS in Britain has been widely criticized on the grounds that it named no names, and no single individual has been brought to book in relation to the unnecessary deaths of thousands of patients; but, though this may not make it excusable, it is difficult to apportion blame to individuals when one is talking about the failure of a vast system. Greed is clearly another factor. Quite apart from the fact that the majority of acts of corruption are presumably largely brought about by greed, there can be little doubt that an economic system which gives a large majority of people, directly or indirectly, an interest in wanting share prices to increase at all costs has a lot to do with the problem.

Advances in technology, despite the advantages they have brought, have also exacerbated the distance between a business or service and its customers, as anyone trying to negotiate a telephone tree in Bangalore in order to call out a telephone repairman in Dorset can testify. Increased specialization in the workplace and a weakening in the provision of a common general education have also surely played their part: there simply isn't the same extent or degree of common understanding and competence that there used to be. Individuals are increasingly detached from their surroundings and from each other.

Alienation, materialism, and greed are both partial causes and consequences of our situation. It may be difficult to discern the precise pattern of cause and effect, but it is hardly necessary: the fact is that in our global (i.e., very big, very far-flung, and interconnected) world and economy, we have become estranged, suspicious, disaffected, and materialistic. What does it matter whether our materialism leads to our selfishness and isolation, or the latter leaves us little option but to retreat into acquisition? Either way we have an esurient society. While we are envious of those with more than ourselves, and condemn the bonuses of the really rich with true indignation, most of us are nonetheless inclined to both hang on to and justify our own relative prosperity and to accept any bonus ('merit increase' in our little world) that comes our way. The reforms that are desperately needed, we cry out for; but Not In MY Back Yard.

There is also an intellectual explanation of our problems, and that is that we have a confused over-reliance on science. Scientific research, of course, is both intrinsically amazing and in practical terms of incalculable benefit. But not everything has a scientific explanation, and not everything that does in principle can in practice be scientifically demonstrated. We also live in a world of values: moral values certainly, but also spiritual values, notions of achievement and failure, beauty and ugliness, honor and dishonor, passion, compassion, cruelty, creativity, and integrity. Yet, despite the ubiquity and acknowledged importance of values in our lives, our understanding and perception are for the most part concentrated on the physical and empirical. So we are mechanistic in our approach to life and fatalistic in our attitude. In time, we seem to believe, research (which will be of a fundamentally scientific kind) will reveal to us how to ensure a successful marriage, how to sort out the economy, how to perfect our teaching, how to write the great American novel, and how to avoid depression. In the meantime, if you can't get a response from the importunate taxman, or if you find no recognition of your concern for beauty or fairness at the local town hall, you call it Kismet. That's the way things are.

As if this misplaced over-confidence in scientific research and the ill-assorted companion belief in matters being beyond our control were not worrying enough, there is also a glaring contrast between our assumption of a scientific certainty about life in general and our acceptance of a moral relativity. We seem to take for granted the crudest of fact/value distinctions, as if everything was either an empirically demonstrable truth ('facts') or a matter of opinion ('values'), and as if there were therefore no place for the question of the truth or otherwise of claims such as 'Dickens is worth reading', 'You are my dear friend', or 'I am emotionally inspired by this music'.

If education has an urgent remit, it should be to instill in future generations an awareness of the nature, value, and *limits* of science; the ability to distinguish knowledge from truth so that it can be understood that some things may be true that cannot be known to be so; a taking to heart of the Aristotelian dictum that one must expect different degrees of certainty in respect of different kinds of question; and an appreciation of the fact that certain questions have many plausible answers, but 'many' is not 'any', so that it is seldom the case that 'it is *just* a matter of opinion' or that *any* opinion is as good as another.

In short, we need to fight against relativism and fatalism, and to promote recognition of the fact that we can and should take responsibility for our futures.

POISON IVY LEAGUE

One of the lesser reasons that I accepted the invitation to move to Simon Fraser University in Canada in 1982 was that it then had a ceiling to its salary scale: after appointment one competed with one's colleagues for biennial salary increases until one reached the maximum possible, and there one remained, regardless of achievement, production, or reputation. The cap was relatively modest, but most people reached it relatively early, and, so the argument went, one's lifetime earnings were likely to be comparable to those where the rewards could be greater but the path slower and more uncertain. This has changed and (in line with most universities) we now follow alleged market forces and pay some senior scholars a great deal more than others.

I cannot claim to speak for the psychology of all, but I think it plausible to suggest that just as there is every reason to suppose that suitable, qualified, and able candidates could be found to take over as CEO of British Airways, Barclays Bank, or the Royal Mail without being paid a ridiculously inflated salary, despite the insistent rhetoric that denies this, so it is untrue that money is needed to attract or keep the best academics. It does not require a background in psychology to know that many people would happily continue working in a university earning the same maximum salary as others of similar, or even lesser, distinction, provided they felt well treated and appreciated, but that they begin to feel aggrieved and ready to move, even if continuing to earn the same salary, when some colleagues are being paid considerably more.

The Canada Research Chair program was a particularly vivid example of this blind assumption that higher salaries are the only, or even the significant, determinant in attracting and retaining personnel of quality and repute. Worried about a lack of research initiative (on what grounds?), the Canadian government decided that it could somehow improve the quality of scholarship by providing a great deal of taxpayers' money to be distributed to the best researchers. The obvious and complex question of how to assess quality was ignored. And the outcome was inevitable: the universities began to play musical chairs. Professor X at University A saw an opportunity to double her income by accepting a chair at university B. Professor Y at university B, naturally discomfited, decamped to take up a chair at university C (or perhaps even B). And so on. But did Canadian scholarship improve? Indeed, although confusing quantity with quality is an error too often encountered, one may query whether scholarship even 'increased'. The project simply increased the cost of research for no discernible benefit whatsoever.

The CRC program was also clearly skewed towards the sciences, disciplines in which attracting large research funding is sometimes a necessity. In this respect the program was not atypical: most thinking and policy-making these days is driven by a view dictated by scientific lenses. But funding, indeed even the idea of research in the manner of the sciences, is often wholly inappropriate in arts and humanities departments. Studying Shakespeare is as important as studying the human genome, but it does not require the funding or the paraphernalia of research assistants, labs, release from teaching, etc. So much should be obvious. Yet universities, while often providing less central support for the arts on the grounds (correct) that they require less, inconsistently and incorrectly continue to rate both departments and faculty in the arts and humanities by reference to such things as the funding they bring in or the number of graduate students they can support.

Equally detrimental to learning and scholarship has been the trend towards bureaucratic management. Gone are the days of academics themselves taking on major administrative positions because they recognized an obligation to take their turn in such a role (and because there was widespread feeling that scholars as a whole should be responsible for their own community). Now we are in the hands, at the top, of celebrity ex-politicians and the like, and at the next level down of professional apparatchiks. These are people whose interest and talent, insofar as they have any, is in organization and control as such, rather than in inspiring and leading, specifically, a university. These are not people with well-thought-out and determined academic or educational aspirations, who see their job as facilitating, maintaining, and where necessary improving the unique qualities of a university. They are people who see themselves as possessed of generic skills of innovation, people management, and the like, in short 'leadership', without any sense that running an educational establishment might be importantly different from running a canning factory.

Technology has not helped here. One effect of new electronic systems of administration and organization has been a further distancing between the rank and file and management. The fact that one seldom meets anybody face-to-face these days depersonalizes the whole business and tends to distance individuals from the process and issues at stake. Technological advances have also tended to distance anybody from personal responsibility: where there is no personal contact it is hard to pin responsibility on anyone. Beyond this, the contemporary obsession with the paraphernalia of vision statements, mission statements, learning objectives, protocols, and so forth, both reinforces the scientific outlook and further divorces the university from an understanding of the individual, the human, the particular, and the ideal of searching for truth and self-awareness. Insistent demands for accountability, unexceptionable in principle, become monstrous curbs on freedom of thought, as do well-intentioned policies on harassment and equity. The institution appears to be more frightened of litigation than of losing a Nobel prize winner. Put simply: the procedures are now driving and dictating the ends.

I must add here a remark about 'professional' schools, and this brings us back to issues of size and money. Not long ago, professional schools were looked down upon in many universities as not being truly academic in nature. That may still be the attitude, perhaps justified in many cases, of individual faculty, but it is not the view of administrators, who now see professional schools as being of particular value. This is essentially because they bring in a lot of money in a variety of ways. For example, graduate education students often pay higher fees than others and are willing to do so because they can get salary increases related to their academic qualifications. Business schools are often generously supported in terms of scholarships, grants, and facilities by business companies. Pharmaceutical companies have a great deal of money, and they are often prepared to invest it in various medical and paramedical departments. For the same reason we see universities unconscionably pursuing foreign students who are willing to pay inflated fees, although in many cases their lack of language ability makes it questionable whether they should be taking up university time and space at all (and, in so doing, excluding local students). This trend is redefining the university.

There is of course nothing wrong with that in itself; the nature of the university has evolved and changed throughout its history and there is no *a priori* reason why it should not become a center for professional schools. But what is currently happening is not the product of some clear and well-thought-out plan. It is a knee-jerk response to a felt need to get more money. The problem is that running an institution dedicated to preparing people for a specific profession, and to some extent funded by that profession, is quite different from providing an education for the academically and intellectually suited, at the expense of the public. If we could accept them for what they are, we could finance excellent liberal arts colleges for a great deal less than we currently spend on maintaining our universities. But universities are caught between providing a liberal education and preparing people for a profession, while seemingly unaware of the fact.

Finally, we too, just like other businesses around the world, are complicit in the bonus culture. As already noted in respect of prizes, we seem to feel that doing the job for which one is paid is somehow deserving of a further reward. University lecturers and professors are paid to teach to the best of their ability and to make as solid a contribution as they can to developing and spreading understanding of their subject matter. They are also paid quite generously, if one takes into account the hours and other working conditions. Why, then, should they expect some kind of material reward for seemingly teaching well or producing a seminal book or important discovery? It is as if we were to give the already particularly well-paid senior surgeon a further prize for performing operations without mishap, or the plumber a bonus for mending the tap without causing much flooding.

Stuck as we are in this commercially orientated, anti-humanistic, and even anti-intellectual culture, one priority for philosophy of education might be to focus more on issues and problems in higher education. In many ways our schools, though perhaps not unfairly blamed for certain shortcomings in preparing students for university, do a more honest and better job than the latter.

TO SIR WITH LOVE

The current Secretary of State for Education in England and Wales, Michael Gove, appears to want to remove teacher education from the universities. This would be to reverse a trend and the course of a battle that has been waged throughout my career. I have some sympathy with Gove on this issue, but it is one on which I have been changing my mind slowly and cautiously over the years.

I was originally a strong supporter of the philosophy of education party line, which was that we needed to get future teachers *educated* in respect of education and teaching, as distinct from merely trained or prepared in terms of techniques of discipline and instruction. And to do that, to truly educate them in respect of education, it was felt that it was important to bring the operation into the university. I still accept that as an ideal. But the reality is nowhere near the ideal. A great deal of what goes on in university departments of education bears little or no relation to the kind of scholarly inquiry and contemplation that we associate with the university and that was originally envisioned as the aim of placing teacher preparation in universities.

Much of the research undertaken is an unnecessary and shallow reflection of *bona fide* scientific or philosophical research, conducted by individuals who are poorly educated themselves and often lacking adequate disciplinary background. The research that superficially most resembles the real thing, namely empirical research, is for the most part an inappropriate aping of the ways of true science. I have engaged in this argument many times elsewhere and will not repeat it here. Suffice it to say, that while I believe that there is a little of real significance and practical use that could be established scientifically as true of human interactions (such as necessarily constitute educational encounters), there certainly isn't much that has been incontrovertibly established. It is simply false to pretend that we have a science of teaching, leadership, assessment, or anything else important in education.

Very few of those who profess to teach philosophy of education today have any formal qualifications in philosophy itself, and many have only a slight, if any, background in philosophy of education. But having written a Master's thesis, purportedly of a philosophical nature, in a typical education department, is simply not adequate grounding for teaching philosophy (whether of education or anything else) in a university. And it is unconvincing to claim that the bulk of work in philosophy of education is philosophically illuminating or of any great practical use.

The dream is not of something impossible. There could be (*has* been at some times and places) a department that involved students in serious study of the history of education, that explored the insights and claims of sociologists and psychologists at the same time as scrutinizing the nature and limits of these types of inquiry, and that involved them in strenuous analytical examination of key concepts such as giftedness and intelligence. But by and large that does not appear to be what is happening, essentially because neither the university nor departments themselves need to worry about that while they can bring in students, money, and even repute by claiming to pass on expertise in the running of schools, design of curriculum, and 'best practice' for control and teaching in the classroom. So, *pace* Chris Winch and Richard Pring in particular, each of whom has an honorable and enviable record of fighting for the retention of education departments and faculties in universities, I think, as I say, that Gove has a point.

The dream of the 1960s has failed. Philosophy of education, which in the thinking of pioneers such as Richard Peters was essential to the wider plan of an educated teaching profession, has been largely squeezed out of the curriculum, a fact that may seem at odds with the increase in membership of professional societies, the number of books and articles published, and the attendance at conferences around the world, but which is nonetheless true. Prospective teachers do not, for the most part, get a thorough grounding in philosophy of education, they do not give deep thought to the nature of the enterprise, they do not reflect deeply on the theories and ideas of Plato, Rousseau, or Dewey, they do not question the findings of empirical researchers, they do not even question the coherence and meaning of contemporary policy documents and directives. Philosophers of education themselves, perhaps because they are often not formally trained as philosophers, all too often write articles which, far from helping to sort out the 'mush' that Peters rightly saw around him, actually add to it.

Part of the reason for this loss of ground is obviously that the powers that be do not see any practical value in philosophy—perhaps because it does not give enough clear directive answers, certainly because it raises awkward questions. Governments and other administrators look only for direct measurable payoffs, with a clear and distinct emphasis on each of those three words. They are not prepared to consider indirect benefits (such as lifelong gains in terms of sustained intellectual curiosity), the non-measurable (such as appreciation of beauty or passion for accuracy and truth), or ends that are not 'payoffs' in any recognizable sense but simply good states of affairs (such as finding life immensely fascinating and rewarding). Philosophy is also often dismissed as being of 'the ordinary language' variety which in turn is wrongly glossed as 'just about words' or etymology. But as I have already pointed out neither assumption is correct: few if any philosophers can really be correctly characterized as simply 'ordinary language' philosophers, and even those who are, such as perhaps J. L. Austin and, in some moods, John Wilson, were not remotely inclined to confuse etymological with conceptual points.

Ironically, there is nonetheless a job to be done at the level of language: it would be good for example if people could be brought to understand the danger of talking about education in inappropriate terms such as the language of business; and it would be good if people would stop making facile and false claims such as that 'education' is derived from the Latin word 'educere', meaning 'to lead out', and that therefore education should be seen as a process of leading or drawing out what is within the individual child, with the conclusion that we should embrace modes of teaching that avoid instruction. Everything in this argument is wrong. 'Education' does not necessarily derive from 'educere'; for all we know, it may equally derive from 'educare' meaning 'to train' (as of plants) or 'to rear' (as of animals). Second, both Latin words in fact have a variety of meanings ranging from those that imply, in either case, 'bringing forth' to those that imply 'cultivating' or 'training'. Third, etymology, when reliable, may suggest ideas to us, but it cannot be used as an argument for drawing a substantive conclusion about contemporary meaning: the fact that 'happiness' derives from the word 'hap' (meaning 'chance' or 'luck') does not establish the conclusion that happiness is entirely a matter of chance. Finally, even if it were agreed that 'education' means 'leading out', what that means in practice for teaching remains entirely unclear until we have a better understanding of the nature of mind, knowledge, and human understanding.

But, more generally, I suggest, most administrators in their ignorance simply confuse philosophy with an undisciplined weaving of theoretical models. To them, philosophy is simply idealistic (to be contrasted with feasible) theorizing (to be contrasted with demonstrated truth, which in turn is to be conflated with 'empirically established'). Whatever the precise reasons, there cannot be much doubt that the policy line adopted by administrators and government involves a mechanistic view of human behavior and consequently a purely scientific approach to explaining and determining it. The only thing that is remotely able to challenge the dominance of the scientific view is the equally suspect ideological approach.

Officialdom's fear or suspicion of theory does raise the question of the role of theory, and in particular the distinction between engaging in theory in the sense of pursuing theoretical or abstract and to some extent ideal understanding, and in the quite different sense of adopting an explanatory framework. The latter is dangerous, as I have already noted. But to pursue theoretical questions, such as what would happen if such and such were the case, without any prior commitment to some agenda, is quite different. In any case, to engage in philosophy in the Western analytic tradition is not to adopt some metaphysical view and to proceed to interpret the world in the light of it. We must get away from grand theories and start trying to *make sense* of particular claims, as distinct from attempting to verify or falsify them (which may, but will not always, come next).

OVER MY SHOULDER

I have made it clear in the foregoing, I hope, that while I think that our society, our universities, and our education departments are all in many ways in poor shape, I nonetheless believe strongly in the potential of academia in general and philosophy of education in particular; and I believe that human beings are capable of pulling themselves together and improving the world. I have not said much about any misgivings I might have about the small part that I have played in the human comedy. But it seems appropriate on an occasion such as this to ask myself, finally, in looking back, what regrets or concerns I might have.

I sometimes wish that I had not spread my fire so widely and that I had not moved around to the extent that I have between philosophy, philosophy of education, and education, not to mention ancient history. (Perhaps also that I had not moved about geographically.) More specifically, it might have been wiser to concentrate on, say, Plato or Utilitarianism. Or, again, I might have focused on and gone more deeply into fewer topics, be it empirical research into teaching, generic skills, the nature of analytic philosophy, happiness, or inclusion, rather than attempted to have my say on them all. In other words, to use the jargon of today, I diversified too much. This has had two direct consequences. First, and less importantly, I think that it has led to my work being less effective in the marketplace. It seems that establishing a niche, becoming associated with a particular line, even a catchphrase, enhances one's profile no end. (We are, after all, close to comedy here.)

But second, and this is the real concern, I think it has led to my work being less searching, less thorough, or simply less good than it might have been. Given the dangers of specialization (including failure to see the wood for the trees and becoming prisoner to a methodology and an explanatory view of the world) there are admittedly things to be said in favor of my scattergun approach. However, on balance I believe that, had I focused more, I might be more personally satisfied about where I stand, what I think, and what I have achieved. Whereas in fact I confess to being less than certain what it all amounts to and even what I really believe. But then perhaps life, including education, just is very complex, confused, and muddled, and I should be grateful that I did not fool myself or others with any grand explanations, theories, or answers to extremely complex and difficult questions.

In general my views on Plato have not changed, though in certain particular respects they have. For instance, I would no longer try to argue that in the *Republic* Plato assumed that all children would initially be regarded as potential philosopher-kings and that it is only through the educational process that distinctions are made between artisans, auxiliaries, and rulers, or that there would be no actual slavery (although there is no specific textual evidence to rule either of these views out). On the other hand, I maintain the view that to represent Plato as a protofascist, as Russell, Crossman, and Popper did, is ridiculous and fails to recognize the clear fact that Plato is sincerely concerned for the well-being and contentment, the 'eudaimonia' or flourishing, of all citizens. It is simply outrageous to identify such thinking with the tyrannical aspirations of a Stalin, Hitler, Pol Pot, or Mao.

Having said that, I have become, philosophically, more liberal as time has passed. That is to say, while, like many ageing people I may be getting personally and psychologically more intolerant, particularly of stupidity, hypocrisy, unkindness, and pretension, I am more inclined to recognize and argue for the vital importance of maintaining political freedom, particularly freedom of thought and expression, in the face of political correctness and other assorted do-gooders, not to mention fanatics of all persuasions, and tyrannical and oppressive regimes. None of us can avoid the tensions that in practice occur between the demands of freedom and equality. But I have always been more of an egalitarian than some of my critics recognize. I do not believe in the wisdom of seeking for equality of outcome, and I am not bothered in the slightest by moderate differences in material wealth, type of work, or style of life. But like most decent people I am appalled (and mystified by the alleged need for) the kind of wealth and lifestyle differences we increasingly see. I am a straightforward believer in equality of opportunity combined with a generous safety net for the less successful and fortunate.

That is one of the reasons that I am passionate about education in principle and hold the particular view of it that I do: I believe that the right kind of education gives individuals the best chance of having some control and choice over the kind of life they may lead. My insistence on refusing to be politically correct and on the desirability of a society in which we are permitted to say things and, within limits, to act in ways that cause offence, and my objection to talking in terms of 'rights' and attributing rights to every species of flora and fauna, should not be confused with a lack of concern for the lowly prawn or daffodil, or for lack of sympathy with those who are upset by some joke or, to them, strange viewpoint, nor for not caring equally for all persons. But the concept of personhood should not be extended to other species, at least not without engaging in further weighty argument (though the principle of compassion should be), while caring about people should not be confused with loving them, liking them, or treating them with kid gloves. In general, commitment to equality should not get in the way of noting difference. And overall I would argue that we live in times where a bit more honest recognition of differences of various kinds is called for.

If I may continue briefly in this self-absorbed, not to say self-congratulatory, vein, I would add that I am fairly pleased with my work over the years on the nature of philosophical analysis. There is nothing particularly original in this work, but it is important that people get it right, and novelty is not all it is cracked up to be. I am reasonably satisfied with my work exposing the generic fallacy, and I still think we need to be vigilant about the dangers of generic ideas of leadership, teaching, football management, conducting, and the like. I stand by my arguments against a mechanistic view of human nature and my criticisms of scientism, which combine to repudiate the idea of a science of teaching. I believe that we should look at teaching more in terms of the kind of character that is needed to achieve ends as varied as helpfully instructing, enthusing, delighting, and puzzling students, etc., than in terms of specific methods and techniques said to be necessary, but generally on no good evidence, to achieve such ends. And I do not regret my emphasis on the importance of curriculum content. Whether my current view of what should be studied in schools is correct, I'm by no means certain; but that we should approach the broad question of what we should do in schools by thinking in terms of what we think is worth understanding, as opposed to thinking in terms of developing mental processes, for example, or of developing certain skills, is, I think, undoubtedly true.

I have my critics, as we all do, and I have had my disappointments. But I shall end on a happy note that fortunately comes naturally to me. One of the real joys of my life has been to work alongside colleagues and friends such as those who have so kindly contributed to this volume. I shall never forget the evening, nor the place (New College Buttery), when John Gingell casually remarked to me that he intended to organize what has become this *Festchrift*. I was overcome by surprise and with emotion then; I am overcome with emotion now. I humbly and gratefully accept the honor implied, but I see it as a tribute to friendship (I hope deserved in some measure) rather than as a (certainly undeserved) tribute to scholarship. For 'not ee'n love should rank above true friendship's name', and at least some of us know the value of something.

REFERENCES

Murray, C. (2003) *Human Accomplishment: The Pursuit of Excellence in the Arts and Sciences*, New York: HarperCollins.

Bibliography of Works by Robin Barrow
(in reverse chronological order)

BOOKS

2008 *Plato* (London and New York, Continuum).
2007 *An Introduction to Moral Philosophy and Moral Education* (London and New York, Routledge).
2006 *What Use is Educational Research? A Debate* (with Lorraine Foreman-Peck) (London, Impact, imprint of PESGB).
1993 *Language, Intelligence, and Thought* (Hants and Vermont, Edward Elgar).
1991 *Utilitarianism: A Contemporary Statement* (Aldershot and Vermont, Edward Elgar).
1990 *Understanding Skills: Thinking, Feeling and Caring* (London, ON, Althouse Press; London, Falmer Press).
1986 *A Critical Dictionary of Educational Concepts: An Appraisal of Selected Ideas and Issues in Educational Theory and Practice* (with Geoffrey Milburn). (Sussex,Wheatsheaf). 2nd edition, 1990 (Sussex, Harvester Wheatsheaf).
1984 *Giving Teaching Back to Teachers: A Critical Introduction to Curriculum Theory* (Sussex, Wheatsheaf; New Jersey, Barnes & Noble; Ontario). 6th printing, 2004 (London, ON, Althouse Press).
1982 *Language and Thought: Re-Thinking Language across the Curriculum* (Ontario, Althouse Press). 3rd printing, 1983.
1982 *Injustice, Inequality and Ethics* (Sussex, Harvester; New Jersey, Barnes & Noble). 2nd printing, 1983.
1981 *The Philosophy of Schooling* (Sussex,Wheatsheaf; New York, John Wiley). 2nd edition, 1983. 6thprinting, 1988. (Sussex, Harvester Wheatsheaf).
1980 *Happiness* (Oxford, Martin Robertson). As *Happiness and Schooling* (New York, St. Martin's Press). Republished 2012 (London and New York, Routledge).
1978 *Radical Education: A Critique of Freeschooling and Deschooling* (London, Martin Robertson; New York, John Wiley & Sons). Republished 2012 (London and New York, Routledge).
1978 *The Canadian Curriculum: A Personal View* (London, ON, Althouse Press). 4th printing, 1983.
1978 *Plato's Apology: A Critical Edition and Translation* (St Andrews, University of St. Andrews Press). 2nd printing, 1980.
1976 *Common Sense and the Curriculum* (London, Allen & Unwin). 4th printing, 1983. (Spanish Translation, 1979). Republished 2012 (London and New York, Routledge).
1976 *Plato and Education* (London, Routledge & Kegan Paul). 2nd printing, 1979. Republished 2012 (London and New York, Routledge).

1976 *Greek and Roman Education* (London, MacMillan). 2nd edition, 1982 (Edinburgh,Thomas Nelson & Sons). 8th printing, 1987. 3rd edition, 1996 (London, Duckworth).

1975 *Moral Philosophy for Education* (London, Allen & Unwin). 3rd printing, 1979. Republished 2012 (London and New York, Routledge).

1975 *Plato, Utilitarianism and Education* (London, Routledge & Kegan Paul). Republished 2010 in International Library of Philosophy of Education (London and New York, Routledge).

1975 *Sparta* (London, Allen & Unwin). 3rd printing, 1979.

1974 *An Introduction to the Philosophy of Education* with R. G. Woods (London and New York, Methuen). 2nd edition, 1982 (London and New York, Methuen). 3rd edition, 1988 (London and New York, Routledge). (Spanish translation, 1978). 4th edition, 2004 (London and New York, Routledge).

1973 *Athenian Democracy* (London, MacMillan). 2nd edition, 1976. (Greek translation, 1975). 12th printing, 1986. Republished 1999 (London, Bristol Classical Press).

EDITED BOOKS

2010 (with Richard Bailey, David Carr, and Christine McCarthy), *Handbook of Philosophy of Education* (London, Sage).

2006 (with Patrick Keeney), *Academic Ethics* (London, Ashgate).

1993 (with Patricia White), *Beyond Liberal Education: Essays in Honour of Paul H. Hirst* (London, Routledge).

1982 *Philosophy and Education* (Sussex, Falmer Press).

CHAPTERS IN BOOKS

2014 'Compulsory Common Schooling and Individual Difference', in *Education and the Common Good*, ed. Marianna Papastefanou (London, Springer).

2014 'Empirical Research in Education: Why Philosophy Matters', in *Philosophy of Education: Introductory readings,* ed. William Hare and John Portelli (Alberta, Brush Education).

2014 'Swansong: The Price of Everything', in *Education and the Common Good: Essays in Honour of Robin Barrow,* ed. John Gingell (New York, Routledge).

2014 'What Should be Taught in our Schools and Why?', in *Commonwealth Educational Partnerships, 2012/13,* ed. R. Jones-Parry and A. Robertson (Cambridge, Nexus).

2013 'Living with Uncertainty, While Maintaining Educational Values', in N.S.S.E YEARBOOK, 2013, ed. Robert Bostrom and Hugh Sockett (New York, Teachers College Press).

2012 'The Changing University, Lifelong Learning and Personal Fulfillment' (with P. Keeney), in *Second International Handbook of Lifelong Learning, Part 1,* ed. David Aspin et al. (London, Springer).

2012 'Universities, New Technologies and Lifelong Learning' (with P. Keeney), in *Second International Handbook of Lifelong Learning, Part 2,* ed. David Aspin et al. (London, Springer).

2011 'Was Peters Nearly Right about Education?', in *Reading R. S. Peters Today: Analysis, Ethics and the Aims of Education,* ed. Stefaan E. Cuypers and Christopher Martin (Oxford, Wiley-Blackwell).

2011 'L'Endoctrinement', in *L'Education, Collection Corpus,* trans. and ed. Normand Baillargeon (Paris, Flammarion).

2008 'Common Schooling and the Need for Distinction', in *The Common School and the Comprehensive Ideal,* ed. Mark Halstead and Graham Haydon (Oxford, Wiley-Blackwell).

2008 'Does the Question "What is Education?" Make Sense?', in *Philosophical Foundations of Education, 8th edition,* ed. Howard A Ozmon and Samuel M. Craver (Columbus, OH, Pearson).

2008 'Or What's a Heaven For?', in *Leaders in Philosophy of Education: Intellectual Self-Portraits.* ed. L. J. Waks (Amsterdam, Sense Publications).

2006 'On the Teaching of Classics', in *Theoi Doron,* ed. P. Brown, T. Harrison, and S. Instone (Herts, Gracewing).

2002 'Lifelong Learning: A North American Perspective' (with P. Keeney), in *Lifelong Learning: Education across the Lifespan,* ed. Mal Leicester and John Field (London, Falmer Press).

2001 'Lifelong Learning and Personal Fulfillment' (with P. Keeney), in *International Handbook on Lifelong Learning,* ed. David Aspin and Judith Chapman (London, Kluwer).

1999 'Being a Bit Pregnant: How Philosophical Misconceptions Lead to Stillborn Empirical Research', in *From Roaring Boys to Dreaming Spires,* ed. Ron Rembert (New York, University Press of America).

1999 'Or What's a Heaven For? The Importance of Aims in Education', in *Aims in Education,* ed. Roger Marples (London and New York, Routledge).

1998 'Educational Psychology and Timing in the Curriculum', in *Philosophy of Education: Major Themes in the Analytic Tradition, Vol. IV,* ed. P. H. Hirst and Patricia White (London and New York, Routledge).

1998 'Curriculum Design', in *Philosophy of Education: Major Themes in the Analytic Tradition, Vol. IV,* ed. P. H. Hirst and Patricia White (London and New York, Routledge).

1997 'Language, Definition, and Metaphor', in *Reason and Education: Essays in Honour of Israel Scheffler,* ed. Harvey Siegel (Boston and London, Kluwer).

1996 'The Lost Content', in *Ring Some Alarm Bells in Ontario,* ed. G. Milburn (London, ON, Althouse Press).

1995 'Philosophy of Education: Past, Present and Future', in *Logical Empiricism in Educational Discourse,* ed. D. Aspin (Amsterdam, Butterworth).

1991 'Creativity', in *Computers in Education 5-13,* ed. P. Jones and J. Grimshaw (Milton Keynes, Open University Press).

1991 'Censorship and Schooling', in *Freedom and Indoctrination in Education,* ed. B. Spiecker and R. Straughan (London, Cassell).

1991 'So Much for the Mind', in *Reform and Relevance in Schooling: Dropouts, Destreaming and the Common Curriculum,* ed. D. Allison and J. Paquette (Toronto, Ontario Institute for Studies in Education).

1990 'Culture, Values and the Language Classroom', in *Culture and the Language Classroom,* ed. B. Harrison (Hong Kong, British Council Modern English Publications).

1990 'R. S. Peters', in *Four Prominent Philosophers of Education,* ed. W. Hare (Nova Scotia, Dalhousie University).

1989 'Some Observations on the Concept of Imagination', in *Imagination and Education,* ed. K. Egan and D. Nadaner (New York, Teachers College Press).

1988 'Dogmatism', in *Papers in Philosophy of Education,* ed. W. Hare (New Jersey, Barnes & Noble).

1984 'The Paradigm to End Paradigms: Reorientating Curriculum Research for the Secondary School', in *Curriculum Canada,* ed. R. Enns and G. Milburn

(Vancouver, Centre for the Study of Curriculum and Instruction, University of British Columbia). .

1983 'The Teacher of Classics and the Teaching of Philosophy', in *From Didaskalos: An Anthology*, ed. J. Mingay and J. Sharwood Smith (Bristol, Bristol Classical Press).

1979 'A Critique of Freeschooling and Deschooling' and 'Forms of Knowledge', in *Philosophy of Education*, ed. M. Ayim (Lexington, Massachussetts, Ginn).

1978 'Back to Basics', in *Schooling in Decline,* ed. G. Bernbaum (London, MacMillan).

1976 'Competence and the Head', in *The Role of the Head,* ed. R. S. Peters (London, Routledge & Kegan Paul).

JOURNAL ARTICLES

2010 'Was Peters Nearly Right About Education?', *Journal of Philosophy of Education* 43. Supplement 1.

2009 'Dictating Democracy', *Journal of Thought* 42(1).

2009 'Is Public Education in Mortal Danger?', *Prospero* 15(4).

2009 'Academic Freedom: Its Nature, Extent and Value', *British Journal of Educational Studies* 57(2), June.

2008 'Education and the Body: Prolegomena', *British Journal of Educational Studies* 56(3), September.

2007 'Common Schooling and the Need for Distinction', *Journal of Philosophy of Education* 41(4).

2006 'Can We Force People to be Democratic?', *Ethical Record* 3(9).

2006 'Empirical Research into Teaching', *Interchange* 37(4).

2006 'Offence and Respect: Some Brief Comments', *Journal of Moral Education* 35(1).

2006 'Judging the Quality of Human Achievement', *Education and Culture* 22(1).

2006 'Moral Education's Modest Agenda', *Ethics and Education* 1(1).

2005 'Why We Educate', *Prospero* 11(2).

2005 'Philosophers Revisited', *Interchange* 36(4).

2005 'On the Duty of Not Taking Offence', *Journal of Moral Education* 34(3).

2005 'Education: The Frustration', *Prospero* 11(1).

2004 'Publicity, the Public and Professors', *British Journal of Educational Studies* 52(3).

2004 'Language and Character', *Arts and Humanities in Higher Education* 3(3).

2003 'In Mere Despair', *Prospero* 9(4).

2001 'Inclusion vs. Fairness', *Journal of Moral Education* 30(3).

2000 'The Poverty of Empirical Research in Education', *Journal of Moral Education* 29(3).

2000 'Include Me Out: Some Thoughts on Inclusion', *European Journal of Special Needs Education* 15(3).

2000 'Leadership in Public Schools: Did Behaviorism Ever Die?', *Prospero* 6(1–2).

1999 'The Higher Nonsense: Some Persistent Errors in Educational Thinking', *Journal of Curriculum Studies* 31(2).

1999 'The Need for Philosophical Analysis in a Postmodern Era', *Interchange* 30(4).

1997 'Language, Definition, and Metaphor', *Studies in Philosophy and Education* 16(1–2).

1997 'Trends and Topics in the Philosophy of Education in Britain and North America', *Journal of Shanghai Institute of Education* 52(2).

1996 'Moral Education: The Need for Clearer Thinking', *International Review of Education* No. 42.

1996 'The Leisure of the Theory Class', *Studies in Philosophy and Education* 15(3).
1996 'Cultural Reproduction and Education', *Journal of East China Normal University* 51 (1).
1995 'Not Guilty as Charged: A Rebuttal of Logical Empiricism', *Paideusis* 8(2).
1995 'Keep Them Bells A-Tolling: Normal Distribution and Intelligence', *Alberta Journal of Educational Research* (Special Issue).
1994 'Teacher Education', *Interchange* 25(4).
1995 'A Common Education', *Canadian Journal of Education* 20(3).
1995 'The Erosion of Moral Education', *International Review of Education* 41(1-2).
1993 'Denominational Schools and Public Schooling', *Interchange* 24(3).
1992 'Developing Intelligence', *Paideusis* 5(2), Spring.
1991 'Understanding "Understanding Skills"', *Paideusis* 4(2).
1991 'The Generic Fallacy', *Educational Philosophy and Theory* 23(1).
1990 'The Role of Conceptual Analysis in Curriculum Inquiry: A Holistic Approach', *Journal of Curriculum and Supervision* 5(3).
1990 'Teacher Education: Theory and Practice', *British Journal of Educational Studies* 38(4), November.
1989 'Politics, Reason and Religious Education', *Ethics in Education* 9(1).
1989 'A Place for Religious Education in the School Curriculum?', *Ethics in Education* 8(5).
1988 'Over the Top: A Misuse of Philosophical Techniques?', *Interchange* 19(2).
1988 'Multiculturalism', *Ethics in Education* 7(4).
1988 'Context, Concepts and Content: Prescriptions for Empirical Research', *Canadian Journal of Education* 13(1).
1987 'Skill Talk', *Journal of Philosophy of Education* 21(2).
1987 'Should Teachers be Told How to Teach?', *Ethics in Education* 7(1).
1987 'Conceptual Finesse', *Canadian Journal of Philosophy of Education* 1(1).
1986 'Socrates Was a Human Being: A Plea for Transcultural Moral Education', *Journal of Moral Education* 15(1).
1986 'Empirical Research into Teaching: The Conceptual Factors', *Educational Research* 28(3).
1986 'The Concept of Curriculum Design', *Journal of Philosophy of Education* 20(1).
1986 'Philosophy and the Classics', *Journal of the Joint Association of Classical Teachers*. 20 (2)
1985 'Patterns and Purposes: The Logic of Curriculum Design', *Teacher Education* (April).
1985 'The Non-Negotiable Curriculum', *Westminster Studies in Education* No.8.
1985 'Misdescribing a Cow: The Question of Conceptual Correctness', *Educational Theory* 35(2).
1984 'The Logic of Systematic Classroom Research: The Case of Oracle', *Durham and Newcastle Research Review* 10(53), Autumn.
1984 'Teacher Education and Research: The Place of Philosophy', *Proceedings of American Philosophy of Education Society* (1984).
1984 'Teacher Judgement and Teacher Effectiveness', *Journal of Educational Thought* (August).
1984 'How Married Are You, Mary Ann? Educating for the Real World', *Oxford Review of Education* 10(2), July.
1984 'Problems in Research into Group Work', *Durham and Newcastle Research Review* (Spring).
1984 'Does the Question "What is Education?" Make Sense?', *Educational Theory* 33(3-4).

1983 '"There is No Conversation": On Teaching Plato's Meno for Purposes of Communication', *Hesperiam* (Winter).
1983 'Prolegomenon to Curriculum Theory', *Canadian Journal of Education* 8(1).
1982 'Studying Ancient History', *History and Social Science Teacher* 17(4).
1982 'Five Commandments for the Eighties', *Educational Analysis* 4(1).
1981 'Philosophic Competence and Discriminatory Power', *Journal of Philosophy of Education* 15(2).
1978 'The Moral Education Issue', *History and Social Science Teacher* 13(2).
1978 'Being and Feeling Happy', *Proceedings of American Philosophy of Education Society*.
1977 'Plato and Politics', *Didaskalos* 5(3).
1977 'On Teaching Athenian Democracy', *Didaskalos* 5(3).
1975 'The Teacher of Classics and the Teaching of Philosophy', *Didaskalos* 5(1).
1974 'What's Wrong with the Philosophy of Education?', *British Journal of Educational Studies* 22(2), June.
1974 'Who Are the Philosopher Kings?', *Proceedings of the Philosophy of Education Society of Great Britain* (July).
1974 'Religion in the Schools', *Educational Philosophy and Theory* (March).
1973 'On Misunderstanding Philosophy', *Education for Teaching* (Autumn).
1972 'Examinations in Classical Studies', *Didaskalos* 4(1).
1967 'Corvo on Corvo', *The Idler.*
1965 'The Nineties: A Way of Life?', *The Idler.*

ENCYCLOPEDIA, HANDBOOK, AND COMPANION ENTRIES

2014 'The Persistence of Ancient Education', in *A Companion to Ancient Education*, ed. Martin Bloomer (Oxford, Wiley-Blackwell).
2014 'The Concept of Education', in *Sage Encyclopedia of Educational Theory and Philosophy*, ed. Denis Phillips (London, Sage).
2013 'Value Theory', in *Bloomsbury Encyclopedia of Utilitarianism*, ed. James E. Crimmins (New York, Continuum).
2013 'Plato', in *Bloomsbury Encyclopedia of Utilitarianism*, ed. James E. Crimmins (New York, Continuum).
2010 'Schools of Thought in Philosophy of Education', in Sage *Handbook of Philosophy of Education*, ed. Richard Bailey et al. (London, Sage).
2007 'Roman Education', in *Encyclopedia of the Ancient World* (Oxford and New York, Facts on File Publications).
2004 'Inclusion vs. Fairness', in *The RoutledgeFalmer Reader in Philosophy of Education*, ed. Wilf Carr (London, Routledge).
1992 'Philosophy of Education: The Analytic Tradition', in *The International Encyclopedia of Education*, 2nd edition, ed. Torsten Husen and Neville Postlethwaite (Oxford, Pergamon Press).
1990 'Curriculum Theory and Values', in *Handbook of Educational Ideas and Practices*, ed. N. J. Entwistle (London, Routledge).

MISCELLANEOUS (INCLUDING SELECTED REPORTS, INTERVIEWS, RECORDINGS, AND PERFORMANCE SCRIPTS)

2011 'Classical Education', a report commissioned by Oxford Analytica on the educational policies of Greece and Rome and their implications for today.

2010 'Happiness, Plato and Education: Some Personal Rethinking', *Vox* Issue 13—Autumn.

2010 'Public Education at the Brink', *Teacher* 22(4).

2010 Foreword to Alexander Mosley's *Aristotle* (London, Continuum).

2007 Program Notes for Presentation House Theatre's (Vancouver) production of Oscar Wilde's 'An Ideal Husband'.

1999 'Controversial and Conservative: Some Comments on Teacher Education', *Distinguished Visiting Lecturer Series* (Winnipeg, University of Manitoba).

1989 'Some Thoughts on Words', *C.A.C.S. Newsletter* (February, 1989).

1981 'Educational and Curriculum Theory: Two Lectures: i) Theory and Practice in the Training of Teachers, ii) Justifying What We Teach' (Vancouver, University of British Columbia).

1978 'A Conversation with Robin Barrow', video interview conducted by John McPeck, produced by Geoffrey Milburn, in *Conversations with Educators* series (London, ON, University of Western Ontario).

1974 'Happiness', *Philosophy of Education Society of Great Britain, Conference Papers*, (January).

1973 'The Trouble with Clary', *London Association of Classical Teachers' Bulletin* 13.

1965 'Too Young to Understand/Foolish Tears' (music by Andrew Lloyd Webber).

1962 *Socrates Swings,* libretto (based on A. C. Malcolm's *Oh Men of Athens*; music by Andrew Lloyd Webber).

1961 *The Bishop of Antigua*, libretto (music by Andrew Lloyd Webber).

EDITED SERIES

Issues and Ideas in Education (Oxford, Martin Robertson). 1979–82.

Greek and Roman Topics (London, Allen & Unwin). 1975–8.

Didaskalos: The Journal of the Joint Association of Classical Teachers 5(1–3), 1975–1977.

London Association of Classical Teachers Bulletin, 1970–1972.

GUEST EDITED JOURNALS

1998 *Canadian Journal of Education* 13(1), On Educational Research.

1982 *History and Social Science Teacher* 17(4), The Relevance of Greece and Rome.

1982 *Educational Analysis* 4(1), On Philosophy and Education.

Contributors

Robin Barrow was educated at Westminster School and Christ Church, Oxford, where he read classics and philosophy. He has a PhD from then University of London for his thesis on Plato's moral and political philosophy. He held a personal readership at the University of Leicester, UK, before being appointed professor of philosophy of education at Simon Fraser University, Canada, in 1982, where he was also dean of education from 1992–2002. The author of twenty-three books (and editor of three), and over one hundred academic papers, he was elected a Fellow of the Royal Society of Canada in 1996.

David Carr is professor emeritus at the University of Edinburgh where he was formerly professor of philosophy of education in the Moray House School of Education from 1999 to 2009. He currently holds a half-time postretirement position as professor of ethics and education at the University of Birmingham, UK. He is the author of several books on the philosophy of education and numerous papers in philosophical and educational journals.

Paul Hager is emeritus professor of education at University of Technology, Sydney. His main scholarly interest is the emerging field of philosophy of adult and vocational education. His work centres on topics such as informal workplace learning, professional practice, and group learning.

Ruth Jonathan is emeritus professor of educational theory and policy at Edinburgh University and an Honorary Fellow in the School of Social and Political Studies (of whose Graduate School she was for nine years the founding director). From 1997–2007 she was an Extraordinary Professor at the University of the Western Cape, South Africa, and an advisor to the Council on Higher Education there, involved in the democratic transformation of educational provision, access, and oversight.

Mike McNamee is professor of applied ethics at Swansea University. He completed a PhD in the philosophy of physical education in the early

1990s, amid wide-scale changes to initial teacher education, which made the subject less congenial to philosophical reflection. He then moved to the field of sports where he pioneered the subject of sports ethics. For the last decade he has taught medical ethics and has combined both sports and medicine in his ethics scholarship. He is editor of Routledge's Sports Ethics series, and is the founding editor of *Sport, Ethics and Philosophy*.

Richard Pring is first professor of educational studies at the University of Oxford, and director of the Department of Educational Studies, 1989–2003; lead director of the Nuffield Review of 14–19 Education and Training for England and Wales, 2003–2009 (report published in 2009); latest book, *Life and Death of Secondary Education for All* (Routledge, 2012).

Harvey Siegel is professor of philosophy at the University of Miami. He specializes in epistemology, philosophy of science, and philosophy of education.

Richard Smith is professor of education at Durham University. He is currently chair of the Philosophy of Education Society of Great Britain. His most recent books are (with Paul Smeyers and Paul Standish) *The Therapy of Education* (Palgrave Macmillan, 2006) and (with Paul Smeyers) *Making Sense of Education and Educational Research* (forthcoming, Cambridge University Press). His principal research interests are in the philosophy of education and the philosophy of social science.

Christopher Winch is professor of educational philosophy and policy in the Department of Education and Professional Studies, King's College, London. His main interests are in the philosophy of education and in professional and vocational education. He has worked in further, primary, and higher education. Among many books and articles he has published *Dimensions of Expertise* (Continuum, 2010), *Key Concepts in the Philosophy of Education* (with John Gingell, 2nd edition 2008), *The Philosophy of Human Learning* (Routledge, 1998), and *Quality and Education* (Blackwell, 1996). He has worked in primary, further, and higher education and served as head of department at King's from 2008–2012.

Index